Biology Brought to Life

A Guide to Teaching Students to Think Like Scientists

Jo Handelsman
University of Wisconsin–Madison

Barbara Houser
University of Wisconsin–Madison

Helaine Kriegel
University of Wisconsin–Madison

This project was supported, in part,
by the
National Science Foundation
Opinions expressed are those of the authors
and not necessarily those of the Foundation

The cover photograph shows release of zoospores from a sporangium of *Phytophthora sojae*. Photograph by Fred W. Schwenk, Kansas State University. Concept for cover design by Jocelyn L. Milner.

ISBN 0-697-35594-2

Printed in the United States of America by Times Mirror Higher Education Group, Inc., 2460 Kerper Boulevard, Dubuque, Iowa, 52001

A Times Mirror Company

10 9 8 7 6 5 4 3

Brief table of contents

Brief table of contents

Table of contents

Table of contents

Table of contents

Table of contents

Acknowledgments

The authors are indebted to many people for their contributions to this book. Here we mention some of the key players who helped make it possible.

Luis Sequeira
for his collaboration and contributions to the early stages of the project

Doug Maxwell
for his fierce defense of academic freedom and individuality

Paul Williams
for paving the way

Craig Grau
for his ideas, friendship, and shared love of students and legumes

Bob Goodman and John Andrews
for their critical reviews of parts of the manuscript

Caitilyn Allen
for the bacterial DNA demonstration, camaraderie, and many good ideas

Marleen Lippert
for friendship and support and for always finding a way to get things done

Jan Phelps, Harriet Irwin, and Caitilyn Allen
for testing the desk-top biology exercises in their classrooms and providing critical feedback from their students

Michael Lange and Wm. C. Brown Publishers
for believing in the future of biology education

Kier Klepzig, Stu Utley, Mara McDonald, Alvea Bridges, Albert Herrod, Brian Manske, Sandy Stewart, Khoosheh Gosink, Jocelyn Milner, Jon Fritz, Gary Roberts, Ken Todar, Craig Grau, Susan Hirano, Eric Stabb, Paul Williams, Ann MacGuidwin, David Johnson, Mike Strand, Elizabeth Blackson, and so many others
for their innovations, inventions, and ideas that make the desk-top experiments work

The National Science Foundation, and especially Bill Cohen, Terry Woodin, and Herb Levitan

for generous financial support and for a vision of the future of education

The University of Wisconsin-Madison Department of English, and especially Charles T. Scott

for seeing the unusual connection between English as a Second Language and Plant Pathology

The University of Wisconsin Center for Biology Education, and especially Lillian Tong

for financial support accompanied by enthusiasm and belief in the project

The University of Wisconsin Undergraduate Teaching Improvement Council

for financial support for collaboration with Jan Phelps and Harriet Irwin

The Department of Plant Pathology, University of Wisconsin

for being a home and family to biology education

Our Students

for teaching us so much about teaching

and

Robert Goodman, David Houser, and Bob Esser

for their enthusiasm and affection for us and our book, for provoking us to find our publisher, and for joining us on the journey

Chapter 1 - Introduction

The challenge for biology teaching: A national mandate

Society's need for excellence in science education has never been greater. Well-trained scientists will be needed to solve the increasingly complex technological issues of the next century wisely, and a scientifically literate public will have an increasing need to understand the scientific issues that affect their lives. Ironically, even as our national need for scientists and scientifically literate citizens is intensifying, interest in science among students is declining (National Research Council, 1990; Raizen, 1991). The numbers of women and minorities in science are not increasing rapidly enough to match their predicted majority in the work force by the turn of the century (Shalala, 1995; Tobias, 1992). To meet our national needs, science must be accessible to everyone regardless of gender, ethnicity, or career interest.

Science educators face a dual challenge: We must attract more students to careers in science, and we must enable non-scientists to confront the technological issues of the 21st century with knowledge and understanding. The spotlight is on the state of science education.

Biology is central to the dual challenge since many of the greatest personal and societal decisions of the future will involve health, the environment, and agriculture. Coupled with the visibility and centrality of biology is the rapid generation of new knowledge in the field. Biology teachers confront a swiftly evolving discipline that presents both exhilarating opportunity and a sometimes overwhelming flow of new information, techniques, and applications. The last decade has brought genetic engineering, molecular forensics, biodiversity, and infectious disease to the public eye. Most biology teachers have scrambled to incorporate new topics and illustrations into their courses to keep them current and lively. But we need to prepare our students to integrate and evaluate advances in science and technology after they leave our courses as well. To help non-majors become literate in biology and to educate the new generation of biologists, teachers at the college level need a variety of well-tested tools and approaches to teaching and learning. We need to train students in the process of analysis and critical thinking so they can successfully face the deluge of information, decisions, and problems they will be confronted with in life or in careers as biologists.

Introductory courses in biology provide a critical forum for addressing the dual challenge. It is in these courses that teachers can excite students about careers in biology or turn them off to further training in science; it is also in these courses that we have an opportunity (often the *only* opportunity) to convince non-science majors that they are capable of thinking about scientific information and ideas. Therefore, focusing attention on introductory courses can have benefits in attracting students to careers in science and in building a scientifically literate citizenry. But some students come to our introductory courses thinking of science as rigid and dull. We can replace this image with the reality of the constant and rapid process of change that typifies science and that is generated by debate and challenge. We can convince students of the dynamic nature of our discipline by actively involving them in the workings of science.

In this book we describe successful teaching methods based on the scientific method, logical thinking, and active learning. The premise underlying this approach is that if beginning students learn these skills, they will be able to think and work as scientists. Those who continue with science careers can specialize, adding the needed vocabulary and techniques of their chosen field to a strong structural scaffolding based on an understanding of the scientific method. Those who choose not to become scientists will have learned valuable thinking skills that will help them interpret what they read and hear about science and make rational decisions about the issues that affect their lives. This approach to science education through logical thinking, problem solving, hypothesis formulation, experimentation, and data analysis stimulates both beginning and experienced students and allows them to be full participants in the fun of doing science.

Biology teachers are supported in the goal to involve students actively in science by a national mandate. Many influential entities in science policy (including the National Science Foundation, the National Academy of Sciences, and the American Association for the Advancement of Science) have advocated taking the steps necessary to create a scientifically literate public and to attract more people to careers in science through promotion of active learning in the science classroom.

Exciting times lie ahead. The reform of science education is challenging, but innovative teachers are receiving enthusiastic support from funding agencies, the government, and the public. Most importantly, the rewards for introducing students to the exhilaration of scientific discovery are well worth the effort.

A strategy for biology teaching: Inquiry, cooperation, and skills

If we are to make our students truly scientifically literate, we should invite them to participate in the process of doing science. If our invitation is to be credible, it must be issued in an environment that is supportive, cooperative, and inclusive. Therefore, we need to incorporate into our classrooms the process of scientific inquiry, not just the information resulting from it, and learn how to construct classroom cultures that foster mutual respect and seek active participation from every member. Engaging students in the process of scientific investigation and the intellectual debate that accompanies it requires a classroom culture that motivates learning, teaches analytical skills as well as information, and captures the spirit of curiosity and questioning. This can be accomplished by building a classroom community. In this book, we define a community as a group that shares an activity with a feeling of unity and individual participation without the loss of individuality. Such an environment can enhance learning for all students but is particularly important for those who traditionally have been alienated from science.

Overcoming barriers to change

Students may initially resist active learning in biology classes. Many of them enter biology courses believing they should be passive receptacles for information because they have nothing to offer biology. It is our challenge as teachers to convince all students that they can be active, contributing members of the community of biologists in the classroom. To overcome their passivity, we need to provide students with a supportive environment that encourages them to take an active role. Students who feel accepted and valued as members of a community will take a responsibility for their own learning. If their initial attempts to contribute ideas are treated with respect, they will contribute again. Before long, they will be hooked on the fun and excitement of participating in a community of biologists—debating, hypothesizing, and learning.

You may hesitate at the thought of challenging your students to be active members of the classroom community. Perhaps you feel you have had little experience in managing an active class or worry about losing control of the class. But the rewards of active learning are immediately evident for the teacher as well as the student. The joy of teaching in a classroom community is in watching the students discover the true excitement of biology and become sophisticated thinkers, exchanging ideas with one another. Just as biologists learn from each other, developing, refining, and challenging ideas cooperatively, so students learn from and with each other. Furthermore, students learn complex thinking skills—problem-solving, divergent thinking, critical analysis—better in cooperative groups than individually or competitively (Johnson and Johnson, 1978; Okebukola and Ogunniyi, 1984; Duren and Cherrington, 1992). One of the goals in this book is to help teachers become familiar and comfortable with these powerful approaches to teaching so that they can discover in their own classrooms how simple and rewarding active learning can be for everyone.

A major barrier to teaching and learning biology is that some students lack the necessary skills for learning in science courses. To be successful in achieving scientific literacy for a diversity of students, we must directly face the inadequacy of our educational system in teaching the practical skills or fostering the confidence and independence needed for learning science. Bright, competent students who are successful in humanities courses often express frustration at their inability to master material, extract key concepts, or prepare for exams in their science courses. An understanding of the skills and attitudes needed to learn science can improve our teaching and help our students develop better strategies for learning. This book is designed to identify the necessary skills and provide practical strategies to build those skills when they are lacking.

Classroom community and women, minorities, and "others"

A democratic society needs scientifically literate citizens of diverse ethnicity, gender, culture, and class. The future will demand the citizenry to have more scientific knowledge to be involved in decisions that affect human health and the health of the environment. But in the past, science has not attracted all people in proportion to their representation in the general population (Kahle and Lakes, 1983; Linn and Hyde, 1989; Cipra, 1991). Since the inception of education, women and ethnic minorities have been underrepresented in science, and this situation continues today (Collea, 1990; Kahle and Danzl-Tauer, 1991).

Science needs diverse scientists to remain vigorous and dynamic. In every field of science, in every era, there have been great scientists who did not resemble their contemporaries either in personal or intellectual traits. The leaders in science are those who are not trapped by current dogma or conventions, but instead bring a different perspective or approach to old problems. Progress in science depends on people such as Einstein, Galileo, Mendel, or McClintock, who have uncommon ideas and the confidence to pursue them. And yet, due to budget constraints and tradition, our educational system rigorously selects for scientists who, like many of their members, can perform well in a competitive environment, on multiple choice exams, and who can absorb and memorize countless facts and not change the status quo. Imagine the face of science if we systematically encouraged those who seem different from the standard scientist of the day!

To meet our responsibility to generate a scientifically literate citizenry and to attract a wider range of human types to science, we need to construct an educational system that accommodates and encourages people who do not fit the current mold of the scientist. We need to provide an environment in which people who reject competition as part of learning can flourish, an atmosphere that stimulates individuality, creativity, and curiosity. Most importantly, we need to accommodate various learning styles. In classrooms that are genuinely inclusive, students who see systems in their entirety should be as successful as their classmates who see the component parts. Those who prefer intuition should find a place alongside the deductive reasoners.

Meeting the needs of diverse students is facilitated by diverse teaching methods. Many methods may enhance learning, but some are particularly well-adapted to teaching biology. Incorporating cooperative learning and open-ended investigation into traditional classrooms may help the non-traditional student find a place in science and can enhance the creativity and problem-solving ability of the science major. Furthermore, we can teach students to appreciate their own learning styles to help them become informed and self-aware, thereby taking an essential step toward becoming successful learners.

About this book

The goal of this book is to provide teachers with strategies for teaching scientific inquiry, using active learning in a community through innovations in content and pedagogy. The methods we describe are not the only successful ones for teaching biology, but the ones we describe have been successful in a variety of biology courses and are particularly easy to incorporate into established courses. They can be added in small pieces to complement existing lectures, laboratories, and discussions. We describe strategies for using cooperative learning in lectures, labs, and outside of class. We present open-ended experiments that help students learn how to apply the scientific method by proposing hypotheses and designing experiments to test them. We present approaches for enhancing the learning skills that students need to complete science courses successfully. The methods we present have application to a wide range of learning environments—large or small classes for majors or non-majors in any college or university. The strategies are designed to improve the scientific literacy of all students and to attract diverse students to careers in science.

We developed the exercises presented in this book in a biology course for non-majors, and we have incorporated some of them into majors' and graduate biology courses as well. Our non-majors' biology course, called "Plants, Parasites, and People," started off as a traditional course with two lectures and one discussion section per week. The students were interested in the material, but lacked a sense of how the scientific information we presented was generated. We had trouble getting them to look at assigned reading, to stay for even a moment after the bell rang, or to attend the discussion section. Most disturbing was that only a few students answered questions we posed in class. Even fewer asked questions.

There were three turning points in the development of the teaching methods and philosophy embodied in this book. The first event occurred one semester when we brought a sick plant and a few simple tools to class and asked the students to design and conduct an experiment to determine the cause of the symptoms. Suddenly, the classroom was buzzing with discussion.

Students were grinding plant tissue, asking questions, demanding information, and staying long after the bell had rung. Many arrived early at the next class session and eagerly looked at the petri plates they had prepared to see what had grown on them. We discovered what many educators learned before us—that students learn far better from doing biology than by being told how someone else did it. With that realization behind us the next step was to incorporate lots of investigative experimentation into the course. Since we were constrained by a low budget and large class, we developed the simple experiments described in this book, which require a minimum of equipment and can be conducted with many students at relatively low cost.

The second turning point in our teaching was the casual use of a cooperative learning technique in lecture. At the beginning of a lecture on etiology of plant disease, we asked the students to form groups and list what they thought might cause plants to get sick. The groups reported back to the entire class, and we recorded the answers on the blackboard. The results were stunning. First, the students' list of possible causes was longer than the list in the lecturer's notes—the students had come up with ideas that had not occurred to us. Second, some of the most creative ideas were from students who had never before spoken in class and from some who had done poorly on exams. Third, during the rest of lecture the students asked many questions and seemed more interested than usual. Hmmmm. This got us thinking about what we were missing with the exclusive use of the lecture teaching style in the classroom. We soon developed a variety of cooperative learning exercises for regular use in lecture. We consistently observe that attendance improves, the students sleep less, and they ask many more questions when we use cooperative learning in lecture.

The third turning point came from working with a student who was bright, attentive, and hardworking but who consistently failed exams. One day, in a desperate attempt to help her figure out why she was not successful on exams, one of us asked to see the notes she had taken in lecture that day. From a 50-minute lecture, she had taken only three lines of notes. We came to realize that this young woman, and many other students we have known, simply lacked the practical skills critical for success in college science courses. That realization led us to identify the necessary skills. We then developed exercises designed to help students improve their learning and academic skills.

We wrote this book to share our experience with other teachers. In the field of science education, we have a habit of rediscovering each others' wheels. We have learned much of what we know about learning and teaching from many thoughtful colleagues and students. This book is, in part, our way of repaying the academic community for the lessons it has shared with us. By sharing our discoveries, strategies, successes, and failures, we hope to help other teachers find their way, perhaps a bit more quickly, to the joy of being a teacher in a classroom of active learners who are ready to face the world with knowledge and curiosity.

References - introduction

◆ Cipra, Barry (1991) They'd rather switch than fight. *Science*, 254: 369–370.

◆ Collea, Francis P. (1990) Increasing minorities in science and engineering: A critical look at two programs. *Journal of College Science Teaching*, Oct: 31–41.

◆ Duren, Phillip E. and April Cherrington (1992) The effects of cooperative group work versus independent practice on the learning of some problem-solving strategies. *School Science and Mathematics*, 92: 80–83.

◆ Johnson, David W. and Roger Johnson (1978) Cooperative, competitive, and individualistic learning. *Journal of Research and Development in Education*, 12: 3–15.

◆ Kahle, Jane Butler and Lynnette Danzl-Tauer (1991) The underutilized majority: The participation of women in science. In: *Science Education in the United States: Issues, Crises and Priorities*, Majumdar, Shyamal K., Leonard M. Rosenfeld, Peter A. Rubba, E. Willard Miller, and Robert F. Schmalz, eds., Ch. 41. Easton, PA: The Pennsylvania Academy of Science.

◆ Kahle, Jane Butler and Marsha K. Lakes (1983) The myth of equality in science classrooms. *Journal of Research in Science Teaching*, 20: 131–140.

◆ Linn, Marcia C. and Janet S. Hyde (1989) Gender, mathematics, and science. *Educational Researcher*, 18: 17-27.

◆ National Research Council (1990) *Fulfilling the Promise: Biology Education in the Nation's Schools*. Washington, DC: National Academy Press.

◆ Okebukola, Peter A. and Meshach B. Ogunniyi (1984) Cooperative, competitive, and individualistic science laboratory interaction patterns—Effects on students' achievement and acquisition of practical skills. *Journal of Research in Science Teaching*, 21: 875–884.

◆ Raizen, Senta A. (1991) The state of science education. In: *Science Education in the United States: Issues, Crises and Priorities*, Majumdar, Shyamal K., Leonard M. Rosenfeld, Peter A. Rubba, E. Willard Miller, and Robert F. Schmalz, eds., Ch. 3. Easton, PA: The Pennsylvania Academy of Science.

◆ Shalala, Donna E. (1995) Ensuring scientific literacy. *ASM News*, 61: 384–385.

◆ Tobias, Sheila (1992) Science education reform: Broadening the agenda. *Molecular Biology of the Cell*, 3: 1195–1197.

Chapter 2 - Desk-top biology

Open-ended explorations into the biological world

Why doing biology helps students learn biology

Biology is the study of life. Biological literacy demands understanding the processes of that study. Biology teaching should therefore incorporate the process of scientific inquiry, not just the information resulting from it. The biology classroom can be enriching as well as enjoyable when it includes hands-on experimentation, which is central to being a biologist. Unfortunately, experimentation is often excluded from introductory biology courses for non-science majors because labs are considered unnecessary, inappropriate, or too expensive. Laboratories for biology majors often stress techniques and equipment instead of the scientific method, inquiry, and challenging ideas. To foster curiosity and an understanding of the study of life, we need courses for majors and non-majors that involve students in experimentation without extensive laboratory facilities. The exercises presented here can be conducted in laboratories or on a desk top in non-laboratory classrooms, they utilize simple and inexpensive materials, and they can be used to teach a range of biological concepts. The exercises can be adopted directly as described here or they can be adapted and modified for other uses or to illustrate other concepts.

Why these topics

Biology fascinates human beings. It is therefore not difficult to make a biology course attractive to a wide spectrum of people by emphasizing what is interesting to most of us: how things work, the mystery of the unknown, the unpredictability of organisms, the aesthetics of the biological world, the tremendous variation on a few biological themes, the interplay of theory and applications to human welfare, and the thrill of discovery. The experiments presented in this chapter are intended to capitalize on these aspects of the biological world.

What students need from their first or only course in biology is a grounding in concepts and processes. If they pursue a major in biology they will gain exposure to the breadth of organisms and techniques for studying them in higher level courses. Their first course should provide the structural framework on which to build. If they take only one biology course and move on to major in another field, then they do not need techniques as much as they need an understanding of the process of biological thought and discovery. Furthermore, many students are alienated by sophisticated equipment, dissections, and other trappings of the traditional introductory biology classroom. We have therefore designed these experiments to focus on the essence of biology—the organisms themselves and the scientific method—and not the tools, such as respirometers or electrophoresis apparatus, used in advanced study of organisms. The experiments primarily utilize lower organisms because they pose fewer ethical and legal problems than do captive or dead higher organisms. Moreover, lower organisms provide malleable systems in which life events occur quickly—in a time frame that is practical for a course. We have striven to illustrate the major concepts of biology (genetics, evolution, cell biology, ecology, and physiology) with examples of plants, animals, and microorganisms, but you will find an emphasis on the lower organisms to facilitate rapid turnaround time, large populations for adequate sampling in a small space, and visual appeal. It is essential, when using these experiments in a general biology course, to make comparisons and connections to other examples of the concepts illustrated in each exercise. For example, Experiments 5 and 6 use bacteria and plants to illustrate the concepts of genetic variation, selection, and change in gene frequency. The experiment can be completed in a week. It would be difficult to match the rapidity of the events in these experiments using animals, but it is essential to provide the students with, or ask them to provide, analogies with larger or slower-growing organisms to ensure that they understand the universality of the concept.

We have chosen to highlight microorganisms in these exercises for three reasons: First, there is no question that microbiology is the field of greatest expansion in biology today. The recognition that the vast majority of biodiversity is microbial, that infectious disease will likely shape the survival of the human race in the next century, that microbes run all of the major geochemical cycles on Earth, and that the unity of biology is much greater than we imagined before DNA sequencing was routine (making microbial systems good models for most biological questions) has revolutionized the way biologists view their science. Microbes are increasingly visible in newspapers, in journals, such as *Science* and *Nature*, and in the funding priorities of major agencies, such as the National Science Foundation and National Institutes of Health. In light of this increased importance of microbes, it is likely that many teachers of introductory biology courses will be scrambling to put more microbiology into their syllabi in the coming years.

Second, these exercises with an emphasis on microbes provide instructors access to new examples for their teaching. Although most of the genetic and biochemical diversity of the biological world is found among the microorganisms, most biology courses, text books, and lab manuals emphasize the morphological and behavioral diversity of plants and animals. We find that the prominence of microorganisms in the popular press has stimulated student interest in this area of biology, and we find that many biology teachers are searching for laboratory materials involving microorganisms to diversify their courses.

Third, microbes and plants are ideal for the inquiry-based approach. By using these malleable and forgiving organisms as experimental subjects, few ethical issues arise, equipment and space costs are minimized, and teachers can maintain their sanity while supplying students with appropriate materials to test their hypotheses.

How to use this chapter

The experiments in this chapter are organized in a standard format to give teachers the information they will need to understand underlying concepts, set up labs, and guide students as they carry out their experiments. Experiments 2 through 10 are arranged roughly in order. Those at the beginning are technologically simpler, based on simpler concepts, and more prescribed; those at the end are technologically more complex, based on harder concepts, and more open-ended. In the beginning, students are given hypotheses to test. Later on, they formulate their own. It is not necessary to do these experiments in the exact order we have given them here, but it is best to start with some at the beginning of the chapter so students can get used to working with laboratory materials, collecting data, and thinking like scientists with relatively simple problems. It is best to save the later experiments until students are confident in the lab. Each of the experiments is designed to illustrate the scientific method, and we indicate in the text which aspect of the method can be highlighted in each experiment.

We suggest beginning with Pet Microbes for several reasons. Students are immediately intrigued by the idea of having a microorganism for a pet. As they start to learn about their pets, they are drawn into the fun and excitement of doing science. Also, this experiment takes time to do. Students work on it throughout the semester, applying concepts, as they learn them, to the characterization of their pets. Pet Microbes is especially good for reinforcing concepts studied in other experiments.

The teacher's manual for each experiment begins with the corresponding pages from the student manual so teachers can look at the experiment from the student perspective. We give a brief overview of the main points of the experiment, followed by an expanded discussion of what students will learn, as well as the experiment's greatest strengths and conceptual challenges. The next section is a sort of cookbook with a complete list of materials teachers will need for preparations and students will need for labs, with a timetable and instructions for setting up each part of the lab. We offer tips on how to guide students through each experiment including examples of hypotheses to test, ways of observing and collecting data, common problems and their solutions, and questions to guide student thinking and discussion. At the end of each experiment, we have included references for additional information, such as standard reference books for microbe identification, historical overviews, or more complete discussions of biological principles. Each experiment is intended to be complete and ready to use, but we encourage teachers to try their own variations, using organisms and materials available to them.

Notes on managing the class

The open-ended experiments described here require a different type of teaching than many of us are familiar with. We suggest the following general format for your class session.

1. Ask the students to read the appropriate part of the student manual before coming to class.

2. Start the class with a very short lecture in which you provide the key background information, state the challenge, and provide basic instructions for how the class period will be spent. This should take 5 to 10 minutes.

3. Ask the students to form groups to make an observation about the materials provided, develop a hypothesis, and design an experiment to test the hypothesis. Ask them also to identify any methods they need to learn to test their hypothesis.

4. Put the following table on the blackboard and collect each group's ideas. This is a good time to ask, "Does that experiment really address your hypothesis?" or "Are there any other controls you need to include?" or "How will you know if the effect is due to your treatment?" to help the students refine their experiments.

Group	Observation	Hypothesis	Experiment	Methods needed
Group #1				
Group #2				
Group #3				

5. Encourage critiques and questions about the experiments.

6. Briefly describe the methods the students have identified.

We find that the group process is an important part of these experiments. Individually, many students are not confident enough to deal with the challenge of experimental design. In groups, students are generally able to function at a higher cognitive level, and they support each other in the effort to learn how to do science. Do not underestimate your students! We have been amazed to find how creative and thoughtful non-science majors at the college level and even precollege level can be about conducting scientific experiments. If you have never given your students the opportunity to work in groups on hard scientific problems, try it. You will likely be surprised at the results. (See Chapter 3 for more on the theory and practice of group work.)

One of the key features of the approach we describe here is that the students request to learn the methods they need to do the experiments. We find that students learn much more this way than if we start the class with a demonstration of a new technique before they realize its context in their own experimentation. Providing methods on demand is also a good lesson in how science progresses: Methods are developed because they are needed, and scientific exploration is often limited by the lack of methodology.

The two most common problems we encounter with this method of teaching laboratory science are (1) the students think they do not have enough knowledge to design an experiment, and (2) they think there is only one right answer. To convince them that they have enough knowledge, remind them that the problem they are trying to solve either has not been solved or was only solved recently. Someone had to do the experiment, probably with less knowledge than the students themselves have. Good examples are Koch, who demonstrated that microorganisms cause disease at a time when it was not known that this was true (see Experiment 5, page 63), or the demonstration that bacteria cause ice nucleation, which was discovered in the 1970s. We attempt to help the students see that they are doing real science, and real science means not knowing the answer before you do the experiment. Analogies can make this point sharply. For example, in Experiment 5, we make an analogy with human medicine—in trying to diagnose a patient, a doctor will be faced with the same dilemma facing the students when they examine their sick plants.

Students often think that if their observation, hypothesis, or experiment is different from someone else's, then one of them must be wrong. We try to dispel this notion by first reassuring them that there is never only one good experiment. The excitement of science is that each of us finds the question that excites us, and there are unlimited interesting questions to ask. We also congratulate the class on the diversity of experiments stating that it shows the creativity and individuality of the class members.

Suggested timetable for a typical class session

The following is a breakdown of time usage for a small class of 15 to 20 students working in groups of three to five members. If your class is larger, you may want to modify this plan by having only some of the groups report to the entire class.

Overview and presentation of challenge	5–10 minutes
Group work to design experiments	10–15 minutes
Group reports to entire class	12–15 minutes
Demonstrate needed methods	5 minutes
Conduct experiments	15 minutes

We have conducted these experiments in 50-minute sessions successfully. If you have longer class sessions then you will have more time for discussion, questions, or variations on the experiments.

Calibrating to your budget

College biology courses typically have budgets between $2 and $40 per student. If you are fortunate to teach a course at the top end of this range, you will have more than enough money for supplies for every student to conduct all of the experiments and variations on them described in this manual. If you have $10 to $20 per student, you should be able to comfortably supply groups with sufficient materials to conduct all the experiments with adequate replication. If your budget is at the lower end of the range, you may want to conserve supplies in a number of ways. Your students can work in larger groups, the groups can share materials for controls to reduce duplication of materials, or you can have the groups agree on a single class experiment. We believe that the exercise of making observations, developing a hypothesis, and designing an experiment should be used repeatedly throughout the semester even if the students do not actually conduct all of the experiments in the lab. You may decide to use a mixture of "drylab" and "wetlab" experiments based on expense.

Some of the experiments, such as "Bread Mold" and "Vulnerability," cost only a few pennies per student once you have a few simple supplies, such as the fungal cultures, aluminum pans, and spray bottles. If you wish to conduct some of the more expensive experiments, such as "Pet Microbes," for which a budget of $2 per student is comfortable, and you do not have a large enough budget to cover them, consider asking the students for contributions. We have found that students are very willing to contribute $2 to $5 each to support a meaningful laboratory experience. Such a fee should enable you to conduct all of the experiments described in this book. Of course, some students cannot afford such a fee, and some institutions prohibit soliciting such a fee, so this may not be appropriate for all teaching settings. If all else fails, take some of the key references from the previous chapter, such as the reports from the National Academy of Sciences and American Association for the Advancement of Science, to your most sympathetic administrators and state your case. Tell your administration that you have a mandate from key scientific bodies to teach biology with active student participation, and you need their support to do so. Describe to them the education reform movement that is sweeping the country (and that they should want to join), convince them of the need for a scientifically literate public, and impress upon them the thriftiness of the experiments described here, and you will have an unbeatable argument!

The well-equipped student

Since many of our students have had little or no experience with microbiology, we have found it necessary to show them basic sterile techniques early in the course. Students learn to think about the importance of maintaining sterility and to avoid touching or breathing on sterile surfaces. In addition, they learn techniques such as the three-way streak to obtain individual microbial colonies (see Appendix II, page 220) and removal of a sterile toothpick from the box by picking it up in the middle to avoid contaminating the tips of the other toothpicks.

Some supplies are used so often in the desk-top experiments that we keep them available on each student table all the time. We list them here as general supplies and will not list them again in the materials sections when they are needed for specific experiments. Supplies that are frequently needed for teacher preparations are listed in "The well-equipped classroom" on the next page.

General supplies for students

- alcohol burner
- small receptacle for used toothpicks
- small receptacle for waste
- aluminum cake or bread pan
- box of sterile toothpicks
- bulbs for Pasteur pipettes
- sterile microfuge tubes in a sterile, covered container
- microfuge tube holder (a plastic 35-mm film can with 2 or 3 holes drilled in the lid works well)
- small plastic soda bottle with top cut off to use as a container for
    - forceps
    - tube of sterile water
    - pencils
    - waterproof marking pens
    - tube of sterile glass Pasteur pipettes
    - glass rod

The well-equipped classroom

The experiments described here work well in a standard biology laboratory. However, it is not necessary to have a large, fully outfitted laboratory to do them. Ingenuity and creativity on your part can do much to overcome a small budget or lack of space. To preserve the peace of mind of both you and your students, you will want at least some space for lab preparation, storage, and conducting experiments. It will be invaluable to have a small, out-of-traffic area to grow plants, prepare culture plates and other materials for the experiments, and to store supplies and students' experiments in progress. Each group of students will also need work space in which to carry out their experiments. A bench-, desk-, or table-top where the group can gather works well.

The experiments require some but not a lot of equipment. Less expensive alternatives can substitute for high-priced equipment. For example, a pressure cooker can be used as a substitute for an autoclave to sterilize media and other supplies (see Appendix III, page 234). And while it is valuable to have at least one compound microscope and one dissecting microscope for use by the whole class, it is not necessary to supply a microscope for each group of students. You may think of other substitutions you can make, such as using jars or bottles with tight-fitting lids instead of purchasing desiccators, Erlenmeyer flasks, or specimen bottles. Use whatever works best for your situation.

A number of supplies will be needed for more than one experiment. We have included them in the list below. Having extra materials in stock will make preparations for the experiments easier.

General supplies for teachers

- aluminum foil
- chlorine bleach
- cotton balls—sterile
- culture media—potato dextrose agar, nutrient broth, nutrient agar
- Erlenmeyer flasks—125-ml
- 95% ethanol
- filter paper disks—9 cm, sterile
- glass rods or spreaders
- microcentrifuge tubes—0.5 and 1.5 ml
- paper towels
- Parafilm
- pencils for micro mortars and pestles
- petri plates—9 cm, sterile
- pipettes, 9 inch
- plastic bags, small
- plastic sprayer bottles
- potting soil
- toothpicks—sterile and non-sterile
- transfer loop
- vermiculite
- water, distilled water—sterile

Safety essentials

Many experiments in this book use microorganisms to illustrate processes and concepts in biology. We have purposefully not designed experiments that require human pathogens, but in some experiments we have used plant pathogens to illustrate concepts of disease. In addition to using specific plant pathogens in experiments, you and your students may encounter pathogenic microorganisms as contaminants or when culturing soil samples. It is important that students learn basic safety practices for working in a microbiology laboratory to minimize contact between themselves and the microorganisms they are studying.

Students often get contaminants on their culture plates. When students use good sterile technique, they will minimize but probably never entirely eliminate contamination. Most of the time the contaminants are likely to be the same organisms used in class, but sometimes a contaminant with unknown behavior and characteristics will grow. All microorganisms, known or unknown, benign or pathogenic, should be treated with respect, using good sterile technique.

Because soil is the natural habitat for a number of animal and plant pathogens, some of the organisms that grow when students culture soil samples in the "Biodiversity" experiment may be pathogenic. It is a good idea to remind the students to handle their cultures with care.

Some class members may have allergies to bacteria or fungi. These allergies may be aggravated when suspensions of microorganisms are sprayed. Spraying the suspensions inside a hood or cardboard box (see page 47) and keeping culture plates closed and sealed with Parafilm reduces the number of microorganisms in the air and decreases the possibility of plate contamination and allergic reactions.

Parafilm is an excellent material for sealing culture plates. It keeps the culture medium on the plates from drying out. It protects the culture from outside contaminants and keeps the culture organisms securely inside the plate. It is especially important that pet microbe plates be sealed with Parafilm if students plan to carry their pets in their backpacks or take them home for observations. All microorganisms should be returned to the instructor and disposed of at the end of the course.

In general, students should always be careful when working with microorganisms. They should not eat or drink while doing experiments, and they should wash their hands after handling inoculated culture plates, infected plants, or soil samples.

If your institution has special rules for disposing of laboratory wastes, you should follow them. Otherwise, we suggest that you provide small receptacles on student work tables for disposal of contaminated toothpicks and other waste materials (see "General supplies for students," page 15). You can autoclave these waste materials and discard them. Used culture plates can be autoclaved or soaked in a 30% bleach solution for 30 minutes and discarded.

Experiment 1: Pet microbes
A lesson in taxonomy

What's in a name? Names help us communicate a lot of information in a few words. They provide a shorthand to refer to individuals or groups of individuals. It is much easier to refer to "the Curie family" than it is to describe all of the characteristics of the family. A short name, such as Marie Curie, quickly communicates the identity of an individual who can be distinguished from most other individuals without a lengthy description of her attributes, when and where she lived, and what she did.

In biology, names of organisms communicate information as well. When we talk about *Homo sapiens* (human beings) or *Felis catus* (house cats), the two-part scientific name (or binomial) conjures up lots of information and images. Imagine how difficult it would be to communicate ideas without names. Without the precision of names, every time we wanted to talk about an organism we would have to describe all of the characteristics that distinguish it from other organisms.

Taxonomy, or the scientific classification of organisms, attempts to group organisms by their evolutionary relatedness. Therefore, a name communicates information about the organism's characteristics as well as what creatures are related to it. The binomial assigned to each organism contains a genus designation, which indicates the broad group of which it is a member, and the species designation, which indicates the specialized group of organisms that are similar in most respects. In higher organisms, members of a species can intermate and produce fertile offspring whereas members of different species cannot.

When we isolate an organism from nature, we must describe its properties to determine its name. If the organism has been described before, there may be a wealth of information about it. If it has not been described before, then finding out what microorganisms it is related to may provide some key hints about its role in the natural world. This means describing what it looks like, what its habits are, who it is related to. It also requires learning how to keep it alive. The aim of this project is to help you develop the skills to work with and name unfamiliar organisms.

Challenge

In this project, you will be issued a nameless microbe to keep as a pet for the duration of the semester. It is your job to determine how to take care of and feed your pet microbe, to describe it, to determine its effect on other organisms, and to attempt to classify it. In addition, you must find out who else in the class has the same pet microbe. You will need to find a way to describe your pet microbe in such a way that others will recognize it.

Final report

Your final report on your pet microbe should contain the following:

- a pure culture of your pet microbe
- a description of your pet microbe
- a discussion of the effect of your pet microbe on plants, lower animals, or other microbes
- a classification of your pet microbe (fungus or bacterium? genus/species?)
- a list of the other students in the class who have the same pet microbe
- your future plans for your pet microbe

Assistance with pet microbes

We will help you work with your pet microbes. If you need culture media, plant material, or a microscope, please ask an instructor. We will also post a list of the students in the class, with a blank next to each name in which students can fill in the properties of their pet microbes. You can use this list to find other students with the same pet. Feel free to ask for help or materials to care for your pet microbe at any time.

Experiment 1: Pet microbes
A lesson in taxonomy

In this experiment, students will investigate an unknown microorganism, observing and documenting its physical and behavioral characteristics and relationships with other organisms to help discover its identity.

The experiment will take place over many weeks, perhaps throughout the semester. It is a valuable exercise for reinforcing concepts learned in other experiments and lecture. Students will want to keep in mind that materials and techniques they will use and concepts they will learn elsewhere in the course may be helpful in identifying their pet microbes.

What students will learn

affection for biology, independence, curiosity, communication, taxonomy

One goal of the Pet Microbes exercise is for students to develop affection for an organism. Students who care about their subject want to learn more about it. Pet Microbes gives them an opportunity to get to know a microorganism slowly, carefully, and at their own initiative throughout the semester. To complete the assignment, students must learn basic ideas about taxonomy and morphology of microorganisms. In addition, they must learn practical skills that will enable them to communicate with other students, use a microscope, describe their observations, and test their hypotheses.

The most important feature of this experiment is the freedom it gives the students to follow their own interests and to be creative and curious. Some students are insistent about matching their pets to known taxa of bacteria or fungi and spend hours in the library combing microbiology textbooks. Others are fascinated with feeding anything they can find to their microbe or feeding their microbe to other organisms. Still others sit glued to the microscope, enthralled with the mysterious new world they have discovered. Pet Microbes helps students find their individual styles of doing biology.

Learning highlights and conceptual challenges

forming attachments; compassion, caring, curiosity; "Where do I start?"

Though a microbe might seem to make a strange pet, the idea of having a pet microbe captures students' imaginations and appeals to their sense of humor from the beginning. As the semester progresses, students develop strong attachments to their microbes. The emotional investment is evident in their requests for media to feed their pets, their concern about taking proper care of their pets, the intensity of their questions about their pets' behavior, and the amount of discussion about names for the pets. (We were surprised to learn at the end of one semester that most of the students had named their pets, giving them all human names!)

Although we advise our students to keep their pets in the classroom, some students take them home. These pets often suffer casualties in backpacks, on radiators, and in any number of situations associated with student life. In one extreme case, we had to comfort a student who arrived in class on the verge of tears because he ran over his pet with his bicycle. These experiences bring out a wonderful side of our students. They demonstrate compassion, caring, and curiosity. The emotional involvement inspires them to find out more about their pets and, in the process, they learn biology.

The open-endedness of the Pet Microbe exercise is its greatest strength, but for some students, its most intimidating challenge as well. The more confident students plunge in, acting like detectives, ferreting out their pets' secrets, demanding tools and information from their teachers, and inspecting the microbe pets of their classmates. The less confident students can be overwhelmed by the choices that confront them. These students may avoid dealing with the project or they may ask desperately, "But where do I start?" We have found that asking simple questions of these students gets them started. Questions such as, "Do you think it is a bacterium or a fungus? Why do you think that? How would you test your hypothesis?" are usually enough to direct a student who is overwhelmed by Pet Microbes. Remind your students that they are doing what biologists have done for centuries and will continue doing far into the future: They are describing a piece of the natural world previously unknown to them. About half-way through the semester, it is very helpful to distribute a list of the Latin names and brief descriptions of all the microbes in the class. This narrows the choices from all organisms in the microbial world to a manageable set of possibilities. However, we strongly encourage teachers to avoid the temptation of distributing the list early in the semester because the challenge of dealing with the unknown is a powerful learning experience.

Materials needed for teacher preparations

For each student, prepare 1 microbe culture on 1 petri plate. Make some extras in case of lost or damaged plates. Any of the following microbes may be used:

- Bacterial cultures (see page 250 for sources):
  Bacillus thuringiensis
  Erwinia carotovora
  Pseudomonas aureofaciens
  Rhizobium tropici
  Xanthomonas campestris

- Fungal cultures (see page 251 for sources):
  Botrytis cinerea
  Colletotrichum trifolii
  Fusarium graminearum
  Rhizoctonia spp.
  Saccharomyces cerevisiae
  Trichothecium roseum

HINTS: These microorganisms are generally safe to humans but should not be ingested. Students like microbes with colorful, interesting growth. **Avoid *Rhizopus*. It has aerial spores and will contaminate everything!**

- Potato dextrose agar plates for growing fungal cultures (pages 229, 249)
- Nutrient agar plates for growing bacterial cultures (pages 228, 249)

Materials needed for students

- microscope (compound and dissecting scopes, 1 each for the class is ideal)
- culture plates with a variety of media, such as nutrient agar, potato dextrose agar, PDA+streptomycin, V-8 agar, Rose Bengal agar, 50% tryptic soy agar

Any or all of these would be helpful:
- plant materials
- soybean looper larvae
- other microbes to test for antagonism, such as *E. coli* or the other pet microbes

Characteristics of pet microbes

Organism	Characteristics in culture	Interactions with plants or animals	Interactions with other microbes
Fungi *Botrytis cinerea*	Gray and white fuzzy growth on PDA; forms grape-like clusters of spores	Causes rot of onion bulbs, storage rot of many vegetables	
Colletotrichum trifolii	White, fuzzy growth on PDA; orange areas where spores form; spores oval	Causes anthracnose on alfalfa	None noted
Fusarium graminearum	White/pink fuzzy growth on PDA; brilliant red pigment; spores canoe-shaped with vertical lines	Causes grain rot on corn	Inhibits *Xanthomonas*; inhibited by *Bacillus*
Rhizoctonia solani	White, fuzzy growth on PDA; mycelia branched	Causes root rot of young seedlings of pea	
Saccharomyces cerevisiae	Cream-colored colonies on PDA; cells spherical	Ferments plant material; produces CO_2 from sugar, grape juice, and bread dough	
Trichothecium roseum	Peach/salmon growth on PDA; abundant spores - oval, bisected latitudinally	Grows abundantly on bread	
Bacteria *Bacillus thuringiensis*	Cream-colored, irregular, matte colonies on NA; heat resistant spores (will grow after boiling)	Kills soybean loopers and other Lepidopteran insects	Inhibits *Fusarium*; inhibited by *Pseudomonas*
Erwinia carotovora	Shiny, white colonies on NA; grows with or without O_2 (under mineral oil overlay)	Causes soft rot of vegetables—potato, cucumber slices	Inhibits *Fusarium*
Pseudomonas aureofaciens	Orange colonies on NA; metallic sheen on TSIAA	None known	Inhibits *Bacillus*; produces antibiotic
Rhizobium tropici	Shiny, white colonies on NA	Induces nitrogen-fixing nodules on roots of bean plants	

Xanthomonas campestris	Shiny, yellow colonies on NA; produces abundant polysaccharide (slime)	Causes black rot of cabbage	Inhibited by *Fusarium*

Teacher preparations prior to lab period

Fourteen days before the lab period

1. Prepare enough potato dextrose agar plates for fungal cultures and/or nutrient agar plates for bacterial cultures so that each student will have one culture plate. Make a few extras.

Twelve days before the lab period

1. Transfer the fungi to the PDA plates.

2. Number all plates sequentially. Make a master list with plate numbers and identities of microorganisms so you will know which organisms are supposed to be growing on the plates.

Four days before the lab period

1. Transfer the bacteria to nutrient agar plates.

2. Number all plates sequentially. (Make sure the bacterial plates have different numbers from the fungal plates.) Make a master list with plate numbers and identities of microorganisms so you will know which organisms are supposed to be growing on the culture plates.

Note: You will need to allow time during many lab sessions throughout the semester for students to work with their pet microbes. As they learn techniques and information from new experiments in the course, they will want to apply them to the identification of their pets.

How to guide students

During class

1. Allow students to select their pet microbes and remind each student to record the number of his/her culture plate.

Data collection

Trait	Materials/possible expts	Data
description	microscopes, eyes	descriptive
growth habits	media	growth rates, diameter of colonies, total area per unit time
interactions with plants/animals	fruits, vegetables, seeds, plants, insects	rotting, killing, wilting
interactions with other microorganisms	different media, other microbes	clear areas between colonies indicating growth inhibition; overgrowth of some colonies on others; growth enhancement of organisms

Troubleshooting and dealing with problems

Problem	Solution
apparently contaminated culture	1. Be sure that the organism has not simply entered a different growth phase with a different color or growth habit. 2. If the plate really is contaminated, have the student streak a fresh plate with a bit of the culture taken from an area as far from visible contamination as possible. 3. Use media inhibitory to bacteria (Rose Bengal) or fungi (cycloheximide).

Questions to guide discussion

- ♦ Is the pet microbe a bacterium or fungus? How do you know?
- ♦ What is your hypothesis? How can you test it?
- ♦ What are the key distinguishing characteristics of a bacterium as opposed to those of a fungus?
- ♦ How can you find out what effect your microbe has on plants or animals?
- ♦ What would you like to know about your pet?
- ♦ Where might your microbe live in the natural world?

Sources of information

Students will need access to good, comprehensive texts in microbiology, plant pathology, and mycology to help them identify their pet microbes. We have included examples of texts our students have found to be helpful.

♦ Agrios, George N. (1988) *Plant Pathology*. San Diego, CA: Academic Press, Inc.

♦ Brock, Thomas D., Michael T. Madigan, John M. Martinko, and Jack Parker (1994) *Biology of Microorganisms*, 7th ed. Englewood Cliffs, NJ: Prentice Hall.

♦ Kendrick, Bryce (1992) *The Fifth Kingdom*, 2nd ed. Newburyport, MA: Focus Texts.

Experiment 2: Bacterial ice nucleation: An unusual adaptation to the environment
A lesson in experimental design

One of the great challenges in science is separating what we *believe* to be true from what we *know* to be true. It is often easy to accept and integrate into our understanding of the world new information that is consistent with what we believe to be true. But science is full of surprises. Often new knowledge is in conflict with our beliefs, which may be based on religion, culture, past personal experience, or existing scientific knowledge. A vivid example of a society's reluctance to accept a new idea was the struggle to introduce the theory of the solar system, which was in conflict with the entrenched belief that the earth was the center of the universe. To gain acceptance for new ideas that challenge current beliefs, scientists must present logical arguments supported by well-designed and carefully executed experiments. The more an idea challenges the status quo, the greater the requirement for data to support the new concept.

Sometimes it is difficult for us to imagine how hard it was for people of another time to accept a new theory because that theory has now become so much a part of our own experience and, therefore, seems so obvious. For instance, the concept that contagious disease is caused by germs or microorganisms is familiar and integrated into 20th century experience. Therefore, it may be difficult to imagine the time when people preferred to believe that disease was caused by gods, weather, evil spirits, or bad luck. Clear, careful experiments convinced the world that bacteria do indeed cause disease. (See Experiment 5 for a discussion of this topic.)

The reluctance to accept new ideas and the power of good experiments is illustrated by the story of bacterial involvement in ice formation. At first it seems like a startling concept, so let us examine it in some detail.

At normal atmospheric pressure, pure water is a liquid above 0°C. Below -40°C, it is a solid that we know as ice. Between 0°C and -40°C, pure water will be a liquid unless it is provided with an **ice nucleus**, or template on which an ice crystal can be built. The better the ice nucleus (or the more it looks like an ice crystal), the higher the temperature at which the water will freeze. An ice crystal is the best ice nucleus and will nucleate freezing at 0°C, whereas dust particles are less efficient and will nucleate freezing at -8°C and below. One of the best ice nuclei is the bacterium *Pseudomonas syringae* (*Ps*), a common leaf-inhabitant in temperate environments. *Ps* will nucleate ice formation at temperatures as high as -2° or -3°C.

Ps has serious implications for agriculture. Without the bacterium on their leaves, many plants can withstand weather conditions in which the temperature dips a few degrees below 0°C. The water on the surface of the plant simply **supercools** (or cools below the freezing point without freezing) and when the air warms up, so does the plant. Supercooling usually does not damage plant tissue. However, if *Ps* is on the leaves of the plant, the bacterium can act as an ice nucleus, and ice crystals may form and damage the plant tissue. In contrast to supercooling, freezing is very damaging to plant tissue. The damage to leaf tissue can kill the plant or greatly reduce its productivity by decreasing the photosynthetic capacity of the plant. *Ps* is responsible for large crop losses during the times in the growing season when temperatures may drop below 0°C for short periods, such as at night.

Key concept

Certain bacteria can act as ice nuclei and promote ice formation, causing damage to plant tissue.

Challenge

You will be provided with a culture of *Ps*, water, a water bath at -6°C, and bean leaves. **Design an experiment to test whether *Ps* is active as an ice nucleus and to determine the effects of supercooling vs. ice formation on plant tissue.**

Key questions

☞ **Why do you think bacteria evolved the ability to nucleate ice formation?**

☞ **How did performing this experiment affect your understanding and acceptance of the concept of bacterial ice nucleation?**

☞ **Why do *Ps* bacteria on the leaf surfaces promote frost damage to plants?**

☞ **What is a "control" and how did you use a control in this experiment?**

Experiment 2: Bacterial ice nucleation: An unusual adaptation to the environment

A lesson in experimental design

In this experiment, students will examine the role of bacteria in ice formation. They will gain an understanding of the importance of solid experimental evidence in the acceptance of new, and sometimes counterintuitive, ideas.

Bacterial ice nucleation is a simple experiment that can be completed and analyzed in a single class period. The students are given two hypotheses to test:

- Certain bacteria can serve as nuclei that initiate the formation of ice in supercooled water.
- Ice formation causes damage to plant leaves.

Students must design experiments to test the hypotheses and identify appropriate experimental treatments and controls. In this experiment, students are presented with the hypotheses or questions, leaving them free to focus on experimental design. This is a first step toward more complicated subsequent experiments in which they must develop their own hypotheses as well as the experiments to test them.

What students will learn

scientific method, controls, the wonder of biology

This exercise introduces students to the scientific method and how it is used to challenge our human biases about the way the world works. The students are presented with the concept of bacterial ice nucleation, a phenomenon that seems unbelievable to most people when they first encounter it. After designing and conducting a carefully controlled experiment that definitively shows that bacteria do, in fact, initiate the formation of ice, the students should discover the power of the scientific method, the irrefutability of good scientific data, and the wonder of biology.

Learning highlights and conceptual challenges

*The **bacterium** causes ice to form?!!!!!!!!!!!!!!!! Water freezes at -40°C? Say WHAT!!!!?*

The ice nucleation experiment is appropriate for the beginning of the semester because it is technically simple and the experimental treatments and controls are fairly obvious. In addition, it has a substantial "gee whiz" factor. The ice crystals form immediately after adding the bacteria and grow from the bacterial drop to the bottom of the test tube before your very eyes! Most people are amazed when they see bacterial ice nucleation for the first time. The immediate response from students is to demand to repeat the demonstration.

We have found two major challenges in teaching ice nucleation. First, most students do not understand, and initially will not believe, that pure water freezes at -40°C. Someone in class is bound to say, "Don't you mean 0°C?" The problem is that most of us have been taught about the freezing point of water *under equilibrium conditions*, i.e., when there is an ice crystal present. Given a perfect ice nucleus in pure water, the freezing point of water is 0°C. Most of us will never encounter really pure water so we will never observe water as a liquid below about -10°C. Many chemicals and contaminants, such as dust particles, will act as ice nuclei at temperatures below -5°C, though few are as effective as the ice nucleating bacteria, which are very active at -2° to -3°C. So be sure to stress that the freezing point of *pure* water is -40°C and that less pure water is unlikely to supercool below -8° to -10°C.

Make sure that students are convinced that supercooling does occur by having them read the temperature of the thermometer in the ice bath and note that the water is in a liquid state even though its temperature is below 0°C. Do not put a thermometer directly into the tube because many thermometers have irregular surfaces that act as ice nuclei, and the water in the tube may freeze and break the thermometer. Some students might have observed that the water in ice cube trays often goes below 0°C before it freezes. (Sometimes this analogy falls flat because none of the students have made ice cubes.)

The second challenge in this experiment is learning the definition of a control and how to choose the appropriate control in an experiment. Many students think that a control is a way of regulating or keeping constant the conditions of the experiment. The concept of eliminating variables is new to many of them. Usually, a series of questions starting with, "How will you know that. . ." helps them realize that to assign responsibility for ice formation to the bacteria, they must have the right controls.

Materials needed for teacher preparations

Pseudomonas syringae pathovar *syringae* Ice^+ culture (page 250)
Escherichia coli culture (page 250)
nutrient agar glycerol (NAG) slants - 2 for each group of students, plus some extras, (page 228)

1 transfer loop

Materials needed for students

Number per group:

1	*Pseudomonas syringae* pathovar *syringae* Ice^+ nutrient agar glycerol (NAG) slant
1	*Escherichia coli* nutrient agar glycerol (NAG) slant
5	bean leaves[1]
10	clean tubes about half full of distilled water
1	ice bath at -6°C (see page 34 for instructions on how to make an ice bath)

Supplies needed per group for ice bath:

	ice
300 ml	95% ethanol
	thermometer
	ice bucket

[1]Leaves of any highly frost-sensitive plants such as tomato, tobacco, or *Impatiens* will do. If you decide to use plant materials other than the ones suggested here, you should test them first for frost sensitivity.

Teacher preparations prior to lab period

Before the semester begins

1. Obtain a plate or broth culture of *Pseudomonas syringae* pathovar *syringae* that has the Ice^+ phenotype ***and***

2. Obtain a plate or broth culture of *Escherichia coli*. *E. coli* is a control to show that not all bacteria initiate ice nucleation.

Five days before the lab period

1. Streak enough NAG slants with either *Pseudomonas syringae* or *Escherichia coli* so that you will have one slant of each per group, plus a few extras. Incubate at room temperature for 48 hours.

2. Store the slants in the refrigerator until they are needed.

A few days before class

1. It is a good idea to check the ice-forming activity of the *Pseudomonas* culture. To do this, you will need to make up a -6°C ice bath and carry out the procedure described on page 34. When you put a few drops of the *Pseudomonas* suspension in a tube of supercooled water, ice should form within a few seconds if you have an active culture.

   Sometimes a *Pseudomonas* culture will not initiate ice formation even though you have used an Ice^+ bacterial strain. If ice does not form when you add your culture, test backup cultures and use the best ones for class.

A few hours before the lab period

1. Pipette 1 to 2 ml of distilled water over the surface of each slant. Agitate each tube on a Vortex mixer until the bacteria are detached from the slant surface and suspended in the distilled water. Pour the bacterial suspension from the slant culture into a clean test tube. Pour the bacterial suspension

from the *E. coli* culture into another clean test tube. Each group of students will be supplied with one tube of *Pseudomonas* suspension and one tube of *E. coli* suspension.

Two hours before the lab period

1. **Preparing the ice bath -** Make one -6°C ice bath for each group of students as follows:

   a. Fill a one-gallon ice bucket or styrofoam cooler about 2/3 full of crushed ice.

   b. Pour 200 to 300 ml of 95% ethanol into the ice and place a thermometer in the ice-ethanol mixture. Allow the bath to reach a temperature of -6°C.

   c. If the ice bath is not cold enough, add more ethanol. If it is too cold, add water or ice. To make sure the temperature is the same throughout the ice bath, stir the ice-ethanol mixture frequently and measure the temperature at various locations in the ice bath.

2. Place 10 clean tubes containing distilled water in each ice bath and make sure the ice bath temperature remains at -6°C.

   After about 30 minutes, the temperature of the water in the tubes should be approximately -6°C. The water in these tubes will be supercooled. Check the tubes for freezing. Some tubes may have contained an ice nucleus (scratches on the glass may provide an ice nucleus) and the water will freeze in these tubes. Remove frozen tubes.

3. Recheck the ability of the *Pseudomonas syringae* culture to cause ice formation by putting a few drops of the culture into one of the tubes of supercooled water. Ice should form within a few seconds.

How to guide students

During class

1. Students will design experiments to test the hypotheses they have been given or hypotheses they have generated on their own. The experiments should test for an association between a given treatment and a result and should eliminate other variables.

Possible hypotheses students might want to test

Given:
1. Certain bacteria cause ice nucleation in supercooled water.
2. Ice crystals are destructive to plant tissues.

Others:
3. *All bacteria* cause ice nucleation in cold water.
4. Supercooled water is destructive to plant tissues.

Examples of treatments and controls

A fundamental scientific concept students will learn by doing this experiment is the importance of using controls to pinpoint which variables affect experimental outcomes. Choosing the right controls is not always easy, but it is crucial for ruling out variables that are unrelated to observed outcomes.

1. A **positive control** will show whether it is possible to get the anticipated result under the experimental conditions used. An ice crystal should serve as an excellent ice nucleus at the temperatures used in this setup. When an ice crystal is added to a test tube of supercooled water, ice should form instantly.

2. A **negative control** will show that the anticipated result will not occur under every possible condition, but is associated with a particular variable. Neither dust, plant material, nor a few drops of the broth culture containing *Escherichia coli* should act as ice nuclei at the temperatures used in this experiment. When any of these are added, the supercooled water should remain in a liquid state.

3. Under the **experimental treatment** conditions, if the temperature of the ice bath remains evenly distributed at or below -6°C, a few drops of *Pseudomonas* added to a test tube of supercooled water should cause ice to form instantly.

4. **Other treatments or controls** Students might want to test other conditions for inducing ice nucleation, such as adding bacteria plus plant material, nutrient broth alone, a few drops of supercooled water, or other substances to the tubes of supercooled water.

Data collection

Experimental condition	Visual observation
Hypothesis 1: *Pseudomonas syringae* initiates ice nucleation.	
Treatment	
Pseudomonas	ice formation
Controls	
ice crystal	ice formation
E. coli	no ice formation
nutrient broth only	no ice formation
others	??
Hypothesis 2: Ice formation causes damage to plants.	
Treatment - plant materials with ice nuclei	limp, damaged plants
Control - plant materials in supercooled water	turgid, undamaged plants

Troubleshooting and dealing with problems

Problem	Possible explanation	Solutions
no ice formation	1. bacterial culture inactive	1. pretesting can avoid this
	2. ice bath too warm	2. add more ethanol to bath
	3. temperature not uniform throughout	3. stir ice bath and carefully check temperature at multiple locations
	4. not enough culture used	4. add more culture
	5. unknown	5. test the system by adding a chip of ice (the best ice nucleus)
ice forms with water alone	1. water tubes have been contaminated with *Pseudomonas*	1. try again with another tube
	2. tubes have scratches inside or are not clean	2. use clean, scratch-free tubes

Questions to guide discussion

To begin a discussion about what students expect to happen in this experiment, you could start with very open-ended questions such as these:

- What do you think you will observe?
- Why do you think this will happen?
- How will you know this is the right explanation and not something else?

However, open-ended questions are sometimes met with blank stares and furrowed brows. Students may need to be asked more specific questions, such as the following ones to help them aim their thoughts in the right direction and choose the right controls for their experiments:

- How will you tell whether it is the bacteria or the medium they are growing in that causes ice to form?
- Are you convinced that bacteria cause ice nucleation? Why?
- How can you tell whether it is cooling or ice formation that damages plant tissue?

Sources of information

Information about ice nucleation can be found in two scientific areas: Chemistry (the supercooling of water and ice formation) and microbiology (how and why *Pseudomonas syringae* is thought to function as an ice nucleus and the importance of ice nucleation in biotechnology). These references provide a good background.

◆ Brock, Thomas D., Michael T. Madigan, John M. Martinko, and Jack Parker (1994) *Biology of Microorganisms*, 7th ed. Englewood Cliffs, NJ: Prentice Hall.

◆ Gurian-Sherman, D. and S.E. Lindow (1993) Bacterial ice nucleation: Significance and molecular basis. *Federation of American Societies for Experimental Biology Journal*, 7(14): 1338-1343.

◆ Lee, R.E., G.J. Warren, and L.V. Gusta, eds. (1995) *Biological Ice Nucleation and its Applications*. St. Paul, MN: American Phytopathological Society Press.

Experiment 3: Bread, mold, and environment
A lesson in biology and the environment

An organism's potential is defined by its genes. Whether the organism achieves that potential is defined by its environment. Tree height is limited by water, people's heights are influenced by nutrition, the thickness of cats' fur is affected by light, flower color is affected by metals in the soil, bacterial behavior is affected by the presence of other bacteria. Every organism responds to a profusion of signals from the physical, chemical, and biological environment that shape its anatomy, physiology, behavior, and longevity. The complexity of the interplay between the environment and genetic potential is exemplified by the debate over human intelligence and behavior. How much of who we are is defined by our genes and how much is a result of our environment?

The environment is a critical player in the occurrence of human disease. For example, people who live in crowded cities are more likely to develop tuberculosis than are rural people, and the incidence of dental caries caused by bacteria is influenced by ingestion of certain elements and compounds. The environment also affects plant disease. For example, the Great Famine that resulted from loss of the potato crop in Ireland occurred in the year 1848, which had a very wet, cold growing season. Irish potato plants succumbed to a pathogen that requires cold, wet conditions to infect plants.

An infectious pathogen and a susceptible host are not sufficient for disease to develop. The environment must play its part as well. Temperature, moisture, concentrations of chemicals, antagonistic or beneficial microbes, and numerous other factors must be aligned properly for the infection and spread of a pathogen. This concept is described by the **disease triangle**, which is a graphical representation of the contributions of the three partners—the pathogen, the host, and the environment—to the disease process.

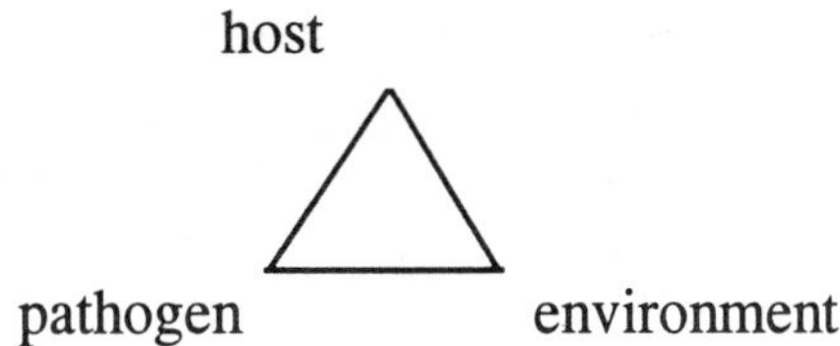

This experiment provides an analogy for the disease triangle. Instead of using a pathogen/host system, we will study the interaction between *Penicillium*, a fungus that causes bread mold, as the pathogen; bread, acting as the host; and the environment. The similarity to the disease triangle is that each partner plays a role in the growth of the mold on the bread. The analogy is not perfect, however, because disease requires a living host, and bread is not alive.

Penicillium is a famous genus of fungi whose members have many different properties. The first antibiotic discovered by Alexander Fleming in 1929 was **penicillin**, produced by a species of this fungus. Other species of *Penicillium* produce molecules that are toxic to humans, known as mycotoxins. Some species of *Penicillium* are plant pathogens, some are responsible for the flavor of certain kinds of cheese, and many grow on plant products in storage. The focus of this experiment is *Penicillium notatum*, a common mold that grows on bread.

Key concept

Growth and behavior of organisms are influenced by the environment.

Challenge

You will be provided with white bread, whole wheat bread, and sourdough bread and a culture of *Penicillium notatum*. **Develop a hypothesis about the environmental factors that might affect the ability of *Penicillium* to grow on bread and design an experiment to test your hypothesis. We will do our best to provide or construct the environments you need for your experiments.**

Key questions

☞ How does growth of mold on bread differ from disease of a living host?

☞ What might be the benefits or risks associated with preservatives in bread?

☞ What factors in the physical environment play a critical role in plant disease?

☞ Based on the disease triangle, what do you think are the major strategies for preventing plant disease?

☞ How might the *biological* environment affect the ability of a plant to be infected by a pathogen?

☞ What factors in the bread might affect growth of the fungus on it?

☞ What environmental factors might affect growth of the fungus on bread?

Experiment 3: Bread, mold, and environment
A lesson in biology and the environment

In this experiment, students will explore a model of the disease triangle, illustrating the interaction of a pathogen, a host, and the environment in causing disease.

The experiment uses materials that are so familiar and is based upon observations that are so simple it may seem that little of importance can be learned from doing it. But do not be fooled by the experiment's simplicity. It provides an open-ended opportunity for posing hypotheses. Often this proves to be the students' favorite experiment of the semester because it allows them such a broad creative, outlet for their ideas.

From this simple experiment, students will learn concepts that are basic to scientific experimentation—using controls to rule out confounding variables and devising measurements to obtain quantitative data—as well as some new ideas about chemicals in food and the environment.

What students will learn

the environment, "chemicals" vs. "natural," quantification and variability

Biological concepts: The bread mold experiment highlights two biological concepts. The first is the role of the environment in mediating interactions between organisms. This principle is key for understanding disease, organismal development, and the role of the environment in realizing genetic potential. The bread mold experiment can be linked to lecture material on ecology, environmental biology, epidemiology, or global change to make the connection between changes in the environment and effects on individual organisms or interactions between organisms.

The second concept is the practical issue of chemicals in food. Many students enter our classes with the attitude that "chemicals are bad." We address this idea with discussions of the fact that living things are comprised of chemicals, that many "natural" chemicals are extremely toxic, and that some synthetic chemicals used in food production and preservation reduce our consumption of nasty fungal by-products such as mycotoxins. If bread with preservatives and "natural," preservative-free bread are used in the experiment, the bread mold exercise can provide a graphic demonstration of the power of preservatives. Discussion following the bread mold experiment is often quite heated and vigorous—the students are adamant in their opinions about the food they eat, and their emotions draw them into considering chemistry, biology, and safety issues in a critical light.

Experimental concepts: The bread mold experiments are simple to design and conduct. This is intentional. The basic simplicity enables the students to spend their mental energy tackling two of the toughest concepts in biological research: quantification and variability. The students quickly realize that their results cannot be described in simple plus or minus terms. (Was there growth or no growth?) Instead they see gradations of mold growth. The bread will often be partially covered, and the different treatments may result in different amounts of coverage. This leads the students to develop methods for measuring the amount of coverage. Some use a subjective rating scale that indicates the density of mold growth, some divide the bread into quadrants and count the number of quadrants that are covered by mold growth, and some attempt to determine the surface area covered by growth. They come to grips with the challenge of measuring and the compromises that are inherent in deciding to use one method or another.

More importantly, the students observe variability in biology. No two slices of bread have exactly the same amount of mold growth. With some careful questioning, the students can usually be led to the concept of replication as a way of ensuring accurate measurements in a variable system. We consider the variability that is inherent in biological phenomena to be one of the most important concepts for students to understand. They will understand the concept by discovering it. Throughout the rest of the experiments they conduct, they will uncover variability in the biological events themselves as well as variability in their own ability to control the conditions of the experiment. Awareness of variability will lead to a better understanding of biology and the limitations and cautions associated with biological research.

Learning highlights and conceptual challenges

familiarity; simplicity; experimental design; controls, controls, controls

The key attraction of "Bread Mold" is that it deals with food in a recognizable form—with mold growing on it. When students see their results, someone is bound to say, "Looks like my refrigerator!" The familiarity and the fact that the experiment deals with food, which seems to have intrinsic fascination for most people, make this an appealing experiment.

The greatest highlight for us is watching the students discover the need for quantification and the issue of variability. People have such a tendency to want the world to be simple and consistent that quantitative concepts and the variability in biology and experimentation are difficult to teach. "Bread Mold" is a first step in helping students deal with these issues.

Perhaps the greatest challenge for the students with "Bread Mold" is in experimental design. Some students immediately state a hypothesis and a clear experimental strategy to test it, whereas many students become lost in the morass of possibilities. "Bread Mold" is much more open-ended than "Ice Nucleation," and some students are intimidated by the choices available to them. Still others want to test many parameters at once (temperature, light, **and** moisture—all with three slices of bread!?) and forget that without all of the appropriate controls and replication, their data will be uninterpretable. It is important to help the students focus on testable hypotheses, inclusion of proper controls, and isolation of variables.

Materials needed for teacher preparations

1 *Penicillium notatum* culture (page 251)
potato dextrose agar (PDA) transfer plates (one per group) (page 249)
sterile distilled water (500 ml per group)
sterile 300-ml plastic plant sprayer bottles (2 per group)
units with various temperatures for incubation—freezer (-20°C), refrigerator (4°C), room temperature (37°C), incubator (40°C)
clear plastic sandwich bags
brown paper lunch bags
oat seeds to create anaerobic conditions (page 48)
desiccator or large jar with tight lid
alcohol burner
ethanol for flame sterilization
10% bleach solution
cardboard box "hood" to reduce contamination of other cultures with *P. notatum* spores

Materials needed for students

Number per group:
5–10 small plastic bags
5–10 sterile paper towels
1 sterile plastic plant sprayer bottle containing 250 ml of sterile water
1 sterile plastic plant sprayer bottle containing 250 ml of *Penicillium* suspension
1 bread piece each: sourdough, "natural" whole wheat, whole wheat with preservatives, commercial white bread with preservatives, Twinkies®

Teacher preparations prior to lab period

Before the semester begins

1. Obtain a culture of *Penicillium notatum* and transfer it to enough PDA transfer plates to have 1 per group.

One day before the lab period

1. **Sterilization procedures -** Sterilize plant sprayer bottles by rinsing with 10% bleach, followed by several rinses with sterile water. To sterilize glass rods, soak for 2-3 minutes in ethanol and then flame, or soak for 20 minutes in 10-30% bleach.

2. **Preparing water sprayer bottles -** Dispense approximately 250 ml of sterile, distilled water into a sterile plant sprayer bottle. You will need 1 bottle for each group of students. **Do this before you work with the *Penicillium* culture to avoid contaminating the sterile water bottle with mold spores.**

3. **Preparing *Penicillium* sprayer bottles -** Pour approximately 3 ml of sterile, distilled water onto the surface of a sporulating *Penicillium* culture. Gently scrape the surface of the agar plate with a sterile, glass rod to dislodge the spores. Pour the resulting mixture into a sterile plastic plant sprayer bottle.

   Repeat this process 2 additional times.

   Dilute the liquid in the sprayer bottle to approximately 200 ml. The final spore suspension should be dark blue-green in color. You will need 1 bottle for each group of students.

How to guide students

During class

1. Supply students with a variety of breads. One piece of each kind per group should be sufficient. Groups can cut these into smaller pieces for use in different treatment conditions. Commercial breads containing preservatives and Twinkies® sponge cakes inhibit fungal growth to a high degree. Sourdough bread inhibits fungal growth to a lesser extent. Organic whole wheat and vegetable breads will usually become well-colonized by *Penicillium*.

2. A control for certain experiments might include spraying some of the bread pieces with sterile water only.

3. **Important point: Students should spray spore suspensions only after all spraying with sterile water alone is finished. This will reduce the possibility of contaminating bread sprayed with sterile water.**

4. The students should put each bread piece in a plastic sandwich bag before spraying. They should spray the bread thoroughly so that each piece is covered with either the spore suspension or sterile water. Once the bread pieces have been sprayed, the plastic bags should be tied tightly.

   To further reduce contamination of the lab with *Penicillium* spores that will lead to problems in future classes, you could have students spray their spore suspensions inside a cardboard box or hood.

5. It is easy to provide a variety of environmental conditions for incubating bread/mold samples.

Condition	**Environment**
cold	Freezers, refrigerators
warm	Incubators, high shelves in the classroom
humid	Place a sterile paper towel saturated with sterile water in the plastic bag with bread.
constant darkness	Place the plastic bag inside a brown paper bag.
anaerobic	Line the bottom of a desiccator with moist oat seeds. Make a small hole in the plastic bag containing the bread sample and place the plastic bag in the desiccator. Seal the desiccator, and keep it in a dark place. The oat seeds will remove oxygen from the air inside the desiccator.

6. Students should be encouraged to develop a semi-quantitative rating of the amount of mold on the various bread samples, such as estimating the proportion of the surface area of the bread covered by mold (see Data collection, page 49).

Possible hypotheses students might want to test

Remember that hypotheses need to be kept simple so that they can be tested.

1. External environmental conditions:
   Warmer temperatures favor mold growth.
   High humidity favors mold growth.

2. Environmental conditions within the bread itself:
   Mold grows best on bread that does not contain preservatives.

Data collection

An important concept for students to learn in this experiment is how to quantify observations to make them objective. In the Ice Nucleation experiment students observed whether ice formed or did not form under various test conditions. However, in most of science there is much more to be observed than simple dichotomous results. Scientists often want to know how great an effect was produced by a given experimental condition, which condition produced the largest effect, or whether two experiments yielded comparable results. To answer questions such as these, researchers must be able to describe experimental observations quantitatively. In this experiment, students are looking at mold growth. They need to be able to record how much or how little growth occurred under various environmental conditions. Here are some ways of quantifying that growth:

Experimental condition	Quantitative Data
Mold growth	1. Examine the total area for each treatment condition. Grade the mold coverage for each treatment on a 1 to 5 scale. 2. Percent coverage - This is easier to do for smaller areas, so students should divide the total area of the bread into eighths or some convenient fraction, estimate the percent of mold growth on each of the fraction areas, and compute the average percent coverage.

Troubleshooting and dealing with problems

Problem	Possible explanation	Solution
too much mold growth to measure	bread samples incubated too long	shorten incubation time
	spore concentration too high	dilute spore suspension
no difference in growth for different conditions	breads all have preser-vatives or none do	provide wider selection of breads
	insufficient variation in environment	use more extreme conditions: very dry, cold (-20°C), or hot (>45°C); ideal = moist at 37°C

Questions to guide discussion

- What controls do you need?
- If you do not include the sterile water control, what will you *not* be able to conclude?
- If all of your bread pieces have some mold on them, how will you decide whether there are differences among treatments?

Plant Pathogen Option: If you prefer to have students study the plant disease triangle with a real pathogen/host system, *Pythium* spp., a pathogen that causes damping-off in seeds and seedlings, and any large, commercially available seeds, such as soybeans or peas, provide an excellent model system. Unlike many pathogens that invade and grow within plants where they cannot be observed, *Pythium* is visible and measurable as it grows over the surface of seeds.

Students can test any of a number of hypotheses describing the optimal environmental conditions for pathogen growth (moisture, temperature, light, etc.), or the effects of the pathogen on the host (altered seed germination rates, reduced germination, susceptibility to secondary infections, bacterial or other fungal growth, or rotting as evidenced by color changes and odors).

Sources of information

♦ Kendrick, Bryce (1992) *The Fifth Kingdom*, 2nd ed. Newburyport, MA: Focus Texts.

♦ *Penicillium and Acremonium* (1987) Biotechnology Handbooks, vol. 1, John F. Peberdy, ed., New York, NY: Plenum Press. [a comprehensive treatment of taxonomy, morphology, physiology, genetics, chemistry and biosynthesis of penicillins and cephalosporins, secondary metabolites and extracellular enzymes]

♦ Raper, Kenneth B. and Charles Thom (1949) *A Manual of the Penicillia*. Baltimore, MD: The Williams and Wilkins Company. [old but an interesting historical overview of early penicillin production]

♦ Stanier, Roger Y., John L. Ingraham, Mark L. Wheelis, and Page R. Painter (1986) *The Microbial World*, 5th edition. Englewood Cliffs, NJ: Prentice-Hall, pp. 666–671.

Experiment 4: Responses to stimuli by simple animals

A lesson in animal behavior

All organisms respond to their environments. One of the distinguishing characteristics of animals is their ability to move in response to stimuli that originate from within their own bodies or from the environment. An animal moving rapidly toward an object it recognizes as food, curling into a ball upon encountering a harmful chemical, or learning from one experience how to react in a future encounter with a similar situation are examples from the repertoire of responses known as animal behavior. Even the simplest and smallest animals exhibit behaviors within their own sensory capabilities. Sow bugs stop moving and curl up when they are touched, bees communicate to other bees the location of a food source, and earthworms and flour beetles learn to negotiate mazes.

In nature, specific behaviors that make it more likely an animal will find food and escape danger, and therefore, reproduce, increase the animal's reproductive fitness. Some of the best-studied behaviors are migration, mating rituals, and territoriality. Successful or adaptive behaviors improve the animal's chances for survival and increase the likelihood that the animal will pass on its genes to future generations. Among the genes an animal gives to its offspring are those that control components of behavior. Thus, behaviors are themselves subject to natural selection pressures.

One of the most challenging areas of animal behavior is distinguishing between **learned** and **innate** behaviors. Innate behaviors are those that are programmed into the animal and do not need to be taught or observed. For example, many mammals have an innate response to snakes that causes them to jump or flee. In contrast, to learn a behavior an animal must have the inborn physical or, in some cases, mental ability to learn it, but then receive instruction, demonstration, or reinforcement. You will never be able to teach a nematode to speak because it lacks both speech organs and the mental capacity. Humans have both the organs and mental capacity for speech, but they will not learn to speak English without the presence of English-speaking people.

The most simple form of learned behavior is **habituation**, which is when an animal learns *not* to respond to a stimulus. For example, the *Hydra*, an invertebrate, initially contracts when touched, but after repeated touching it ceases to respond. More complex animals learn more complex behavior. Birds learn to sing and wolves learn to hunt in a pack. When we study animals in the wild or people in their normal lives, it is difficult to separate learned from innate behavior because we usually cannot determine the individual's past experience. In contrast, certain animals provide excellent laboratory models because we can follow the entire life of the animal in captivity and monitor its total life experience. A vast amount of knowledge about animal behavior has been derived from the study of simple organisms. Bacteria, paramecia, nematodes, and ants have been wonderful models for understanding the behavior of higher organisms.

In this experiment we will examine the behavior of a small free-living nematode, *Caenorhabditis elegans* or an insect, the soybean looper, *Pseudoplusia includens*. In nature, *C. elegans* inhabits soil and feeds on bacteria. Because of its small size and relative lack of complexity, *C. elegans* has served as a model for biologists studying a number of biological systems. The nematode's nervous system, consisting of only about 300 neurons, has been completely mapped by neurobiologists, and relationships between its behaviors and the responses of specific neurons have been documented. The soybean looper is a simple insect that is a pest in agricultural settings and has the advantage of growing on simple substrates and being highly responsive to environmental stimuli.

The behaviors that can be observed in any animal depend on the animal's ability to receive stimuli and exhibit a response. Though animals such as soybean loopers and *C. elegans* lack highly specialized sensory organs (*C. elegans* has no eyes; both the nematodes and loopers lack ears and noses, for example), they respond to a surprising number of stimuli including light, temperature, electric current, gravity, touch, and a variety of chemicals in their environment. The response to environmental stimuli centers around body movement. An inactive animal may begin to move when it encounters a stimulus. One that is moving may move faster or slower in response to a stimulus or stop moving altogether. In addition to changing its rate of movement, the nematode or looper may also exhibit directional movement, being either attracted toward or repelled away from a stimulus. Behaviorists refer to non-directional change in the rate of movement as **kinesis**; directional movement is called **taxis**.

Key concept

Animals behave in response to stimuli.

Challenge

You will be provided with soybean loopers, free-living soil nematodes, *Caenorhabditis elegans*, cultures of *Escherichia coli*, and some common, household substances. **Develop a hypothesis about the nematodes' or loopers' responses to food and other substances in their environment and design an experiment to test your hypothesis.**

Key questions

☞ **How might the behavior of the nematodes or loopers on a petri plate differ from their behavior in nature?**

☞ **How might attraction to or repulsion from certain chemicals help ensure loopers' or nematodes' chances for survival in nature?**

☞ **How might response to light or heat help ensure loopers' or nematodes' chances for survival in nature?**

☞ **How do you think a simple animal such as *C. elegans* is able to detect the presence of *E. coli* bacteria in its environment?**

☞ **How do you think a soybean looper can distinguish between a soybean plant and an oak tree?**

Experiment 4: Responses to stimuli by simple animals

A lesson in animal behavior

In this experiment students will examine the behavior of small, free-living soil nematodes or soybean loopers to observe how these animals respond when they encounter food and other substances.

Why do hummingbirds prefer red? Why are moths attracted to light? Why do cockroaches scuttle around in the dark? Why does a dog turn round and round before settling down on the carpet for a nap? How do squirrels figure out how to get on the feeder to eat the birdseed? These are examples of an amazing array of animal behaviors that pique our curiosity and prompt scientists to study why animals behave as they do. The more complex the animals, the more complex are the behaviors they exhibit. But simple animals also exhibit amazing behaviors, and they can serve as models, making it easier to understand the complex systems of complex animals.

This experiment features two simple animals that serve as biological models. *Caenorhabditis elegans* is a much-studied nematode that lives in soil and preys on bacteria and fungi, keeping microbe populations in check and contributing to soil quality. The soybean looper, *Pseudoplusia includens*, is an agricultural pest, causing extensive damage to soybeans and other plants.

In this experiment students will use their own careful observations of these animals to develop ways to quantify animal behavior, a more elusive task than they have dealt with so far.

What students will learn

animals behave, quantification, model systems

The exercise illustrates the fundamental issues in animal behavior as well as the problems with studying the phenomenon. The students will be challenged to think about the chemical, physical, and biological factors that might affect invertebrate behavior. Experimental design is crucial in this exercise since the students need to develop a method for quantifying behavior at the population level. Controls must be carefully chosen to distinguish random behavior from directed response. If the students choose to determine whether the animals can learn, the experimental issues are more difficult, with controls playing a different and central role in data interpretation. This experiment can be used to develop an appreciation for model systems. Point out to students the experimental and technical challenges of studying behavior of more complex organisms in the real world. (We will return to this topic in Experiment 11.)

Learning highlights and conceptual challenges

innate ≠ learned behavior; animal rights

The highlight of the exercise is the fun of watching the animals respond. There is something irresistibly funny and charming about watching a plateful of loopers all swaying in unison or nematodes making a mad dash for the bacteria on the other side of the petri plate. Expect some good laughs and wide-eyed surprise from this one.

The greatest challenge and the most important part of the experiment is backing up perceptions with real data. It may be obvious that the nematodes like the light or that the loopers look sleepy when they have been in the fridge for a while, but how do you measure this in a way that convinces other people? This will lead the students to develop ways to count, measure, or score behavior. It is a key lesson in objectivity and data collection.

Some students may object to working with the insects or nematodes either because they find the animals repulsive or because they think it is unethical to use animals in research. If a student does not want to handle the animals, help them find a task in the group that does not involve direct contact (designing the experiment, labeling plates, taking notes, or making solutions to test). If a student questions the ethics of working with the animals, use this as a springboard for discussion of ethics of animal use, the differences between animals and plants, and the differences between invertebrates and vertebrates. In general, the objection to use of invertebrates in research is not as emotionally loaded as discussions of use of mammals. Therefore, it is a relatively safe basis for a rational, balanced discussion of animal rights.

With small modifications, this experiment can be done either with free-living soil nematodes, *Caenorhabditis elegans*, or with soybean or cabbage loopers, or both can be used to compare the behaviors of two different kinds of animals under similar experimental conditions.

Materials needed for teacher preparations

Caenorhabditis elegans culture (page 251)
Escherichia coli culture (page 250)
nutrient agar plates (1 for each two groups) (page 228)
soybean or cabbage loopers (*Pseudoplusia includens* or *Trichoplusiani*, 2nd or 3rd) (page 250)[2]
water agar plates (about 12 per group) (page 231)
microcentrifuge tubes (page 250)
10-μm-pore filters (page 250)

Materials needed for students

Number per group:

5 microcentrifuge tubes containing about 100 *C. elegans* per tube
1 *E. coli* plate
water agar plates (these do not need to be sterile)
1 glass tubing (about 7 mm in diameter and 10 cm long for cutting wells in the agar)
test substances and conditions:[3]
inorganics—sodium chloride, potassium chloride, ammonia
organics—fructose, sucrose, glucose, vinegar, coffee, tea, foods
biologicals—pet microbes, plant leaves for loopers - potato, tomato, tobacco, eggplant, or grasses; controls are soybean or cabbage
environmental—light, heat, cold sources

[2]If you cannot locate loopers for this experiment, you can substitute tobacco hornworm larvae, *Manduca sexta*. *Manduca* is available from most educational supply companies.

[3]According to the literature, *C. elegans* is attracted to anions and cations, certain amino acids, alkaline pH values, and colonies of *E. coli*. They will also respond to temperature, light, touch, electric fields, and gravity. Loopers are attracted to soybean leaves and light, they slow down at 4°C.

Teacher preparations prior to lab period

Before the lab period

1. Obtain cultures of *C. elegans* and *E. coli*.

2. Obtain enough soybean or cabbage loopers to have about 8 for each test plate.

Eight days before the lab period

1. Prepare 1 nutrient agar plate for every 3 groups of students. With a glass rod, spread *E. coli* evenly over the agar on each plate. Incubate the plates overnight at room temperature.

Seven days before the lab period

1. Inoculate each culture plate with 5 to 10 *C. elegans*. Incubate at 20°C.

One to four hours before the lab period

1. Pour about 5 ml of tap water onto the agar surface of each plate. Swirl the water to loosen the nematodes. Pour the nematode suspension over a 10-μm-pore filter. Pour 3 tap water rinses through the filter to remove *E. coli* from the nematodes. Wash the nematodes off the filter and into a test tube. Centrifuge the nematode suspension for 10 seconds at low speed. Suspend the nematodes in 0.5 ml of tap water and count under a dissecting microscope. Each agar plate should yield about 2,000 nematodes.

   Put about 100 nematodes in 50 μl of tap water in microcentrifuge tubes and cap the tubes. The students will need one microtube for each test condition.

   Repeat this procedure for each of the nematode culture plates.

   Nematodes suspensions can be stored up to half a day in the cold. If they are kept at room temperature, put them in a shallow dish, swirling the dish occasionally to provide oxygen.

How to guide students

During the first lab period

1. **Testing *C. elegans* for attraction or repulsion to substances:** Using a waterproof marker, the students should mark the bottom of each water agar plate, dividing it into four quadrants. With the glass tubing, they should remove a plug of agar from the center of each quadrant to make a well. The test substances will be placed in the wells.

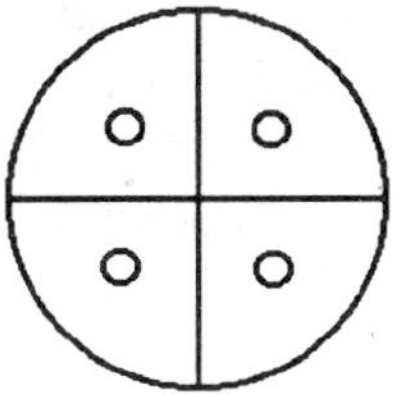

The students should label the quadrants with the names of the chemicals they want to test. They should then place 8 to 10 μl of test substance in each well. One well should be left empty as a control. The plates should remain undisturbed at room temperature for 10 to 30 minutes to allow the test substances to diffuse through the agar.

2. To test the attraction of *C. elegans* to living bacteria, the students should scrape *E. coli* from the surface of a culture plate with a glass rod. Suspend the bacteria in about 0.5 ml of tap water. Place 8 to 10 μl of the suspension into test wells. (Pet microbes or other microorganisms used in the course can also be tested in this way.) Allow the plates to remain undisturbed at room temperature for 10 to 30 minutes to allow exudates to diffuse through the agar.

3. Next the students should carefully pour or pipette the nematodes from one of the microcentrifuge tubes into the center of each test plate. They should observe the nematodes under a dissecting microscope and note the distribution of the worms on the plate surface at 15-minute intervals.

4. **Testing loopers for attraction or repulsion to substances:** The students should set up water agar plates as for the experiment with *C. elegans*. They should place about 8 loopers in the center of each test plate. Alternatively, loopers can be placed in each of several closed vessels containing a choice of different plant materials to determine which plant is most attractive. (We call this the cafeteria experiment.)

Possible hypotheses students might want to test

1. *C. elegans* (loopers) can perceive certain chemicals and alter their behavior in response to the chemicals by moving toward or away from the source.

2. *C. elegans* (loopers) are attracted toward colonies of *E. coli* (cabbage or soybean plants), a common food source.

3. *C. elegans* (loopers) are attracted toward/repelled from (students supply names of chemicals to test).

4. Loopers prefer soybeans to tobacco leaves.

Data collection

Descriptive: location of the nematodes (loopers) on the plate with respect to the test substances, amount of activity or movement, types of movement or behavior

Quantitative: number of nematodes (loopers) in each quadrant at 15-minute intervals.

Troubleshooting and dealing with problems

Problem	Possible explanation	Solution
nematodes or loopers show only random movement	might not have a good enough attractant	use *E. coli* for *C. elegans* and soybean leaves for loopers as positive controls
nematodes or loopers stop moving	they might be dead or paralyzed	check the chemicals to determine whether they are toxic to the animals

Questions to guide discussion

◆ Can you test a chemical that attracts and one that repels nematodes (loopers) on the same test plate? How would you set it up?

◆ What environmental conditions would you want to control when conducting this experiment? Would it make a difference if you did the experiment in the dark or in the light?

◆ How might the nematodes' (loopers') responses to specific substances help ensure their chances for survival?

◆ If the nematodes move toward *E. coli* and they also move toward your pet microbe, can you say for sure that your pet is *E. coli*? Why or why not?

Sources of information

- Croll, Neil A. (1970) *The Behavior of Nematodes: Their Activity, Senses and Responses*. New York: St. Martin's Press.
- Dusenbery, David B. (1980) Behavior of free-living nematodes. In: *Nematodes as Biological Models, Vol. 1, Behavioral and developmental models*. Bert M. Zuckerman, ed. New York: Academic Press.
- Matthews, R.W. and J.R. Matthews (1978) *Insect Behavior*. New York: John Wiley and Sons. (See Chapter 4 for feeding behavior.)
- Romoser, W.S. and J.G. Stoffoloano, Jr. (1994) *The Science of Entomology*. Dubuque, Iowa: Wm. C. Brown Publishers. (See page 440 for discussion of biological control.)
- Thomas, James H. (1994) The mind of a worm. *Science*, 264: 1698–1699.

Experiment 5: Koch's postulates and experimental evidence

A lesson in correlation vs. causation

All people are scientists. We all make observations, look for correlations, develop hypotheses, and then test them. From the beginning of human existence people have been teasing apart the world and advancing the knowledge of how things work by searching for relationships between events. This is such a common part of our everyday lives that many of us do not realize we are doing it. We notice, for example, that when the soil looks dry, our tomato plants wilt—a simple observation. So we develop a hypothesis, such as lack of water causes plants to wilt. We might do an experiment to see if watering the tomato plants prevents wilting. An essential step is observing a simple **correlation**, but the experiment establishes that the lack of water is **causal** to wilting. If the water does not reverse the symptoms, we look elsewhere for cause of the wilting.

In the example in the previous paragraph, the answer was pretty clear because we all know that plants need water, but the obvious answer is not always the right answer. It is all too easy to be misled by assuming that a relationship is causal based on a simple correlation. One of the most difficult challenges in biology is to determine whether events that appear to be related are **causally associated**. Just because two things happen in the same place or at the same time does not mean that one causes the other. For example, there may be an association or **correlation** between the number of telephone poles in a geographical region and the frequency of cancer in that region, but that does not mean that telephone poles cause cancer. Careful experimentation is needed to separate **causation** from **correlation**. An instructive example of such experimentation is the story about the discovery of the role of microbes in causing disease.

To understand the story, we must examine the context in which the experiments were done. As we discussed in Experiment 2, it is not always easy to assimilate new discoveries into our body of knowledge and beliefs. Conversely, it can also be difficult for us to try to imagine what it must have been like in the past when people did not have some of the knowledge that we now take for granted, such as the concept that germs cause disease. It was only through clear evidence from thoughtfully designed experiments that we came to adopt what is now referred to as the germ theory of disease.

By the mid 19th century, the French scientist Louis Pasteur had conducted extensive studies of the role of bacteria in fermentation, and he had shown conclusively that while germs could travel through the air, they were not capable of spontaneous generation. There was also a prevailing assumption at the time that microbes were in some way connected with disease, but whether their presence was a requirement for disease or a result of disease was not clear. Furthermore, many infected tissues contained more than one type of microorganism. This made it difficult to define with certainty the role played in disease by any particular type of bacterium.

The work of Pasteur and others, improved techniques in microscopy, and perhaps most important, the discovery of semi-solid culture media all paved the way for a German physician, **Robert Koch**, to demonstrate for the first time in 1875 that a specific type of bacterium was responsible for a specific disease.

Koch had been studying anthrax disease in sheep, and he noticed that certain rod-shaped bacteria and their spores were characteristically found in the tissues of the sick livestock. He meticulously isolated these bacteria, which he named *Bacillus anthracis*, and grew pure cultures of them in a culture medium consisting of the aqueous humor of cattle or rabbit eyeballs. Next, he introduced the bacteria from the cultures into healthy rabbits. When the rabbits subsequently developed symptoms of anthrax, Koch again isolated the bacteria from the tissues of the rabbits and observed them under the microscope to confirm that they were indeed the same ones he had seen in his original culture.

The steps he used are now known as **Koch's postulates.** Meeting the criteria laid down by Koch is referred to as "satisfying Koch's postulates" and is considered the standard evidence required to show that a microorganism plays a causal role in a particular disease.

Koch's postulates

1. Observe a consistent association between the disease condition and the presence of a specific microbe.

2. Isolate the microbe and grow it in pure culture outside of the original host.

3. Inoculate a healthy, susceptible host with the pure culture and observe disease symptoms that are the same as those in the original host.

4. Isolate the microbe from the inoculated host and demonstrate that it is the same as the microbe from the original diseased organism.

Note: These criteria must be met to firmly establish that a microbe causes disease.

Key concepts

Specific microbes cause specific diseases in plants.

Satisfying Koch's postulates provides rigorous proof that a specific microbe is responsible for a particular disease.

Experiments provide a test for a hypothesis that observations alone cannot provide.

Challenge

You will be provided with a diseased plant and a healthy plant, a microscope and slides, an improvised mortar and pestle to grind up plant tissue, and petri plates with media on which to grow cultures of microbes from the plant. **Design an experiment based on Koch's postulates to identify the microbe that is responsible for the disease.**

Note: See "Pure cultures from single colonies" on page 220 for help with culturing methods.

Key questions

☞ **What is disease? How can it be distinguished from other conditions?**

☞ **What was the cause of the symptoms in your unhealthy plant? What evidence do you have?**

☞ **Why couldn't you simply grind up some of your initial plant tissue, spread it on a second (healthy) plant and see if the disease appeared? Assuming it did appear, what would that show and what would that fail to show?**

☞ **Why is it important to grow a pure culture and to inoculate with bacteria from a single colony?**

☞ **What if the disease-causing pathogen does not grow outside of the host? How might this have changed Koch's understanding of infectious agents? Can you think of any examples?**

Experiment 5: Koch's postulates and experimental evidence

A lesson in correlation vs. causation

In this exercise, students will determine the cause of disease in a plant.

One of the most difficult challenges biologists face is how to distinguish whether two phenomena are related by correlation or causation. Robert Koch faced this challenge in determining the cause of anthrax. His careful experimental work resulted in Koch's postulates, a logical progression of steps to show that a specific disease is caused by a specific organism.

This experiment employs familiar plant disease systems to illustrate Koch's postulates. The students will discover how to use logical thinking to find the real pathogen in a jungle of microbes by isolating microbes from the sick plant and determining which one induces the disease symptoms in a new host plant.

What students will learn

correlation vs. causation, experimental design, deductive reasoning

In this experiment students will learn about the experimental evidence required to establish that a given microorganism causes a specific disease. The exercise emphasizes the difference between correlation and causation and demonstrates the value of carefully designed experiments in establishing causal relationships. The exercise introduces students to plant disease (many are surprised to find out that plants get diseases!) and hones their skills in experimental design, logic, and deduction.

Learning highlights and conceptual challenges

"How can I figure out who is the pathogen?" *"Oh, I get it!"*

We call this a light bulb experiment because it so often makes a light go on in the students' minds. Although we present Koch's postulates in lectures and in assigned reading, it is always in the lab that the students discover for themselves the simple but powerful logic that embodies the postulates and the experiments derived from them. A key feature of the experiment is that the plant material has not been surface-disinfested before the students begin to isolate the pathogens, making conditions of the exercise more like those found in actual experimental situations. Therefore, when the plant material is spread on solid media, a plethora of microorganisms, including the pathogen, will grow. At that point we can always count on one of the students to say, "But how can I figure who in this jungle is the pathogen?" We usually wait to give the student a chance to answer his/her own question or reflect the question back to the student, and we usually are rewarded with that look students get when it dawns on them that the answer is really simple. Then they inoculate healthy plants with each of the colony types and wait to let the microbes tell them the answer to their question.

The biggest challenge in this experiment is convincing the students that the most abundant microorganism is not necessarily the pathogen. Non-pathogenic organisms from the surface of the plant often dominate the culture plates, and some students will inoculate only those organisms onto new plant material. Usually, a few questions such as, "How do you *know* that the yellow one is the pathogen?" will guide students to test a variety of organisms from the plate, enabling them to identify the true pathogen.

Variations on the theme

Depending on class time available, the number of students in class, and accessible sources of plant disease for study, this experiment can be done using one or more of the following plant disease options: black rot of crucifers, root rot of peas, storage rot of onion, or soft rot of potato. If possible, the four pathogens can be distributed among the student groups for study. Students can then compare their observations of different pathogens.

For simplicity, we will give instructions for only one option, black rot of crucifers, in the next section. Preparation instructions for the other three options are given at the end of the experiment. Alternatively, you can use any plant pathogen common to your area.

Three class periods are needed for this experiment: one in which students observe healthy and diseased plant materials and culture microbes from the plants, a second in which they inoculate healthy plant materials with microbes from individual colonies on their culture plates, and a third in which they observe the inoculated plants and interpret the results of the experiment to identify the microbe that is the pathogenic agent.

Option I. Black rot of crucifers - *Xanthomonas campestris*

Materials needed for teacher preparations

Wisconsin Fast Plants kits (page 251)
potting soil
Xanthomonas campestris culture (page 250)

Materials needed for students

Number per group:
(for the first lab period)

4	Wisconsin Fast Plants infected with *X. campestris*
4	healthy Wisconsin Fast Plants (for visual comparison)
5	nutrient agar plates (pages 228, 249)
5	sterile micro mortars and pestles (page 233)
	plant labels or tape

(for the second lab period)

4–8 healthy Wisconsin Fast Plants (3 to 4 days old)

(for the third lab period)

samples of healthy and *X. campestris*-infected Wisconsin Fast Plants

Teacher preparations prior to the first lab period

Before the semester begins

1. Obtain enough Wisconsin Fast Plants seed so that you will be able to supply at least 8 plants per group. Obtain a culture of *Xanthomonas campestris*.

Eight days before the lab period

1. Grow Wisconsin Fast Plants from seed so that you will have at least 4 plants per group.

Four days before the lab period

1. Inoculate the four-day-old Wisconsin Fast Plants by piercing each cotyledon with a sterile toothpick bearing a mass of *Xanthomonas campestris* bacteria. Necrotic lesions with yellow margins will develop on the cotyledons over a four-day period.

   Note: Be sure to keep the inoculated plants physically separated from the uninoculated plants so that the pathogen does not spread to the healthy controls.

How to guide students

During the first lab period

1. Students should first examine both healthy and diseased plant materials and record their observations of the appearances of the plant materials.

2. Students should attempt to isolate microbes from their plants. Encourage students to make isolations from several areas on the infected Wisconsin Fast Plants to help them learn about the distribution of the pathogenic bacteria on the plants. Isolations from the yellow margins of the lesions will most likely yield the pathogen.

   Isolations from healthy plants serve as interesting controls that show students that healthy plants are the home to many bacteria and fungi.

3. Isolations are most likely to be successful if students perform a 3-way streak (page 220) or place a piece of infected plant tissue on a nutrient agar plate. Look for slimy, yellow colonies after incubating the isolation plates at 24° to 28°C for 2 to 3 days.

During the second lab period

1. Students should inoculate healthy Wisconsin Fast Plants with a variety of the microbes they isolated during the previous lab. Encourage students to sample from as many different types of colonies as is feasible. Remind them to describe thoroughly the appearance of the colonies they are using for the inoculations and to note which colony is being used to inoculate which plant.

2. Suitable controls (or additional treatments) for this stage might include no treatment, wounding with a sterile toothpick, inoculation with sterile water, or inoculation with pet microbes.

During the third lab period

1. Students should examine the plants they inoculated during the previous class to determine which microbe caused the symptoms of disease they observed initially in the Wisconsin Fast Plants and which microbes can be ruled out as the pathogenic agent in this system. It is useful to have samples of diseased and healthy plants available for comparison.

Possible hypotheses students might want to test

1. A specific kind of microorganism caused the disease symptoms observed in the plants.

2. The observed symptoms on the plants were caused by physical injury and not by a pathogen.

Data collection - Each of the three class periods devoted to this experiment has its own data collection requirements. Students must carefully observe, measure, and put the pieces together to solve this whodunit mystery.

Period 1: The original sick plant (compare with healthy plants)
Descriptive: symptoms of disease—color, texture, location, etc. of lesions
Quantitative: number of lesions per plant, fraction of inoculated plants that became infected

Period 2: Microbes growing on the culture plates
Descriptive: color, texture, shape, interesting features of each colony
Quantitative: size of colony, abundance of each colony type

Period 3: Inoculated plants (compare with controls—no treatment, wounding with a sterile toothpick, inoculating with sterile water)
Descriptive: color, texture, location, etc. of lesions
Quantitative: presence/absence of lesions, number of lesions per plant, fraction of inoculated plants that became infected

Troubleshooting and dealing with problems

Problem	Possible explanation	Solution
no disease	students did not inoculate with a pathogen	share data among groups; encourage students to inoculate with several organisms—the most abundant is not necessarily the pathogen
no disease	inoculated the wrong part of the plant	try a number of different inoculation techniques and sites on the plant
disease symptoms different from original	inoculated with another pathogen	produces interesting results but does not satisfy Koch's postulates; compare results with other groups

Questions to guide discussion

◆ How do you know you have isolated the pathogen and not just something living on the plant?

◆ How are you going to figure out which microbe, if any, is the pathogen?

◆ How would you demonstrate that a virus is the cause of a disease if you cannot grow it in pure culture?

◆ How will you tell that a microorganism is causing the disease symptoms and not the technique you used (cutting, wounding, etc.)?

Sources of information

◆ Agrios, George N. (1988) *Plant Pathology*. San Diego, CA: Academic Press, Inc. [source of information on specific pathogens and diseases]

◆ Brock, Thomas D. (1988) *Robert Koch: A Life in Medicine and Bacteriology*. Madison, WI: Science Tech Publishers, and Berlin: Springer-Verlag. [see especially Chapter 5 for an excellent depiction of the process of scientific discovery]

◆ De Kruif, Paul (1953) *Microbe Hunters*. New York, NY: Harcourt, Brace & World. [the human side of scientific research]

Other pathogen options for Koch's postulates experiments

II. Root rot of peas - *Rhizoctonia solani*

Materials needed for teacher preparation

pea seed, surface-disinfested (at least 12 seeds per group)[4]
sterile 9-cm petri plates (page 250)
sterile 9-cm filter paper disks (page 250)
Parafilm (page 250)
1 *Rhizoctonia solani* culture on PDA (page 251)

Materials needed for students

Number per group:
(for the first lab period)

12 pea seedlings (14 days old) infected with *Rhizoctonia solani*
3 weak PDA plates (pages 229, 249)
5 sterile micro mortars and pestles (page 233)

(for the second lab period)

10 healthy pea seedlings (7 days old)
sterile 9-cm petri plates
sterile 9-cm filter paper disks
Parafilm

(for the third lab period)

samples of healthy and *Rhizoctonia*-infected pea seedlings

---

[4]Any variety of peas will work. You can find pea seeds in the garden seed section of your grocery store, a garden supply store, or in a seed catalog.

Teacher preparations prior to the first lab period

Before the semester begins

1. Obtain enough pea seed to supply at least 12 pea seedlings per group. Obtain a culture of *Rhizoctonia solani*.

Fourteen days before the first lab period

1. Surface disinfest the pea seeds (see page 235). Germinate the seeds as follows: Place 1 disk of sterile filter paper in the lid, and 1 sterile disk in the base of a sterile, 9-cm plastic petri plate. Dispense enough sterile water onto each of the filter paper disks so that they are damp but not dripping. Place several pea seeds in each dish, seal the dish with Parafilm, and incubate at room temperature for 3 to 7 days at room temperature.

Seven days before the first lab period

1. Puncture the major root of each pea seedling with a sterile toothpick and place a small section (about 0.4 × 0.4 cm) of PDA colonized with *Rhizoctonia solani*, face down, over the wound. If necessary, re-moisten the filter paper. Then reseal the plates with Parafilm and continue to incubate at room temperature.

2. Disease symptoms (brown, mushy roots) will develop over a 7-day period. Some roots may develop elongated, brown lesions.

How to guide students

During the first lab period

1. Encourage students to make isolations from several areas on the root, seed, or shoot to help them learn more about how *Rhizoctonia* is distributed over the seedling. Isolations from the margins between the healthy (white) and diseased (brown) areas of the roots will be most likely to yield the pathogen.

2. Isolations will be more successful if students do a 3-way streak (page 220) or plate small pieces of tissue on weak PDA. Incubate plates at room temperature for about 7 days. Look for white or brown hyphae.

During the second lab period

1. Students should inoculate healthy pea seedlings with the microbes they cultured in the previous lab. Encourage students to sample from as many different types of colonies as is feasible. Remind them to describe thoroughly the appearance of the colonies they are using for the inoculations.

2. Suitable controls (or additional treatments) for this stage might include no treatment, wounding with a sterile toothpick, inoculation with sterile water, or inoculation with pet microbes.

During the third lab period

1. Students should examine the pea seedlings they inoculated during the previous class to determine which microbe caused the symptoms. Samples of healthy and diseased seedlings should be provided for comparisons.

2. The major challenge with this pathogen is that it does not grow as discrete colonies, and, therefore, it may be difficult to obtain a pure culture from the diseased plant.

III. Storage rot of onions - *Botrytis cinerea*

Materials needed for teacher preparation

onion slices or quarters, surface disinfested (2 per group) (page 235)
sterile 9-cm filter paper disks
small, sterile containers—petri dishes, jars, or specimen containers with lids or aluminum foil covers
Botrytis cinerea on PDA culture plate (page 251)
9-inch sterile pipettes

Materials needed for students

Number per group:
(for the first lab period)

1 onion slice, infected with *Botrytis cinerea*
3 PDA plates (pages 229, 249)

(for the second lab period)

1 onion slice, surface disinfested (page 235)
1 sterile 9-cm filter paper disk
1 small, sterile container—petri dish, jar, or specimen container with lid or aluminum foil cover

(for the third lab period)

non-infected and *Botrytis*-infected onion slices

Teacher preparations prior to the first lab period

Before the semester begins

1. Obtain a culture of *Botrytis cinerea*.

Seven to fourteen days before the first lab period

1. Obtain enough onions to supply at least 2 per group.

2. Cut enough onions to provide 1 slice per group. (Save the rest for later labs.) Prepare 1 container with a *Botrytis*-inoculated onion slice for each group of students as follows:

   Place a sterile, 9-cm filter paper disk in a small, sterile container. Dispense sterile water onto the filter paper to thoroughly moisten it. Place an onion slice in each container.

3. Place a small section of PDA colonized with *Botrytis cinerea* (approximately 0.4 x 0.4 cm) on the cut surface of the onion. Cover the container and incubate at room temperature. Disease symptoms (brown, mushy onions covered with white to gray, fuzzy fungal growth) will

become apparent over a period of 7 to 14 days. You will also notice a foul odor if you remove the lid of the container.

3. You should supply one container containing a *Botrytis*-infected onion slice for each group of students.

How to guide students

During the first lab period

1. Encourage the students to isolate material from several areas on the onion to help them learn more about how the *Botrytis* is distributed over the surface. Isolations from the white to gray fuzzy areas will be most likely to yield the pathogen.

2. Isolations will be more successful if students do a 3-way streak (page 220) or plate small pieces of tissue on PDA. Incubate plates at room temperature for about 7 days. Look for white to gray threadlike strands.

During the second lab period

1. Students should inoculate onion slices with the microbes they cultured in the previous lab. Encourage students to sample from as many different types of colonies as is feasible. Remind them to describe thoroughly the appearance of the colonies they are using for the inoculations.

2. Suitable controls (or additional treatments) for this stage might include no treatment, inoculation with sterile water, or inoculation with pet microbes.

During the third lab period

1. Students should examine the onion slice they inoculated during the previous class to determine which microbe caused the symptoms. Samples of infected and non-infected onion slices should be provided for comparisons.

IV. Soft rot of potatoes - *Erwinia carotovora*

Materials needed for teacher preparation

sterile 9-cm filter paper disks
small, sterile containers—petri dishes, jars, or specimen containers with lids or aluminum foil covers
potato slices (2 per group)
1 sterile pipette (6–9 inches long)
1 *Erwinia carotovora* plate (page 250)

Materials needed for students

Number per group:
(for the first lab period)

1 potato slice, infected with *Erwinia carotovora*
3 NA plates (pages 228, 249)
5 sterile micro mortars and pestles (page 233)

(for the second lab period)

1 potato slice
1 sterile 9-cm filter paper disk
1 small, sterile container—petri dish, jar, or specimen container with lid or aluminum foil cover

(for the third lab period)

non-infected and *Erwinia*-infected potato slices

Teacher preparations prior to the first lab period

Before the semester begins

1. Obtain a culture of *Erwinia carotovora*.

Three to seven days before the lab period

1. Obtain enough potatoes to have at least 2 per group.

2. Cut into 2-cm-thick slices enough potatoes to provide 1 slice per group. (Save the rest of the potatoes for later labs.) Prepare 1 container with an *Erwinia*-inoculated potato slice for each group of students as follows:

   Place 1 sterile, 9-cm filter paper disk in a small sterile container. Dispense enough sterile water onto the filter paper to thoroughly moisten it. Place one potato slice in each container. Use a sterile pipette tip to make a hole in the center of each slice.

3. Place a small amount of *Erwinia carotovora* from the culture plate in the hole. Cover the container and incubate at room temperature. Disease symptoms (creamy, tan, slimy rot in the center of the slices) will become apparent over a period of about 3 to 7 days.

How to guide students

During the first lab period

1. Encourage students to isolate material from several areas on the potato to help them learn more about how the *Erwinia* is distributed over the surface. Isolations from the slimy, tan areas will be most likely to yield the pathogen.

2. Isolations will be more successful if students do a 3-way streak (page 220) or plate a small piece of tissue on NA. Incubate plates at room temperature for about 3 to 7 days. Look for creamy white to tan colonies.

During the second lab period

1. Students should inoculate potato slices with the microbes they cultured in the previous lab. Encourage students to sample from as many different types of colonies as is feasible. Remind them to describe thoroughly the appearance of the colonies they are using for the inoculations.

2. Suitable controls (or additional treatments) for this stage might include no treatment, only cutting the hole in the potato slice with a sterile pipette, inoculating with sterile water, or inoculating with pet microbes.

During the third lab period

1. Students should examine the potato slices they inoculated during the previous class to determine which microbe caused the symptoms. Samples of infected and non-infected potato slices should be provided for comparisons.

Experiment 6: DNA, the universal hereditary material of cellular life
A lesson in molecular biology

DNA is the universal hereditary material. It is carried by all organisms, except for some viruses that have RNA rather than DNA. It is transmitted to offspring, and it directs synthesis of proteins that define the organism. Its amazing property is that, in its simple four-letter code, DNA can carry all of the information for the splendid diversity of creatures in the biological world. It is a universal and versatile molecule.

The functional units of DNA are known as **genes**, which code for proteins. At the organismal level, **gene expression** confers characteristics or **phenotypes**. At the biochemical level, when a gene is expressed it directs the synthesis of a **messenger RNA** molecule, which acts as the template on which a **protein** is synthesized. Generally, each gene directs the synthesis of one protein. Gene expression, or production of RNA and proteins, is tightly regulated. Organisms deploy elaborate mechanisms either to shut off expression of genes when their products are not needed or to turn on genes when the gene products will contribute to the success of the organism under certain environmental conditions. One of the key elements involved in gene expression is the **promoter**, which is a small sequence of DNA that is in front of the genes and must be recognized by the cell machinery for genes to be expressed.

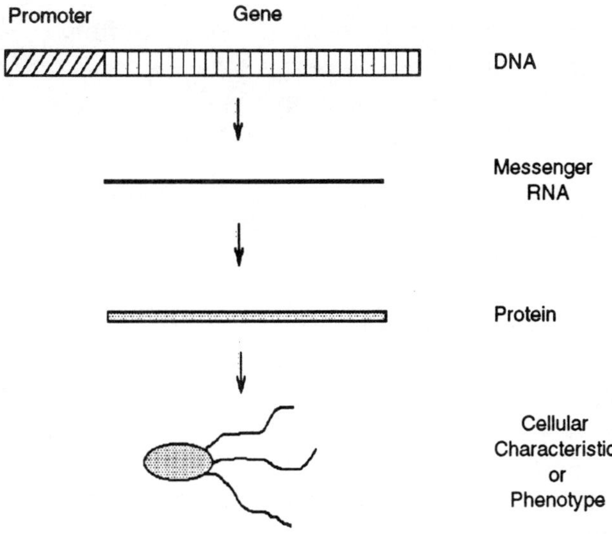

Exchange of DNA between organisms is common and results in organisms with new combinations of traits. These new combinations are the basis for diversity and serve as the fuel for evolution. Plants and animals transfer DNA through sexual reproduction between members of a species. Bacteria exchange DNA with each other through a process known as conjugation. Viruses transfer DNA to plants, animals, and bacteria. They inject DNA (or in some cases, RNA) into their host's cell, which leads to production of more virus and often to the demise of the host cell.

Although the biological world is rich with illustrations of DNA exchange, there is only one example of transfer of DNA between bacteria and higher organisms. ***Agrobacterium tumefaciens*** causes the plant disease known as crown gall by transferring a small, discrete piece of its own DNA to plant cells. The piece of DNA that is transferred from the bacterium to the plant is called the **T-DNA**. The genes carried on the T-DNA are not expressed in the bacterial cell because the bacterial machinery for gene expression does not recognize the promoters on the T-DNA. However, the genes are expressed in the plant cell because the promoters are recognized by the machinery of the plant. The genes code for production of plant hormones and nutrients known as **opines** that can be used as food by *Agrobacterium*. The result is that the plant cells that carry and express the genes on the T-DNA grow large and multiply rapidly, producing a tumor on the plant. The tumor exudes opines, providing an abundant food source for the bacterium. *Agrobacterium* genetically engineers the plant host and turns it into a food factory for the benefit of the bacterium!

The T-DNA carries genes for production of two types of plant hormones, **auxin** and **cytokinin**. In normal plant development, the ratio of these hormones is carefully regulated and certain ratios lead to **differentiation** of shoots and leaves, whereas other ratios lead to differentiation of roots. In plant cells containing T-DNA, the hormones are synthesized in large amounts and at a ratio that results in rapid **undifferentiated** growth, which leads to formation of tumors instead of normal organs.

Key concepts

DNA is the universal hereditary material.

***Agrobacterium* makes a permanent, heritable change in cells of its host through transfer of T-DNA.**

The ratio of hormones produced as a result of expression of the genes in the T-DNA alters plant development and results in tumor formation.

Challenge

> You will be provided with sunflower plants and a strain of *Agrobacterium tumefaciens* that is pathogenic and causes crown gall tumors on plants. **Develop a hypothesis about conditions that favor or disfavor crown gall disease. Design an experiment to test your hypothesis.**

Note: *Agrobacterium* infects plants through wounds.

Key questions

☞ **What benefit does *Agrobacterium* derive from inducing tumors on plants?**

☞ **What do you think would happen if the genes for auxin or cytokinin production were deleted from the T-DNA?**

☞ **Why do you think transfer of DNA between bacteria and plants or animals is such a rare phenomenon?**

Plant transformation by *Agrobacterium tumefaciens*

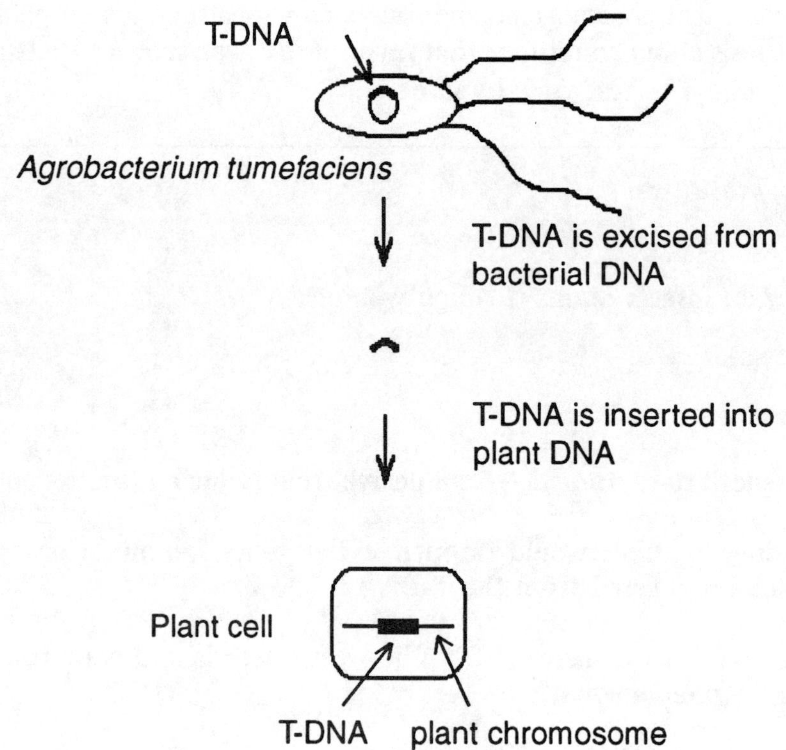

Expression of genes on T-DNA in plant cell
(p = promoter)

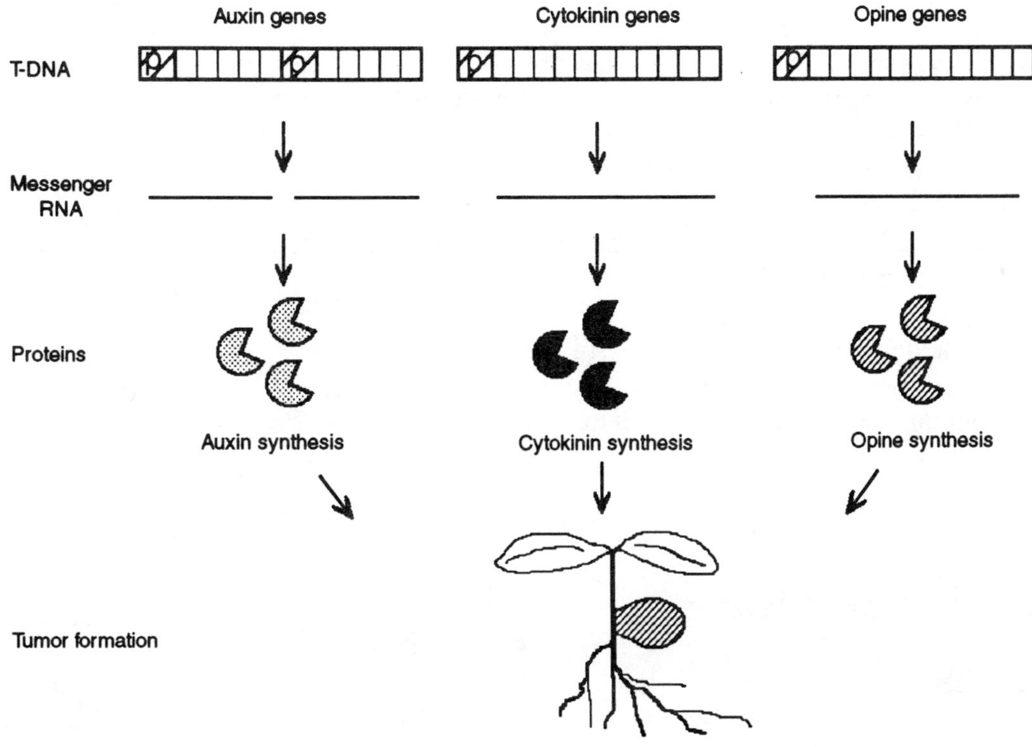

Experiment 6: DNA, the universal hereditary material of cellular life

A lesson in molecular biology

In this exercise, students will inoculate plants with a bacterium that transfers DNA to its host, and they will work with DNA isolated from bacteria.

If there is one concept in biology that is the most fun to teach and that is guaranteed to fascinate the students, it is the concept that DNA is the universal hereditary material. The idea boggles most people's minds for two reasons. First, that a simple, linear molecule—a mere chemical—is our inheritance and encodes the biological features of an individual initially seems impossible, then simply marvelous. Second, that the same molecule is the hereditary material for all cellular life, defining all of the diversity of life on Earth, is stunning. The simple unity of life is perhaps the most humbling concept of all.

In this exercise, students will experiment with *Agrobacterium tumefaciens*, a bacterium that causes plant disease by inserting a piece of its own DNA into the host's chromosomes. In an accompanying demonstration, you may isolate bacterial DNA for the students to touch and experiment with. These experiments appeal to the intellect, the spirit, the senses, and the emotions.

What students will learn

This exercise is designed to get students thinking about both the simplicity and complexity of genes and gene function. The first concept to emphasize is that DNA is the universal hereditary material. The hereditary molecule carried by the bacterium, *A. tumefaciens*, is chemically the same as the hereditary molecule in a plant or a human being. This concept is highlighted by the fact that this bacterium can carry genes that can then be expressed in a plant cell. The second concept is that gene expression is highly regulated and the regulation tends to be specific for types of organisms. This concept follows naturally from the idea that *A. tumefaciens* carries genes that it does not express, but those same genes are expressed when they are inserted into the plant genome. This exercise provides an opportunity to present the concept of gene regulation, promoters, and the organization of prokaryotic and eukaryotic genes. One key point to emphasize is that prokaryotes express genes in operons. Operons are groups of genes that are transcribed from a single promoter resulting in a messenger RNA molecule that encodes more than one protein, whereas eukaryotes carry a separate promoter for each gene, resulting in a single protein produced from each messenger RNA.

Learning highlights and conceptual challenges

we all have it; it's so simple; it's so complex;
the stuff of life?—looks like snot to me! no one's gonna play with my genes!

In the exercise with *A. tumefaciens*, the students are appreciative of the exotic nature of this bacterium. The fact that no other known bacterium has evolved the ability to genetically engineer its eukaryotic host makes this bacterium worthy of attention. The intrinsic cleverness of the life strategy of this organism—to engineer the plant to produce food for the parasite—is intellectually appealing. The fact that interkingdom DNA transfer is occurring under their eyes is exciting to most students. This event brings home sharply the concept that "DNA is DNA"—the chemical is the same whether it comes from a plant, a bacterium, or an animal.

The demonstration of DNA extraction from a bacterium is powerful for most people. (We still get shivers up our spines when we do this demonstration. There is something awesome about playing with DNA.) The students seem to be universally affected by the simplicity of inheritance when they see the DNA molecule in front of them. Ask them to envision DNA polymerase sliding along the molecule, copying it with great fidelity, as they string the DNA on pipettes. Almost every time we have used this demonstration, someone in the class has commented on how much DNA looks like mucous. This provides an opportunity to discuss the chemistry of polymers and that a major contributor to mucous is DNA from lysed lymphocytes. Many students are surprised to learn that they have seen DNA before in their own handkerchiefs!

One of the challenges in this exercise, and in teaching molecular biology in general, is the complexity of gene expression. Whereas the conservation of the central dogma throughout biology provides a certain simplicity and unification to the topic, the multiplicity of mechanisms of gene expression is complex and difficult for students to comprehend. The *A. tumefaciens* experiment provides a simple example of gene regulation—genes that are not expressed in the bacterium are expressed in the plant. The evidence of gene expression is in the tumors that develop on the plant after infection by the bacterium.

This exercise provides an excellent introduction to genetic engineering. Once the students understand the basics of heredity and gene expression, then the concept of gene transfer among organisms is a natural extension. *A. tumefaciens* has often been described as a "natural genetic engineer," but it has also been used by humans to introduce genes of use to us into plants. In fact, this bacterium provided the first and still most popular means to genetically engineer crops.

The controversy over genetic engineering provides an emotionally charged topic to reinforce the basic concepts of heredity and gene expression. The students should be able to understand that given the right regulatory signals, any gene could theoretically be expressed in any organism, independent of the origin of the gene. You may then challenge them to identify the barriers to genetic engineering and to recognize what is feasible with current technology and what is not. This can lead a useful discussion of our understanding of gene expression across species barriers, the complexity of certain genetic traits, and the difference between engineering somatic cells and germ lines.

Expect students to be interested in the ethics of genetic engineering. Many are troubled by the apparent fine line between engineering bacteria to make insulin and changing characteristics in humans. We find it useful to point out that eugenics was used long before genetic engineering was developed, and therefore, the ethical decisions about appropriate use of genetic technology preceded the invention of this set of tools.

Materials needed for teacher preparations

Agrobacterium tumefaciens pathogenic strain (page 250)
nutrient agar (NA) (1 plate per bacterial strain for each group of students) (pages 228, 249)
striped sunflower seeds[5] (page 251)
potting soil
flower pots or other vessels for growing plants

Materials needed for students

Number per group:

4 sunflower plants
Agrobacterium tumefaciens culture

Teacher preparations prior to lab period

Before the semester begins

1. Obtain a culture of *Agrobacterium tumefaciens*.

Four days before the first lab period

1. Plant sunflower seeds. **Note:** These seeds may have a low rate of germination, so plant extra seeds to have at least 4 plants for each group of students.

Two days before the first lab period

1. Plate *Agrobacterium tumefaciens* on nutrient agar. Incubate at room temperature.

---

[5]*Agrobacterium* has a very broad host range and will infect most dicotyledonous plants. Tomato, sunflower, Kalanchoe, and tobacco are particularly susceptible hosts.

How to guide students

During the first class

1. Use a separate sterile toothpick to inoculate each sunflower plant. Leave one plant uninoculated as a control.

   The students should scrape a toothpick tip through the *Agrobacterium* culture and collect a mass of bacteria on the tip. To obtain tumors, students should inoculate by poking holes in the plant stem with the toothpick tip.

During the second class (ten to 30 days later)

1. The students should observe their plants for signs of disease.

Possible hypotheses students might want to test

1. Agrobacterium induces tumors on stems better than on leaves.

2. All bacteria cause tumors on plant tissue.

3. Agrobacterium causes tumors on all plants.

Data collection

1. **Descriptive** - Describe the size, color, shape, texture, location, and other characteristics of the tumors. Describe the appearance of control plants.

2. **Quantitative** - Measure the diameter of the tumors; count the tumors if many form; measure the distance of tumors from the site of inoculation.

Troubleshooting and dealing with problems

Problem	Possible explanation	Solution
no tumors	strain not virulent	precheck strains
no tumors	conditions too dry for infection	spray plant with water after inoculation or put in plastic bag
tumors form in controls stabbed with toothpicks	some plants will form spontaneous swellings as a result of wounding	this is unlikely, but if it occurs, use a different variety of plant

Questions to guide discussion

- ♦ What are the events that must occur for a crown gall tumor to form?
- ♦ What is the evolutionary advantage for *Agrobacterium* of causing crown gall?
- ♦ How would you determine whether DNA transfer had occurred if you were using a strain of *Agrobacterium* that did not induce tumors but could transfer DNA?
- ♦ If you could have *Agrobacterium* transfer any type of DNA to a plant, what trait would you engineer a plant for?

Sources of information

♦ Brock, Thomas D., Michael T. Madigan, John M. Martinko, and Jack Parker (1994) *Biology of Microorganisms*, 7th ed. Englewood Cliffs, NJ: Prentice Hall. Has an excellent section with diagrams (pp. 678–682).

♦ Chrispeels, Maarten J. and David E. Sadava (1994) *Plants, Genes, and Agriculture.* Boston: Jones and Bartlett Publishing International. Chapter 15 has an excellent description of plant genetic engineering and use of *Agrobacterium* (pp. 400–432).

♦ Gasser, C.S. and R.T. Fraley (1992) Transgenic crops. *Scientific American* 266: 62–67.

II. DNA extraction demonstration This demonstration makes a lasting impression on students because it allows them to encounter DNA, not as the abstract concept they have seen illustrated in their biology textbooks, but as a real, tangible substance that they can see and touch.

Materials

	Escherichia coli culture (page 250)
	LB (Luria-Delbruck) broth (page 228)
2	250-ml polypropylene centrifuge bottles
	centrifuge
	100% ethanol (**not** denatured) (page 249)
	TES 8 (page 230)
	SDS (page 249)
	proteinase K (page 249)
	water bath at 42° to 55°C
	50-ml test tubes
	hooked glass pipettes (see below)

Teacher preparations prior to lab period

1. Heat glass Pasteur pipette tips over a gas flame and draw the tips into hooks.

2. Obtain a stock culture of *E. coli*.

3. Grow the *E. coli* overnight in 100 ml of LB broth at 37°C.

4. Place the 100% ethanol in a -20°C freezer overnight. (DNA precipitates in cold, 100% ethanol.)

5. The next day, about 2 to 4 hours before class, pour the bacterial culture into two 250-ml centrifuge tubes.

6. Centrifuge at 6,000 rpm for 10 minutes until a pellet forms. Pour off and discard the supernatant.

7. Resuspend the pellet in 50 ml of TES 8 and transfer to 4 50-ml test tubes. Add 0.5 ml of SDS to each tube (for a final concentration of 1%). Add 40 μl of

Proteinase K (10 mg/ml) to each tube (for a final concentration of about 5 to 10 μg/ml). You have created a detergent and protein-digesting enzyme solution that will break down the bacterial cell walls and release the DNA. Try to provide enough tubes so that each group can have one.

8. Incubate the tubes for two hours in a water bath at 42° to 55°C. The solution in the tubes will be clear and somewhat thickened.

During the lab period

1. Add two volumes of ice cold (-20°C), 100% ethanol. The DNA will precipitate as a gelatinous material.

2. Insert a hooked glass pipette into the tube and, rotating in one direction, wind the DNA onto the pipette.

3. This works well if you demonstrate the technique and then let students try it. The precipitated DNA may be stored in tightly capped tubes of 50% ethanol, or it may be placed on filter paper and dried. (Students enjoy having their own small mass of dried DNA to keep.)

Troubleshooting and dealing with problems

Problem	Possible explanations/solutions
DNA does not precipitate	Make sure the ethanol is cold enough (-20°C).
	Use careful handling throughout the experiment; rinse all glassware with distilled water and avoid touching the insides. This reduces the risk of introducing nucleases.
DNA precipitates as fuzzy, white mass that does not wind on the rod	Rough handling during preparation can result in breakage of DNA strands into short fragments. Handle the solutions containing DNA gently.
DNA slips off the pipette	Make sure the pipettes are very clean; avoid touching the hooked ends before use.

Questions to guide discussion

◆ What is the same about genes in bacteria and in plants? What is different?

◆ What is unique about *A. tumefaciens*?

◆ What are the requirements for successful genetic engineering? (Emphasize the need for gene transfer, appropriate promoters and other regulatory elements, and access to a useful gene.)

◆ Why might it be difficult to engineer plants for multigenic traits such as yield or production of complex chemicals?

Sources of information

◆ Brock, Thomas D., Michael T. Madigan, John M. Martinko, and Jack Parker (1994) *Biology of Microorganisms*, 7th ed. Englewood Cliffs, NJ: Prentice Hall. Has an excellent section with diagrams (pp. 678–682).

◆ Maniatis, T., E.F. Fritsch, and J. Sambrook (1982) *Molecular Cloning: A Laboratory Manual*. Cold Spring Harbor, NY.

Experiment 7: Are chemicals, mutations, and cancer linked?

A lesson in mutation and selection

Life is a collection of chemicals. Thousands of different molecules are required for the cellular functions of every plant, animal, and microorganism. Without chemicals, life would not exist. How, then, has our society developed the notion that chemicals are "bad" and that "natural" things do not contain chemicals? The answer is probably quite complex. Some of the factors that contribute to the answer include the following:

Many human diseases, including certain types of cancer, have been associated with long-term exposure to certain synthetic chemicals (made by people) that are used in industry and agriculture. This has led some people to brand all synthetic chemicals as dangerous.

The most abundant source of "natural" chemicals to which people are continually exposed is food. We may believe that the natural chemicals in food are safe because we benefit from thousands of years of human experience testing and choosing foods. We no longer try to eat many foods that contain toxic chemicals because we can rely on history and lore to warn us of them. The avenging angel mushroom, food spoiled by certain bacteria, and the root of the hemlock plant are far more toxic than many of the synthetic chemicals we are concerned about. However, we have much less experience (only 30 to 40 years) with most of the synthetic chemicals used in industry and agriculture. We are still learning about which ones we should use and which ones to avoid.

The first flush of extensive use of synthetic pesticides in the 1940s and 1950s included some nasty chemicals that were used in large quantities and had negative consequences for the environment. The somewhat indiscriminate approach to agricultural chemicals in the past is currently contributing to the argument made by some people that we should avoid all synthetic chemicals because they have such potential for harm.

In contrast with the popular view and the position taken by the federal regulatory agencies, some people believe we should focus on the activity of a chemical and how much of it we are exposed to, **not** whether it was synthesized in a factory or made by a plant, animal, or microbe.

One of the areas in which this debate about chemical safety has become quite heated is in the regulation of chemicals based on their potential for causing cancer. Many chemicals that are naturally found in the foods we eat show potential for causing cancer in the same tests that have been set up for synthetic chemicals, which has led some scientists to question the relevance of these tests.

The most famous example of a test that predicts carcinogenicity of chemicals is the Ames test, developed by a scientist named Bruce Ames. The test has been used extensively for many years to predict the safety of synthetic chemicals. Recently, Ames and some of his colleagues found that chemicals in many "natural" foods (such as broccoli, potatoes, beer, and mushrooms) show just as much potential for carcinogenicity as many of the synthetic chemicals that alarm regulatory agencies and consumers. Ames has been a vocal advocate of applying the same standards to synthetic chemicals and natural foods. The debate is not finished.

Let us take a closer look at the Ames test. It is based on the following theories and assumptions:

- Normal development of animals and other multicellular organisms depends on the control of cell growth. Cancer is the uncontrolled proliferation of cells in animals.
- The change to a cancerous condition is often caused by a genetic change in the cell.
- Genetic changes in cells can be induced by chemicals that alter DNA, causing mutations.
- DNA is the universal genetic material in plants, animals, and microbes. Therefore, the ability of a chemical to cause mutations in the DNA of a bacterium may be used to predict its ability to cause mutations in human DNA, which, in turn, may be correlated with its potential to induce cancer.

Some definitions that may be useful for this experiment

Streptomycin: the antibiotic that provides the selection; differentiates strains of bacteria that are sensitive (do not grow on streptomycin) from those that are resistant (grow on streptomycin).

Mutagen: a chemical (or a physical phenomenon, such as X-rays) that causes changes in the sequences of bases in DNA; exposure to a mutagen will increase the frequency of mutants in a population.

Mutagenicity: the potential of a chemical for causing mutations or changes in DNA.

Mutant: an organism that differs genetically from its parent, in this case, bacteria that are resistant to streptomycin.

Spontaneous mutant: a mutant that arises from random changes in the DNA; changes can be caused by mistakes during DNA replication, damage from X-rays or ultraviolet light.

Frequency of mutants: the proportion of the population accounted for by mutants; for spontaneous bacterial mutants, the frequency is typically one mutant for a given trait in every million to 10 million cells.

Carcinogenicity: the ability to cause cancer in animals.

Key concept

The Ames test is based on the assumption that mutagenicity is associated with carcinogenicity and that mutagenic activity in bacteria is predictive of mutagenic activity in humans.

Challenge

Mutations in DNA appear at random in a population of bacteria. A chemical mutagen ***increases the frequency*** at which mutations appear. The Ames Test measures the ability of a chemical to increase the mutation rate in bacteria. The mutations are detected by measuring a characteristic that results from changes at the gene level, such as the ability to grow under certain conditions. We will conduct a modified Ames Test. You will be provided with a strain of *Escherichia coli* that is sensitive to (killed by) the antibiotic chloramphenicol. Cultures contain rare mutants that grow in the presence of the antibiotic because of a small change in their DNA that makes them resistant to the action of the drug. Chemicals that cause mutations should increase the frequency of chloramphenicol-resistant mutants in a population of cells.

Bring chemicals to class to test for mutagenicity. Propose a hypothesis about the types of chemicals that are likely to be mutagens and design an experiment to test your hypothesis.

Key questions

☞ **Are there flaws in using the Ames test to predict carcinogenicity?**

☞ **Should we base regulation of food additives on the Ames test?**

☞ **Should we base our choices about which foods to eat on the Ames test?**

☞ **If a major pesticide was very mutagenic in the Ames test, would you advocate that farmers not use it?**

☞ **If your favorite food was very mutagenic in the Ames test, would you stop eating it?**

☞ **If you do not expose a population of bacteria to streptomycin, are there streptomycin-resistant mutants in the population?**

Materials provided

bacterium that is sensitive to streptomycin
agar medium containing streptomycin
glass spreader
filter paper
chemicals and biological materials for testing

Experiment 7: Are chemicals, mutations, and cancer linked?

A lesson in mutation and selection

In this exercise students will use a simple test for bacterial mutants to assess the mutagenicity of household chemicals and food.

Because human beings are not used as experimental animals in potentially dangerous experiments in our society, scientists employ a variety of alternative systems to gather data about the effects of various phenomena on people. Animal models, computer programs, epidemiological studies that correlate conditions with effects, and other systems are commonly used. How closely these non-human systems parallel what might happen in humans is a basic question that must be answered for every system.

In this experiment students apply a modification of the Ames test, a bacterial model that assesses potential carcinogenicity of chemicals, to a number of familiar substances. (The authentic Ames test detects auxotrophic mutations that have reverted back to wild type. We have simplified the test to detect mutants resistant to streptomycin. We find that the logic of this version of the experiment is easier for students to follow.)

Students doing this experiment often make interesting discoveries, for example, that "chemicals" are not necessarily bad, "natural" is not necessarily good, and what's sauce for the bacterium may or may not be sauce for the human. In addition, they will learn important concepts about genetics, mutation, natural selection, and evolution and generate some stimulating discussions about human health issues.

What students will learn

This exercise introduces students to the concept of genetic frequency. Using a simple bacterial model, they estimate a spontaneous mutation frequency and compare it with the frequencies that result when they apply chemicals that are or are not mutagens. Since arguments based on frequencies are the backbone of classical genetics, this exercise is a first step in teaching genetic theory.

The power of the "Chemicals" exercise is the application of the principles to a wide array of human experiences. The students are drawn to the importance of the implications of the experiment, and as a result they want to understand the sophisticated genetics underlying the outcome. For example, the exercise addresses the role of mutations in cancer and the parallel between mutations in bacteria and in animal cells, through its application to the Ames Test for mutagenicity. The current model of cancer is that the condition results from mutations that affect regulators of the cell cycle, leading to de-regulation and uncontrolled proliferation of cells. This is a topic of general fascination to students because of its intrinsic biological appeal as well as its applications to human health.

One of the attractive features of this exercise is that it can be inserted into units on a wide range of biological topics. It fits well with cell biology, genetics, environmental biology, and epidemiology, and it is particularly powerful as an illustration of evolution. Although the analogy with natural selection is not perfect, the selection of bacterial mutants on a culture plate provides students with a graphic image of the ramifications of a rare mutation in a population when a strong selection pressure is applied to the population.

Although experimental design and hypotheses are not the focal point of the experiments that students propose, the use of controls is strongly reinforced by the nature of the genetic phenomenon studied. It is essential that the students include controls with no mutagen to estimate the background frequency of streptomycin-resistant mutants and to determine whether the chemical treatments affect the mutation frequency. The experiment is very effective in highlighting the need for the appropriate control since the results are uninterpretable without it.

Learning highlights and conceptual challenges

hold the mustard? antibiotic-resistant human pathogens; background mutation rates; not all bacteria produce colonies; mutations happen

The "Chemicals" exercise consistently gets students excited about the issue of regulation of food, food additives, and pesticides. Invariably, among the students' treatments, the most effective mutagen is a food, a "natural" product. By far, the most effective mutagen we have found is ground mustard. This is shocking to the students because it challenges their assumptions that the highest mutagenicity will be found in the synthetic chemicals. The fact that human beings eat many excellent mutagens and are, nevertheless, generally pretty healthy is a surprise to the students and stimulates their thinking about the link between mutagenicity in bacteria and carcinogenicity in humans. It also stimulates thought and discussion on the subject of food regulation. The students vigorously debate questions about regulating mutagenic foods, using the Ames test to identify potential carcinogens, and defining appropriate criteria for establishing safety of pesticides and food additives.

Another topic that makes the "Chemicals" exercise particularly relevant to human experience is antibiotic resistance in human pathogens. As students observe the resistant colonies appearing on their plates, it is easier for them to see how infrequent events can have an enormous influence on populations under selective conditions. For example, the streptomycin-resistant mutants appear at a frequency of approximately 1 in 1 million to 10 million cells, which seems quite infrequent. But during the course of an active infection, a human being can easily harbor more than 10 million pathogen cells, which makes it likely that a mutant will be present. For the mutant to be dominant in the population, all we need is a powerful selection for the mutant—and taking an antibiotic supplies that selection.

The most difficult aspect of the experiment is the most important concept: mutation frequencies. There are three components of the concept that are not intuitive for most students. First, it is a surprise to them that there is a background mutation rate. The fact that cells make mistakes in copying their DNA and that X-rays and other physical factors can damage DNA is often new to them. The second idea that needs special attention is the fact that there are many more bacteria on a plate containing streptomycin than actually produce colonies. It helps to explain that we place 10^7 bacteria on a plate and if only 10 colonies grow, these are probably mutants that are resistant to the antibiotic.

The third difficult concept, which is the most important for an understanding of Darwinian evolution, is the idea that mutations occur whether or not selection is present. We find that this issue comes up repeatedly in discussions of evolution, and the lab exercise provides a great opportunity to address it. The students often believe in the Lamarckian concept that mutants develop as a result of exposure to selective pressure. It is important to discuss the randomness of mutations, that they are in the population whether or not they are needed, and that we can observe mutants only when selection pressure prevents growth of the other bacteria. Drawing parallels to the lengths of giraffes' necks, insecticide-resistant insects, and other familiar examples of evolution can be very helpful in reinforcing the concept of selection acting on existing genetic variability in a population.

One extension of the Lamarck problem is that some students think streptomycin is *causing* mutations. It is therefore important to separate the steps in evolution (genetic variation followed by selection) and ask the students to identify each step in this experiment.

Materials needed for teacher preparations

	Escherichia coli culture (page 250)
	50 ml nutrient broth (pages 228, 249)
1	125-ml Erlenmeyer flask (page 250)
1	sterile cotton ball
	aluminum foil
	shaker in a 28°C incubator
	nutrient agar + 5 mg/ml streptomycin plates (2 to 5 per group) (pages 228, 231, and 249)
	Parafilm (page 250)
	alcohol burner
	ethanol for flame sterilization of glass spreaders
4	sterile glass spreaders (page 250)
	ICR-191, acridine mutagen, or another known mutagen (pages 109, 249)

Materials needed for students

Number per group:

5	nutrient agar + streptomycin plates inoculated with *E. coli*
25	0.5-cm diameter, sterile filter paper disks (page 250)
1	bag of "mutagens" (see "How to guide students" on page 108)

Teacher preparations prior to lab period

Before the semester begins

1. Obtain a culture of *Escherichia coli.*

Three days before the lab period

1. Transfer a loopful of actively growing bacterial cells to 50 ml of sterile nutrient broth in a sterile 125-ml Erlenmeyer flask. Seal the mouth of the flask with a sterile cotton ball. Cover the cotton ball and the top of the flask with aluminum foil.

2. Incubate the broth culture at approximately 28°C on a shaker for 1 to 3 days until the culture has reached saturation. *E. coli* in a rich nutrient medium will often reach saturation overnight. A saturated culture of *E. coli* will contain between 10^9 and 10^{10} cells per ml.

3. Sometime before the lab, it is a good idea to test the system by spreading 0.1 ml of a saturated culture on nutrient agar plates that contains streptomycin at 10 μg/ml. At this concentration, expect approximately 100 mutants per plate. If there are 10^8 to 10^9 bacteria on the plate and 100 are mutants, this means that the mutant frequency is 10^{-6} to 10^{-7}.

   Incubate the plates for 1 to 3 days. Then examine them to verify viability of the culture and that mutants arise at a detectable frequency.

4. It is best from a scientific standpoint to do this experiment quantitatively by plating a known number of bacteria, counting the number of mutant colonies, and calculating precise background and chemically induced mutation rates. However, we realize that not everyone will have the equipment to do the experiment quantitatively, so in addition to quantitative methods we have included methods for doing a less rigorous, approximate experiment that is still valuable for teaching students important concepts.

Quantitative method Using a spectrophotometer, determine the absorbance of the *E. coli* culture at 600 nanometers, assuming that an absorbance of 0.1 will be a concentration of 10^8 bacterial cells per ml. You will need to dilute the original culture to determine the absorbance. Calculate the amount of the original culture needed to deliver 10^8 bacteria per plate and spread this amount on the plates.

Approximate method A saturated culture of *E. coli* will yield a concentration of 10^9 to 10^{10} cells per ml. An inoculum of 0.1 ml of *E. coli* broth culture will result in about 10^8 to 10^9 cells per plate. This concentration will produce a lawn of bacteria on plates without streptomycin or about 10 to 100 colonies on plates with 10 μg/ml of streptomycin.

Two to four hours before the lab period

1. Inoculating the test plates: Spread approximately 0.1 ml of bacterial broth culture on the surface of the nutrient agar + streptomycin sulfate plates. Prepare about 5 plates per group. Alternatively, provide the cultures to the groups and have the students spread them on the plates.

How to guide students

During class

1. Students should bring to lab substances they wish to test. Mustard, hot sauce, orange peel, tobacco, and shoe polish have all shown reasonably high degrees of mutagenicity in our labs.

2. Students apply each substance (suspected mutagen) to a filter paper disk. The disks will then be placed on the surface of the nutrient agar plates that have been inoculated with the bacteria.

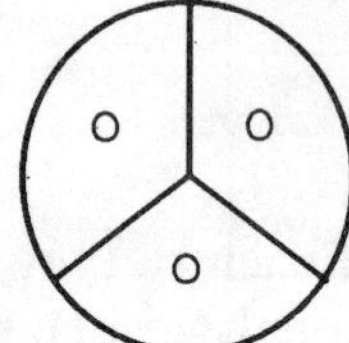

To keep costs down, each culture plate may be used to test 3 to 5 substances. The plate may be divided into sectors by drawing on the underneath side with a waterproof marker, labeling each sector with the name of the suspected mutagen to be tested, and placing the filter paper disk with the test substance in the center of each sector.

3. Seal the plates with Parafilm and incubate, inverted, at room temperature.

4. Examine the plates for bacterial growth after 3 to 5 days. Plates with observable growth should be placed in a 4°C refrigerator until the next lab period.

Possible hypotheses students might want to test

1. Specific substances (list by name) increase the frequency of streptomycin-resistant mutants.

2. Food substances do not increase mutation rates. Household substances do increase mutation rates.

3. Vegetables cause cancer. Cosmetics cause cancer. **Note: This hypothesis is not testable in the experiment described unless the association between mutagenesis in bacteria and cancer is perfect, which it is not. However, some students are likely to propose this hypothesis.**

Controls Students often have to be convinced to include controls in this experiment. However, appropriate controls are vital for interpreting the experimental results.

Control	What will be shown	Plate diagram
NA + strep + bacterial inoculum (no mutagens)	The background mutation rate	
NA + strep (no bacteria) suspected mutagens	Whether bacteria are present in the test substances	
NA + strep + bacterial inoculum filter paper	If the filter paper is a source of mutagenic activity	
NA (no strep) + bacterial inoculum (no mutagens)	Viability of the bacterial culture	
NA + strep + bacterial inoculum ICR-191 acridine mutagen (page 249)	Whether a known mutagen increases the mutation frequency[6]	

Data collection

Quantitative method

1. Tell students how many bacteria were spread on each petri plate and allow them to calculate the background mutation rate.

$$\text{background rate} = \frac{\text{number of streptomycin-resistant mutants}}{\text{number of cells inoculated}}$$

[6]For safety, it is best to set up the ICR 191 test plate yourself, present it as a demonstration, and not allow students to handle this strongly mutagenic substance.

Approximate method Students can compare similarly sized segments of test plates and background plates and report the relative strength of each suspected mutagen. They can also compare the frequency of colonies in areas of the plate near the test chemical with the frequency of colonies on the rest of the plate.

Troubleshooting and dealing with problems

Problem	Possible explanation	Solution
no colonies	bacterial culture not viable	Test the culture ahead of time to make sure it grows.
no mutagens	substances chosen by students are not strongly mutagenic	Develop a collection of substances that work (mustard or basil); encourage students to use them.

Misleading event	Observation	How to avoid
antibiotic inactivated by the test substance	looks like strong mutagenic reaction	Beware of very low or very high pH substances; inactivation of antibiotic can be confused with mutagenesis.
bacteria killed by the test substance	clear zone with no colonies around test disk	Beware of cleaning products, especially disinfectants and petroleum-based products.

Questions to guide discussion

◆ If you see colonies on the plate with the chemical, how will you know if the chemical is a mutagen? (This question highlights the need for a control to determine the background mutation frequency.) Are the colonies located near the filter paper disk?

◆ What causes mutations?

◆ In this experiment, what serves as the selection pressure?

◆ How are the events on your petri plate analogous to evolution? How are they different? (Highlight mutation frequency, selection pressure, change in gene frequency in a population.)

◆ What are the implications of your experimental results for treatment of human diseases caused by pathogens?

Sources of information

◆ Brock, Thomas D., Michael T. Madigan, John M. Martinko, and Jack Parker (1994) *Biology of Microorganisms*, 7th ed. Englewood Cliffs, NJ: Prentice Hall.

◆ Stent, Gunther S. and Richard Calender (1978) *Molecular Genetics: An Introductory Narrative*, 2nd ed., ch. 6. San Francisco, CA: W.H. Freeman and Company.

Experiment 8: The risk of genetic vulnerability
A lesson in selection and evolution

History is punctuated with disease epidemics that have decimated entire races or species of plants and animals. Examples include the destruction of the Irish potato crop in the 19th century by a pathogen, the devastation of the Native American people by the introduction of smallpox virus from Europe, the widespread death in 17th-century Europe resulting from the bubonic plague bacterium, and devastation of the Australian hare by a viral infection. Some scientists have even proposed that the dinosaurs were driven to extinction by infectious disease. More recently, the loss in the United States of the American elm and the chestnut tree was the result of uncontrollable fungal diseases. The 1969 and 1970 corn crop in the United States was affected by a fungus that caused the infamous Southern Corn Leaf Blight. When the majority of members of a population is susceptible to a particular pathogen, that population is **genetically vulnerable**.

Plants and animals resist disease by quite different mechanisms. Mammals have a highly sophisticated **immune response** for protection from disease. The immune response leads to production of **antibodies** that help specialized immune cells recognize and destroy pathogens. **Immunization** involves exposure to a pathogen followed by an immune response that protects against disease on subsequent exposure to the pathogen. Once a mammal is immunized against a pathogen and has the ability to produce antibodies against that pathogen, the immunity lasts a long time, often a whole lifetime. The mechanism of resistance to disease in plants is less well understood, but, in general, plants have **genes for resistance** to disease that do not require preexposure to the pathogen to be active. In contrast to the mammalian immune response, if a plant carries a gene for resistance to a pathogen, the pathogen will not be able to cause disease in the plant even the first time they come in contact.

A striking similarity of disease resistance in plants and animals is **specificity**. In animals, the immune response is highly specific—immunization against one pathogen does not cause immunity to other pathogens. For example, the smallpox vaccine does not induce immunity to measles, and infection by one strain of the flu virus does not protect you when the next flu strain comes along. Similarly, resistance genes in plants are pathogen-specific. A gene that makes a plant resistant to a particular fungal disease will not affect resistance to a virus. A gene that confers resistance to a specific strain of a fungus will not confer resistance to all strains of the same fungal species. Furthermore, most pathogens are specific to the hosts they can infect, attacking one or a few species, although some plant pathogens infect hundreds of different types of plants, and certain viruses infect both plants and insects. The specificity of pathogens for their hosts and the specificity of host resistance has resulted in a complex array of interactions between hosts and their pathogens.

In the plant world, the most devastating epidemics often occur because the plant population harbors little or no genetic resistance to the disease. Disease can be a powerful driving force in evolution by selecting for survival of a subpopulation that is resistant to disease. Genetic resistance to a disease is often found in the area of the world where the host and pathogen have interacted for eons. Plant breeders have been using genetic resistance to disease for the benefit of agriculture for many centuries. Utilizing the tremendous genetic variability present in most crop species, breeders have selected individuals that are resistant to a particular disease, intermated those individuals, and increased the seed from those crosses, continually screening for the ability of the population to survive in the presence of the pathogen. This method has been used to generate **varieties** or **cultivars** that are resistant to the common diseases affecting most of the major crops we use for food and fiber.

Breeding for resistance is the most important strategy for controlling plant disease in modern agriculture. For most of the known diseases of economically important crops, resistant cultivars are available to farmers. However, unanticipated, new disease problems often arise. New strains evolve from old pathogens, and pathogens that do not exist in a geographic region may be imported on plant material or in soil and quickly become a problem. Some of the most devastating epidemics in agricultural history have resulted from farmers planting genetically uniform populations that were uniformly susceptible to an unanticipated and highly destructive pathogen. To protect crops against unknown or unpredicted diseases, farmers often plant a mixture of crop varieties to maximize the genetic variation in the population, thereby increasing the chance that at least some of the members of the population will be resistant to an unforeseen disease problem.

Key concepts

Breeding crops for resistance to disease reduces crop loss due to known diseases.

Most pathogens are host-specific.

Challenge

You will be given two populations of alfalfa plants. One is a population that has not been bred for resistance to anthracnose and the other has been bred for resistance. Anthracnose is a disease caused by the fungus *Colletotrichum trifolii*. You will also be given a culture of *C. trifolii* and soybean plants. Develop a hypothesis and an experiment to test it. Focus on the issues of pathogenicity, resistance to disease, and pathogen specificity.

Key questions

- **What is the importance of genetic vulnerability?**
- **What happens to the frequency of genes for resistance after exposure of a population to a pathogen?**
- **Explain why genes for disease resistance might be pathogen-specific.**
- **How do you explain the evolution of crops that are highly susceptible to certain pathogens?**
- **Compare and contrast evolution with breeding and selection.**
- **How do you think national agricultural policy could be used to reduce the impact of major epidemics on crop production?**

Experiment 8: The risk of genetic vulnerability
A lesson in selection and evolution

In this exercise students will examine the effect of genetic resistance on development of plant disease.

Genetic resistance/vulnerability: The exercise utilizes *Colletotrichum trifolii*, the fungus that causes anthracnose on alfalfa, and two plant species, alfalfa and soybeans, to examine resistance and pathogenicity. Students investigate two populations of alfalfa—one that is almost non-resistant and one that has strong resistance to *Colletotrichum*—to observe two levels of host resistance to the pathogen.

Pathogen/host specificity: Finally, soybean plants are inoculated with the alfalfa pathogens to test the concept of pathogen specificity for hosts. Students will see that the alfalfa pathogen does not infect soybeans.

What students will learn

genetic vulnerability, population genetics, selection pressures, pathogen and resistance specificity

The key conceptual elements of this experiment are genetic vulnerability, population genetics, selection pressures, and specificity of pathogenicity. The experiment provides a graphic demonstration of the power of resistance to disease. This, in turn, can be used to illustrate the influence of genetic variation in populations and the power of selection pressure in changing the genetic structure of the population. The process of breeding and selection for genetic resistance in crops provides a useful process to compare and contrast with evolution and natural selection, providing strong reinforcement for these difficult concepts.

An important element of the experimental system is that the anthracnose fungus ***kills*** the alfalfa plants. This provides a visual illustration of how population genetics are influenced by selection pressures: It is quite obvious that after infection and death of the susceptible plants, the frequency of the gene for resistance to the pathogen is much higher in the surviving population than it was in the initial population. It is simple to see that the dead plants will not reproduce and will not pass on their genes to offspring, whereas the resistant, live plants will be able to do so.

Learning highlights and conceptual challenges

> *"Poor plants!" first variation, then selection;*
> *pathogenicity for one ≠ pathogenicity for all*

The most rewarding aspect of "Vulnerability" is seeing the students begin to understand the meaning of gene frequency in a population. The visual impact of the experiment is electrifying because the anthracnose pathogen is so virulent. The sight of the devastated population of susceptible alfalfa plants always elicits a "wow!" or "poor plants!" from the students. Although the materials and examples are quite different, the concepts in this exercise are closely related to those in the previous exercise on genetic frequencies in bacteria. By drawing comparisons between the two experiments, you can reinforce the population genetics concepts.

The most challenging aspect of teaching with "Vulnerability" is overcoming the students' misconceptions about evolution and resistance to disease. One idea that seems to be prevalent among our students is that traits appear as the result of selection pressure, not that natural selection acts on *existing genetic variation in a population* (Lamarck again!). It is essential to stress that genetic variation for a given trait occurs normally within populations and that we can measure frequency of the trait by applying a selective pressure, such as a pathogen that kills all susceptible individuals.

Another misconception held by many students is that resistance to one disease results in resistance to all diseases. The concept that pathogens are specific for their hosts and that hosts possess resistance that is specific to the pathogen is foreign to most of the students. Using examples from human disease (did having a cold keep you from getting the flu?) can be helpful in sorting out this concept. Including both soybeans and alfalfa plants in the experiment will demonstrate the specificity of pathogens for their hosts.

Materials needed for teacher preparations

8" × 12" pans (2 per group)
soil mixture (½ sand, ½ muck or a standard potting soil mix) to fill the pans
vermiculite (page 250)
alfalfa seed (anthracnose-resistant population, "Arc") (page 251)
alfalfa seed (anthracnose-susceptible population, "Vernal") (page 251)
soybean seed (page 251)
small rubber scraper
Colletotrichum trifolii on crystals (page 251)
PDA plates (pages 229 and 249)

Materials needed for students

Number per group:

2	rectangular pans filled with soil mixture
	alfalfa plants - resistant population, "Arc"
	alfalfa plants - susceptible population, "Vernal"
	soybean plants
1	sterile sprayer bottle containing water
1	sprayer bottle containing *C. trifolii* suspension

Teacher preparations prior to lab period

Before the semester begins

1. Obtain anthracnose-susceptible and anthracnose-resistant alfalfa seed and soybean seed (or seed of another plant species). Also obtain *Colletotrichum trifolii* crystals.

Two weeks before the lab period

Planting alfalfa and soybean seeds:

1. Steam soil 1 to 2 hours and allow it to cool. (Alternatively, use sterilized potting soil.)

2. Fill 2 rectangular pans for each group with soil mixture. In each pan, make 12 shallow parallel rows in the soil, evenly spaced and perpendicular to the long side of the pan.

   Plant one of the pans with alfalfa seed as follows: In the first 6 rows, plant anthracnose-resistant alfalfa seeds, and in the second 6 rows, plant anthracnose-susceptible seeds (60 to 65 seeds per row). Mark the center of the pan and label the populations of alfalfa seeds on each side of the center.

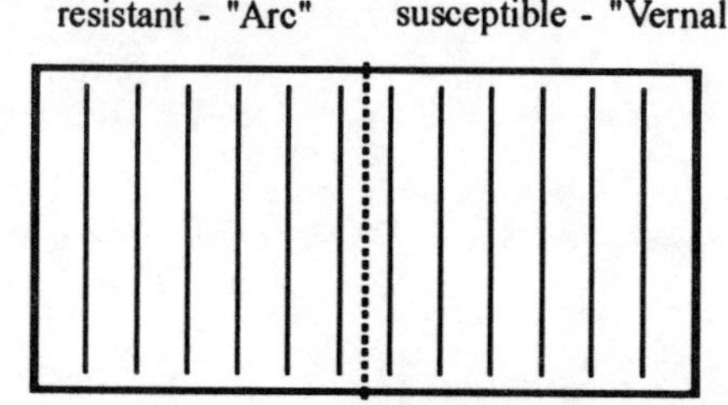

   Plant the other pan with 12 rows of soybean seed. Label the pan containing the soybean seeds. See the diagram on page 120.

3. Cover the rows with a layer of vermiculite approximately 5 mm deep. Moisten the vermiculite and keep it moist during the growth period. Place pans under a grow light or in a well-lighted location for best plant growth.

Prepare *Colletotrichum* cultures:

1. Sprinkle *Colletotrichum* crystals, 5 - 10 per plate, on PDA plates and incubate for 2 weeks at room temperature.

A few hours before the lab period

1. Pour 10 ml of sterile water onto each plate and scrape the spores into a suspension using a rubber scraper. Combine the suspensions from all the plates and filter through cheesecloth. Count and dilute the spores to 10^6 per ml. Plan to have about 10 to 20 mls of suspension per group. You should be able to harvest 10^7 to 10^8 spores per plate, so a few plates will provide inoculum for many plants.

2. Pour the *C. trifolii* inoculum into plant sprayers (one for each group of students).

How to guide students

During class

1. Using sheets of cardboard or stiff plastic to divide the pans containing the alfalfa or soybean seedlings longitudinally into two equal sections, students should spray the plants on one side of each divider with the anthracnose suspension and the plants on the other side of each divider with sterile water. Care should be taken not to contaminate the plants across the divider. The plants should be sprayed from different directions until the suspension thoroughly coats them and begins to run off.

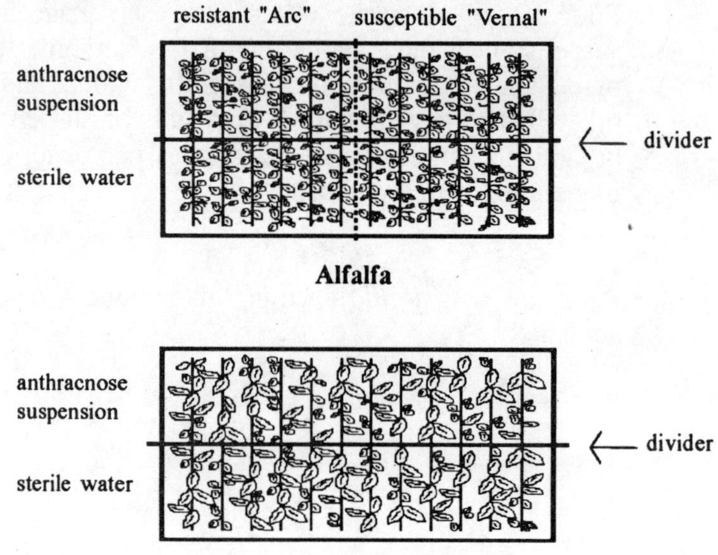

Alfalfa

Beans

Students should count and record the number of living plants in each quadrant of the pans before or right after inoculation.

Place the pans in plastic bags to keep the humidity on the leaf surface high for the first 48 hours after inoculation. This facilitates infection.

Seven to ten days later

1. Students should observe physical differences of plants in each treatment and count and record the number of living plants in each quadrant of the pans.

Possible hypotheses students might want to test

1. **General** - Some plant varieties are more resistant than others to a given pathogen. **Specific** - The alfalfa populations vary in their resistance to anthracnose. One population is susceptible, the other is resistant.

2. **General** - A pathogen that causes disease in one kind of plant does not cause disease in another kind of plant. **Specific** - The anthracnose pathogen is specific for alfalfa. Soybeans are not susceptible to anthracnose.

Data collection

1. **Descriptive** - Note any differences in the general appearance of the plants for each treatment group, such as color, robustness, size, or presence of lesions.

2. **Quantitative** - Count the number of living alfalfa and soybean plants in each quadrant before treating with the pathogen suspensions; after 7 to 10 days, again count the number of living plants for each treatment group; calculate the plant survival or mortality rate.

Troubleshooting and dealing with problems

Problem	Possible explanation	Solution
no disease	not enough spores	check spore concentration by counting spores with a hemacytometer under microscope; err on the high side with spore concentration if you cannot quantify them
	not enough humidity	be sure the plastic bag makes a humid environment (make sure there are no holes in the bag and that it is tightly knotted closed); be sure plants are sprayed until the water runs off the leaves and are then immediately placed in the bags
	culture not virulent	good to precheck culture on alfalfa plants; start from culture stored on silica crystals

Questions to guide discussion

◆ What is the selection pressure in this experiment?

◆ What are the similarities/differences between selection with a pathogen in the lab and natural selection in the real world?

◆ Why do you think many pathogens evolved to be host-specific?

◆ If you were a plant breeder, what would be your strategy for breeding crops for disease resistance?

Sources of information

◆ Agrios, George N. (1988) *Plant Pathology*. San Diego, CA: Academic Press, Inc.

◆ Darwin, Charles (1859) *The Origin of Species by Means of Natural Selection or the Preservation of Favoured Races in the Struggle for Life*. London: Collier Macmillan Publishers. (In Chapter 1, Darwin provides an insightful discussion of the parallels between breeding and evolution.)

Experiment 9: Microbial biodiversity
A lesson in diversity

Biodiversity is one of the Earth's greatest treasures, and it is being destroyed by human activity. Biodiversity is the term used to describe the variety of organisms, which includes the number of species and the genetic variation within species.

Diversity of the biological world has both aesthetic and practical value. A multitude of species create the subtle and complex beauty of the world around us. The diverse organisms in our biosphere contribute to the stability and productivity of our planet. Throughout history, human beings have put members of the biological world to use in ingenious ways as food, fiber, and medicines. Coffee is made from the seed of a tropical bush, french fries are made from a plant discovered high in the Andes, blue jeans are made from the fruits of cotton plants, and drugs for heart ailments are made from foxglove and periwinkles.

One of the alarming consequences of the loss of biodiversity is that we cannot guess today what species will contribute to feeding the world or curing disease tomorrow. Therefore, preserving biodiversity in its totality is a wise investment in the future of our species. Moreover, many people believe that we as a species have a special obligation to preserve the beauty, complexity, and balance of the world around us since we have greater power than any other species over the fate of the planet.

Recently, attention has focused on maintaining biodiversity of plants and animals in the tropical rain forests, which are the source of most of the world's biological diversity. The Environmental Summit in Rio in 1992 highlighted the conflicts between environmental and economic concerns about maintaining biodiversity. Some of the key issues about preserving biodiversity include: Who should take responsibility for preserving natural communities? Who should bear the cost of this preservation? Who should share in the profits derived from organisms taken from the tropical forests of developing countries?

Although biodiversity has been the focus of heated debates and political platforms, little attention has been paid, in all of the international discussion of the topic, to preserving biodiversity of microorganisms, which have provided a rich source of technology for improving human existence since the beginning of civilization. Bacteria and fungi are responsible for all of our fermented food and drink—bread, cheese, sauerkraut, yogurt, soy sauce, wine, beer, and sake—and for many of the antibiotics that have vastly reduced human mortality due to bacterial infections. Penicillin was first discovered in a culture of a common mold, *Penicillium*, and most of our antibiotics are produced by bacteria or fungi that live in soil.

The soil is teeming with bacteria and fungi of great variety (one billion microbes per gram!). Some have been isolated and characterized while many remain an untapped resource that may provide the key to solving nutritional or disease problems of the future. Some estimates show that we have isolated and grown in culture less than one percent of the bacterial species from the soil, suggesting that the greatest untapped source of biodiversity might be right under our feet! Preserving diversity of bacteria and fungi is an imposing task because of the problems inherent in dealing with such diverse groups of organisms, many of which cannot be seen with the naked eye. But preserving them may be as important to the health of our planet as preserving diversity of plants and animals.

One of the challenges of assessing biodiversity of microorganisms is the problem of detecting organisms we cannot see. Walking through a forest, we can look at the flora and fauna and count the numbers of different kinds of birds, ferns, or beetles. But how do we know how many different kinds of microorganisms are there? The most common method is to spread a sample (for example soil, leaves, roots, or insect legs) on a petri plate containing nutrients that will enable a wide variety of microorganisms to grow, incubate the plates, and then count the different kinds of colonies that grow on the plates. This is a powerful method that has contributed substantially to our knowledge of environmental microbiology, but it is important to be aware of its limitations. It detects only organisms that grow on the culture medium, under the conditions chosen, in the presence of the other microorganisms on that particular plate. This is a common problem in science: Our image of the world around us is defined and limited by the methods we use to measure that world.

Key concepts

Soil contains a diverse community of microorganisms.

Culturing techniques detect only part of the microbial community in soil.

Challenge

Bring three different soil samples to class with you. Try sampling a range of soil types from a garden, a beach, a forest, or from different depths. Construction sites and cemeteries are good places to sample deep soil. You will only need a small sample of each (½ teaspoonful). You will be supplied with the materials listed on the next page. **Generate a hypothesis about the microbes in your soil samples and design an experiment to test it.**

Key questions

☞ What do microorganisms require for growth in soil?

☞ Do you think that all soil samples will have the same microorganisms in them?

☞ Can we affect the types of organisms we isolate by the growth conditions we provide them?

☞ What problems are specifically associated with doing a census of microorganisms?

☞ What factors might affect the composition (types of members) of microbial communities?

☞ How might the presence of one species affect our ability to detect another species?

☞ How many times do you think you need to repeat your experiment to obtain an accurate representation of the microorganisms in your sample? How will you know when you have repeated it enough?

Materials provided

test tube
water
glass rod (cleaned with alcohol)
sterile toothpicks
agar plates containing media with various nutrients
incubators with various environmental conditions

Experiment 9: Microbial biodiversity
A lesson in diversity

In this exercise, students will test hypotheses about the nature of diversity of microorganisms in soil.

As citizens of a world that seems to revolve around information bits and highly specialized machines, it is well for us to take a moment to appreciate biodiversity—for its own sake as well as for its practical applications. It is easy to forget that although we do not always live in great intimacy with nature, we still depend on its diverse organisms for nearly every aspect of our lives, from our food, shelter, and medicines, to the air we breathe.

Imagine Earth populated with only a few kinds of plants, a few kinds of animals, and a few kinds of microbes. What a sterile and boring place this would be. And how vulnerable these few creatures would be to changes in the environment.

What students will learn

biodiversity; controls, controls, controls; indirect methods; biological variability; respect for microbes

This exercise is designed to promote thinking about both biodiversity and the indirect, and perhaps inadequate, methods available to measure diversity of organisms that we cannot see or differentiate by eye. The profound variety of organisms that can be cultured from a tiny sample of soil provides a powerful demonstration of the concept of biodiversity. Students must develop methods to describe or measure diversity, which encourages them to observe and become intimate with the organisms they culture. Designing the experiment helps the students understand how the environmental conditions they choose determine which organisms they will detect on the plates. If they culture aerobically, for example, they will see a different part of the community than if they culture anaerobically. This will illustrate the problem of developing an accurate picture of microbial communities given that we can only detect those organisms that grow under a defined set of conditions.

The experiments will emphasize two design issues. The students must be careful to include the appropriate controls to enable them to draw conclusions, reinforcing the principles of use of controls in designed experiments. The exercise can also be used to introduce the concept of biological variability and sampling. The soil is an extraordinarily variable environment, and each sample is likely to give rise to a different subset of culturable organisms. If the students replicate their experiments, they are likely to be able to observe this variability, which will enable them to understand the need for logical sampling and sufficient replication tailored to the variability in a given biological event.

Learning highlights and conceptual challenges

> *"Wow! So many types of critters." "You mean we don't know what's down there?!!!"*
> *"You only get what you look for."*

Two realizations stun the students when they work on "Biodiversity." First, they are overwhelmed by the profound diversity they can detect in the soil. On the right media, they may get 100 easily distinguishable colony types on their plates—exhibiting a wonderful variety of color, morphology, and behavior. Perhaps the most exciting phenotype they observe is the bacterial colony that produces a zone of inhibition around it, on a plate that is otherwise covered with fungal and bacterial growth. From their observations of diversity come an understanding of the challenges these soil organisms face in making their homes in a harsh, nutrient-poor environment. The abundance of organisms, the obvious antagonisms due to competition or antibiosis, and diverse life strategies evolved by soil microbes are concepts vividly illustrated in this exercise.

One of the attractions of this experiment is that the students supply the soil samples—literally bringing a piece of their world to the classroom. This leads to the second surprise in the experiment: how little we know about the microorganisms that live in the soil. The earth around us seems so familiar—we walk on it, grow our crops and forests in it, and bury our dead in it. It is curious, then, that we know of only a fraction of the bacteria that live in the soil. Our knowledge is limited by the tools available to study soil microbiology. The experiments that the students design are a good illustration of how the techniques we use influence which organisms we detect, and little extrapolation is needed to imagine the plethora of microbes likely to be in the soil that do not grow on the media we supply in the lab. This discovery can provide a starting point for a discussion of how we might improve detection techniques and of the general issue of the bias that is inherent in all biological experimentation. The discussion of other techniques for studying soil bacteria can be stimulated with questions that focus on the properties of bacteria such as lipids, DNA sequences, or morphology (if stained properly) that we can detect directly, without culturing. (See "Sources of Information" for references on these new techniques.)

Students are often troubled when they realize that our view of how the world works is influenced by the tools we choose to study it. We find that "Biodiversity" often leads to one of the semester's most stimulating discussions about the limitations of scientific study and the quest for new methods. This experiment can go a long way toward helping students develop an accurate understanding of how knowledge is derived and the challenges and limitations inherent in the process of discovery. "Biodiversity" stimulates students intellectually and emotionally. The open-endedness of the experiment, resulting from the large number of variables that could be tested, presents students with the challenge of focusing their experiment on a clear hypothesis and developing a logical experimental design to test it. This experiment is used late in the semester because it is so challenging in terms of design. Juggling soil type, choice of culture medium, and environmental conditions under which to incubate the medium is quite a task. We can help students to focus by reminding them to state a clear hypothesis and then asking them to describe to the group how their experiment tests that hypothesis. The most common mistake students make in "Biodiversity" is to include too many variables and too few controls, making it difficult to draw conclusions from the resulting data.

You can target questions to provoke thought about this issue. ("How will you know if differences are due to soil type or to temperature?") It is important to *ask* and not *tell* when guiding students through this experiment. If they insist, even after being questioned by you or the other students, on using a set of treatments that will not permit them to draw conclusions, let them do the experiment. We have found that the best way for some students to learn about controls is for them to encounter real data that cannot be interpreted without a control they have omitted from their experiment. Some of the most thoughtful lab reports we have read include comments about the controls that were needed but not included and the conclusions that *might* have been drawn had the experiment been designed better.

Many students confront the concepts of replication and sampling for the first time through this experiment. With the vast numbers of microorganisms to be found in even a small sample of soil, students will observe only a fraction of the many organisms possible each time they culture a subsample. They will learn that the diversity of organisms they observe is limited by both the particular bit of soil they choose and the methods they use for culturing (aerobic or anaerobic conditions, media types, or incubation temperatures). A followup question, "How many different conditions would we need to culture all of the organisms from soil," is useful, if unanswerable, to focus attention on the unknown.

The emotional challenge in "Biodiversity" lies in the discussion of the limitation of scientific investigation. The realization that scientific knowledge is derived from a flawed process, often involving methods with inherent bias, is stunning to many students. Many express amazement that the "facts" in textbooks were generated by a process not unlike the one they use in their Desk-top Biology experiments. We often hear them comment that they thought there were some things that are "simply known" and other things that are "researched." Understanding the source of our knowledge base helps them appreciate its fragility, as well as the centuries of difficult research that contributed to its creation. Be aware that this discussion can be emotionally loaded. For those students who like to be assured that we have definitive, indisputable knowledge of the natural world, this discussion can be disturbing but enlightening.

Materials needed for teacher preparations

potato dextrose agar + streptomycin culture plates (PDA+strep) (5–10 per group) (pages 229, 249)
V-8 agar culture plates (5–10 per group) (pages 231, 249)
Rose Bengal agar culture plates (5–10 per group) (pages 230, 249)
50% tryptic soy agar culture plates (50% TSA) (5–10 per group) (pages 231, 249)
3 or more samples of different soil types (100 g, each) (e.g., sand, forest soil, field soil, swamp muck)
1.5-ml sterile microtubes (page 250) containing 0.5 ml sterile water (5 per group)
glass rods (5 per group)
Parafilm (page 250)
incubators to provide various environmental conditions (see "How to guide students," page 133)
4°C refrigerator

Materials needed for students

Number per group:

1–3	soil samples to test
5–10	culture plates—PDA+strep
5–10	culture plates—V-8 agar
5–10	culture plates—Rose Bengal agar
5–10	culture plates—50% tryptic soy agar
5	1.5-ml test tubes containing sterile water

Teacher preparations prior to lab period

Before the lab period

1. Prepare enough of a variety of media (such as PDA+strep, V-8 agar, Rose Bengal agar, 50% tryptic soy agar) to supply each group with 5–10 culture plates of each kind.

2. Encourage students to bring samples of different soil types to lab. In addition, collect a few grams each of at least 3 different soils.

3. Dispense 0.5 ml of sterile water into sterile 1.5-ml microfuge tubes. Prepare enough water tubes per group so students will have 1 for each soils.

Three to four days after the lab period

1. Examine all plates for the presence of especially fast-growing fungi. If plates appear to be in danger of being overwhelmed by fungal growth, store them in a 4°C refrigerator until they are to be used in the next lab.

How to guide students

During class

1. Students should place a small sample of the soil from which microbes are to be isolated in the sterile water contained in a microfuge tube. Use a sterile rod to thoroughly mix the soil and water.

2. Using the same glass rod, students should streak a drop of the water/soil mixture onto the various culture media. Then using sterile toothpicks, they should complete a 3-way streak (page 220).

3. Seal plates with Parafilm, invert, and incubate in various environments (freezer and/or refrigerator) for cold environment, incubator and/or high shelf for warm environment, humid environment, dark environment, or anaerobic environment (see page 48, no. 5 for specific directions in creating environments).

4. In the second lab, students will examine the microbes growing on their culture plates. Students should be encouraged to develop a semi-quantitative scale for rating the amount of diversity in the soils in response to incubation in the various environments, for example, the number of different colony morphologies and the total number of colonies.

Possible hypotheses students might want to test

1. Surface soil samples have a greater variety of aerobic microorganisms than do deep soil samples.

2. Deep soil samples have a greater variety of anaerobic microorganisms than do surface soil samples.

3. There is a greater variety of microorganisms in rich, forest soil than in beach sand.

4. Microorganisms are evenly distributed through a given soil sample. (Replicate platings of different subsamples, or even of the same subsample, yield the same variety, or number, of microorganisms.)

Data collection

1. **Descriptive** - Characterize the different kinds of colonies growing on each plate, including observations such as colony color, size, texture, surface sheen, regularity of edges, zones of inhibition, or other striking features.

2. **Quantitative** - Count the number of individual colonies growing on each plate, the number of different kinds of colonies on each plate, and the number of each kind of colony. Estimate the relative abundance of each kind (determine the approximate surface area covered by each kind of colony).

   In the discussion, you may want to help the students identify sources of variability in experimental technique, such as measuring soil or plating technique, and discuss the role of experimental variability as well as the intrinsic variability in the soil itself.

Troubleshooting and dealing with problems

Problem	Possible explanation	Solution
plates are overwhelmed by rapidly growing colonies	high concentration of microbes in soil samples; warm temperatures favor rapid growth	store plates in a 4°C refrigerator to slow down growth

Questions to guide discussion

- Do you think you are detecting *all* microbes that are alive in your soil sample? What evidence do you have to support or refute your answer?

- What are the limitations on your conclusions about what microbes are in the soil?

- What methods other than culturing might we use to detect organisms in soil? What properties of bacteria might we detect directly?

- How is our knowledge of the world shaped by the experimental tools we have in hand?

- Do all scientific methods have an inherent bias? Examples?

- What is an example of a very biased method? A less biased method?

- How might some of the undescribed organisms be useful in medicine or agriculture?

Sources of information

- DeLong, Edward F., Gene S. Wickham, and Norman R. Pace (1989) Phylogenetic stains: Ribosomal RNA-based probes for the identification of single cells. *Science*, 243: 1360–1363.

- Holben, William E., Janet K. Jansson, Barry K. Chelm, and James M. Tiedje (1988) DNA probe method for the detection of specific microorganisms in the soil bacterial community. *Applied and Environmental Microbiology*, 54: 703–711.

- Olsen, Gary J., Carl R. Woese, and Ross Overbeek (1994) Minireview. The winds of (evolutionary) change: Breathing new life into microbiology. *Journal of Bacteriology*, 176: 1-6.

- Reid, Walter V., Ana Sittenfeld, Sarah A. Laird, Daniel A. Janzen, Carrie A. Meyer, Michael A. Gollin, Rodrigo Gámez, and Calestous Juma (1993) *Biodiversity Prospecting: Using Genetic Resources for Sustainable Development*. World Resources Institute.

Enrichment exercise on sampling

One of the most difficult concepts to understand and one of the most challenging technical skills to get right in biological research is sampling. How much is enough? What part of the experiment do we replicate? How do we know if we have a representative sample? These are questions that plague quantitative biologists in fields such as ecology, behavior, and epidemiology. We have found that the following simple exercise clarifies the issue of sampling for the students.

1. Give each group in the class a bag of M & M's. Each bag should contain at least 20 pieces.

2. Tell the class that the goal of the exercise is to describe the population of M & M's in the bags.

3. Tell each group to remove one M & M from its bag. The students may look inside the bag to determine how many M & Ms there are of each color, but they should not purposefully pick a certain color. Ask whether one M & M is a representative sample.

4. Tell each group to remove one more M & M and ask whether the groups now have representative samples.

5. Continue this process until the groups agree that they have a sample that reflects the entire population in the bag. There are usually six colors in a bag so adequate samples will likely fall between 5 and 10 pieces.

6. Discuss how much over-sampling is needed to be sure to cover all the colors. For example, if a student pulls out three greens in a row, s/he will need more than six pieces to obtain a representative sample.

7. When the students seem comfortable with the concept of sampling M & M's, make the analogy with sampling microorganisms in soil. Stress the greater challenge in sampling soil since the diversity is much greater than six types. The students will want to know how they would know when they have sampled enough soil. Talk them through how they knew in the M & M's exercise (when new types stop turning up) how much is enough. Sampling strategies are determined empirically in biology, as well as in sampling M & M's.

Experiment 10: Mutualism and antagonism among organisms

A lesson in ecology

Species of plants, animals, and microorganisms interact in many ways. Since they live on a planet with limited resources for supporting life, organisms must often behave in ways that interfere with the normal life processes and reproduction of other species to obtain sustenance for their offspring and themselves. Such negative interactions include **predation** (for example, a lion eating a zebra), **parasitism** (*Phytophthora*, a microorganism causing disease of a potato plant), **competition** (two species of salamanders competing for food, plant species competing for water, or barnacle species competing for space), or **antagonism** or **interference** (the black walnut tree releasing a toxic chemical, juglone, from its roots, which prevents the growth of other plant species such as tomatoes).

Although there are many examples of detrimental interactions between organisms, just as important in biology are the beneficial interactions. Many organisms have developed mutually beneficial and mutually dependent relationships with members of other species. This type of relationship is known as **mutualism**. For example, the parrot fish maintains a fleet of little fish that clean its scales of parasites and receive a nutritious parasite meal for their efforts. Some plants depend on insects, bats, or hummingbirds for flower pollination, providing the animals with nectar or pollen in return.

We often think of microorganisms as the "germs" that cause diseases of plants and animals, but microorganisms can act as both antagonists and mutualists with other organisms. As mutualists they provide many necessary nutrients and protectants that make life possible for higher organisms. Cyanobacteria and fungi team up to form lichens in which the bacteria contribute their ability to convert light energy to food through photosynthesis and to fix nitrogen gas from the air. It is not known what the bacterial partner derives from the relationship, but some bacteria exist only as lichens, suggesting that the fungus provides them with something necessary for life. Cows depend on the bacteria that live in their rumens to degrade the fiber in the hay they eat; humans depend on the intestinal bacterium, *Escherichia coli*, for a steady supply of vitamin K; and termites carry bacteria that supply them with nitrogen. All of these relationships benefit the animal nutritionally, and the bacteria acquire a specialized niche with sufficient nutrients for growth. Bacteria can also assist their hosts in functions other than nutrition. In one unusual relationship, the luminescent bacterium *Vibrio fischeri* colonizes specialized organs below the eyes of certain fish. The bacteria emit light, which is thought to help the host attract prey.

Microorganisms are also responsible for recycling organic nutrients and transforming minerals. For example, fungi decompose organic matter, and bacteria reduce manganese and oxidize iron.

Plants derive nutrients and protection from pests through their interactions with microorganisms. Mycorrhizal fungi invade the roots of plants and increase availability of soil nutrients, most soils contain microorganisms that suppress root disease, and some bacteria produce toxins that kill plant-feeding insects. In one of the most remarkable interactions in the biological world, the soil bacterium *Rhizobium* invades the roots of legume plants, such as alfalfa and peas; induces swellings known as nodules; and provides the host plant with nitrogen for growth. The bacterium, living inside the nodule it induces, obtains nitrogen from the air in the form of dinitrogen gas (N_2), which comprises 80% of the atmosphere around the Earth. Dinitrogen gas is not usable as a nitrogen source by plants, animals, or most microbes, but *Rhizobium* (and certain other bacteria) converts it to ammonia (NH_3), which is readily used by plants for growth.

Human beings have harnessed both mutualistic and antagonistic relationships to improve agricultural production. The best example of mutualism in agriculture is the use of *Rhizobium* and leguminous plants to supply nitrogen to agricultural systems. Leguminous crops do not require nitrogen fertilizer for growth because the *Rhizobium* in the nodules fix sufficient nitrogen for the plants' needs. Not only do the legumes not require the application of nitrogen fertilizer, but the residues of leguminous plants left in a field provide nitrogen for subsequent crops that do not enter into a mutualistic relationship with *Rhizobium.* A widely used antagonistic relationship is one between insects and bacteria that kill them and thereby act as crop protectants. Bacteria are likely to become more prominent in world food production as agricultural producers search for alternatives to chemical fertilizers and pesticides, which have generated vigorous criticism from consumers and the general public because of their potentially negative impacts on the environment and human health.

Examples of bacteria that are antagonistic to agricultural pests:

Bacillus cereus strain UW85 is a bacterium discovered in 1985 at the University of Wisconsin. It produces antibiotics that prevent oomycete pathogens from causing disease of plants.

Bacillus thuringiensis (commonly known as "Bt") is a bacterium that produces a toxin that kills certain insects. Bt is used widely in agriculture to control insect damage on crop plants.

Key concepts

Antagonistic relationships between bacteria and insects or pathogens improve plant health and agricultural production.

Mutually beneficial relationships between plants and microbes contribute profoundly to plant health and agricultural production.

Challenge

Design an experiment to determine the effects of ***either*** *Bacillus cereus* or *Bacillus thuringiensis* on plant health.

You will be supplied with a culture of *B. cereus* strain UW85, alfalfa seeds, and a suspension of zoospores of the oomycete, *Pythium*, which is pathogenic to alfalfa. **Design an experiment that will determine whether UW85 protects alfalfa seedlings from *Pythium*.**

You will be supplied with soybean plants, soybean loopers (insects that can be very destructive to soybean plants), and a culture of Bt. **Design an experiment that will determine whether Bt protects soybeans from damage by the loopers.**

You will also be supplied with a nodulated alfalfa plant so that you can observe the effects of a mutualistic relationship between *Rhizobium* and a legume host.

Key questions

☞ How might mutualistic or antagonistic relationships have evolved?

☞ Why do you think some nitrogen-fixing bacteria will only enter into a mutualistic relationship with certain plant species?

☞ How would you determine whether a plant was deriving benefit from a microbe that had infected its roots or its leaves?

Life cycle of *Bacillus cereus:*

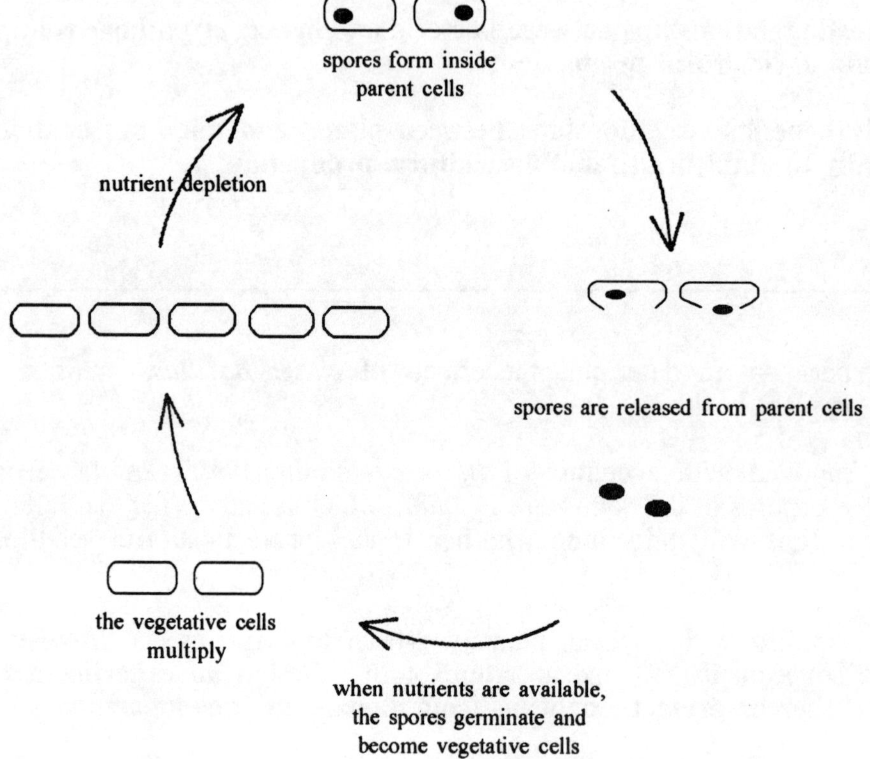

- Under nutrient-rich conditions, *Bacillus* grows as vegetative cells, like other bacteria.
- When the cells run out of food, they sporulate.
- One spore is produced inside each vegetative cell.
- When the spores are fully formed, they are released from the parent cell.
- The spores will survive drying, boiling, and other conditions that destroy vegetative cells.

Pythium - simplified life cycle:

Fine, white mycelium rapidly grows within infected plant tissues.

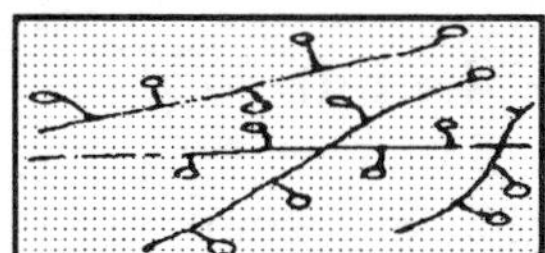

Sporangia form along and at the tips of the mycelial strands (hyphae). The sporangia may produce 3 different kinds of structures.

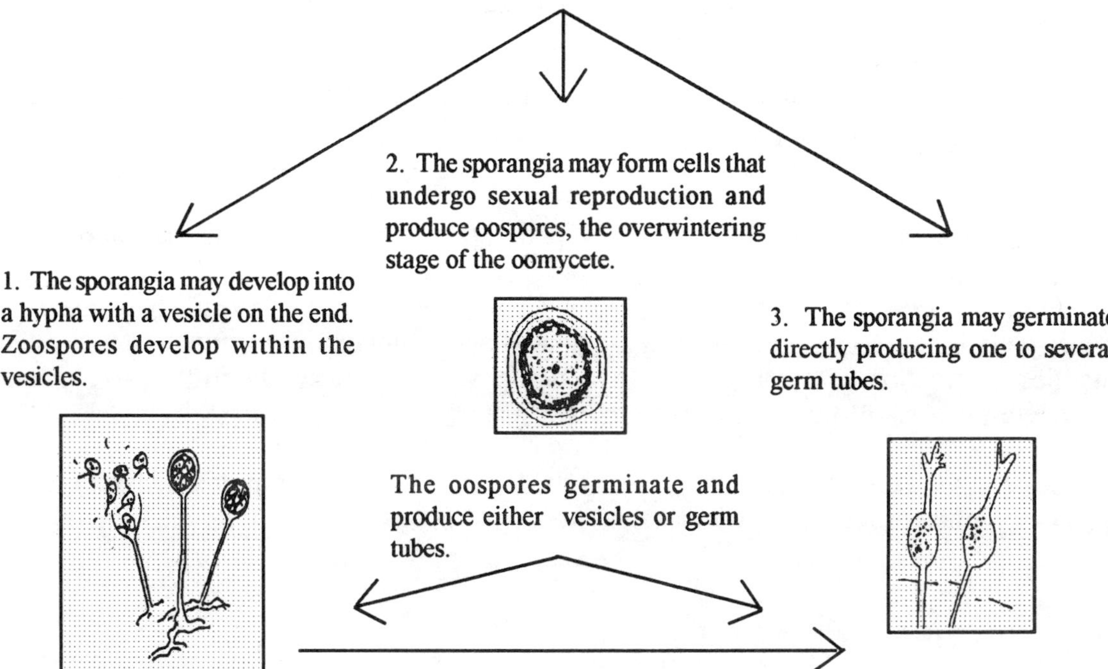

1. The sporangia may develop into a hypha with a vesicle on the end. Zoospores develop within the vesicles.

2. The sporangia may form cells that undergo sexual reproduction and produce oospores, the overwintering stage of the oomycete.

3. The sporangia may germinate directly producing one to several germ tubes.

The oospores germinate and produce either vesicles or germ tubes.

The swimming zoospores are released. They encyst by producing a rigid wall.

The germ tubes invade plant tissues and grow into mycelial strands to begin the cycle again.

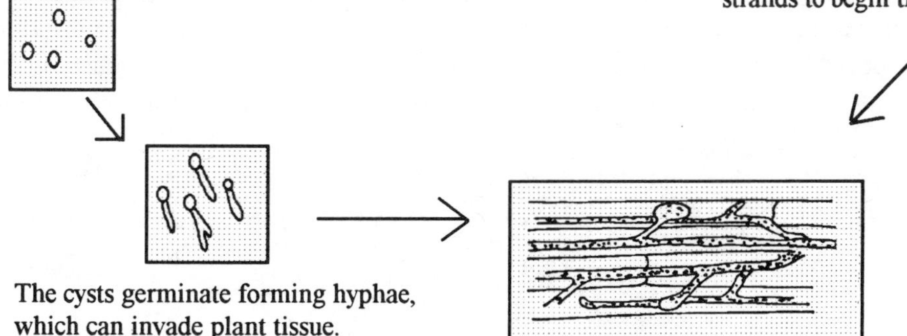

The cysts germinate forming hyphae, which can invade plant tissue.

Experiment 10: Mutualism and antagonism among organisms

A lesson in ecology

In this exercise students will explore the influence of antagonism between bacteria and either insect larvae or an oomycete pathogen on plant health. They will also observe mutualism between root nodule bacteria and their plant hosts.

As we study microorganisms in the lab, growing in pure cultures in petri plates, it is sometimes easy to overlook the fact that in this artificial environment we see only a part of the microbes' whole existence, free from interactions with other organisms. Studying these isolated microbes is like studying a solitary elephant in a zoo. We can learn much from examining the living elephant, but we see an incomplete picture of what elephants in nature are like. In the wild, elephants are not solitary creatures. They live in herds, interacting with herdmates, predators, and plant and animal species that populate the same ecosystem. Elephant behavior is shaped by complex relationships and interactions, both positive and negative, in an ecological dance of survival.

So it is when we study isolated microbes on a petri plate. We can learn much about their morphology, chemistry, and behavior from observing them in culture, but our view is incomplete. Microorganisms in the wild rarely occur in pure cultures. Instead, they are found interacting with other species of microbes, plants, and animals in teeming communities. Studying these interactions, from mutualistic to antagonistic, gives us an opportunity to construct more complete pictures of microbes as they exist in nature.

This exercise allows students to explore a few of these fascinating and complex interactions and invites them to witness some of the dramas that are played out every day in the microbial world.

What students will learn

ecology; it's a cruel world; competition

This exercise illustrates the unusual adaptations that organisms have evolved to deal with the competition. Specifically, it deals with the important biological concepts of mutualism and antagonism. For experiments involving *Bacillus thuringiensis* and soybean loopers or *Bacillus cereus* strain UW85 and an oomycete pathogen, the experimental design is relatively simple, and the necessary controls should be obvious to the students by this point in the semester. The *Rhizobium* interaction is a simple demonstration. Thus, the students should have sufficient time and mental energy to focus on the fascinating biological interactions inherent in the systems being studied. Because mutualism and antagonism are key interactions in any ecosystem, the exercise also provides a platform for discussing individual-, population-, and community-level interactions in ecosystems.

Learning highlights and conceptual challenges

"Poor little loopers" "Go get that plant root....got it!" ethics

If biology is the study of life and death, this experiment is rich with biology. Students often squeal with delight watching zoospores homing in on a root under the microscope, they enjoy observing the behavior of loopers on petri dishes or plants, and they are thrilled by just how dead the loopers look after eating the Bt. The experiment has substantial visual appeal. Loopers are simply fun to watch inching around a plate, and zoospores zooming around a root elicit smiles from even the greatest biophobe. The exercise also stimulates strong emotions. The students seem to be attracted to the "good guy/bad guy" scenario. Some sympathize with the plant and are eager for the bacteria to protect it from the pathogen or insects. Others seem to feel sorry for the loopers and are shocked when they return to find looper carcasses draped on the soybean leaves. These emotional reactions may seem silly at first, but they lead to an intense interest in the subject and ultimately, to learning.

The emotional content also provides the springboard for a discussion of ethics in biology. Oomycetes and loopers may not have the appeal of koala bears and whales, but students often argue that killing them is wrong. This can force all of the students to face the issues of life and death that we all participate in every day by eating food, using medicine or paper, or just sitting under a tree.

Be sure to provide the students with an opportunity to look at the loopers and zoospores under a microscope. We find that many of our students are reluctant to use microscopes, but the appeal of these organisms can help them overcome their reluctance. In addition, provide cultures of Bt on agar plates and encourage the students to put loopers on the plates. In a few days the loopers on the Bt plates will turn black and die, while control loopers on uninoculated agar plates are still going strong.

This exercise is just good fun. Enjoy it!

I. *Bacillus thuringiensis* and soybean loopers

Materials needed for teacher preparations

	soybean seed to grow 4 plants per group
	10-cm flower pots (2 to 4 per group)
1	*Bacillus thuringiensis* broth culture (page 250)
1	transfer loop
	nutrient broth (50 ml per group) (pages 228, 249)
	125-ml Erlenmeyer flask (1 per group) (page 250)
	sterile cotton ball (1 per flask)
	aluminum foil
	shaker in 28°C incubator
	plastic bags (4 per group)
1	colony of second or third instar soybean loopers[7] *Pseudoplusia includens*[8] (20 larvae per group) (page 250)
	plastic bags to cover soybean plants (4 per group)
	rubber bands (4 per group)

Materials needed for students

Number per group:

4	soybean plants with at least 2 true leaves per plant
1	*Bacillus thuringiensis* (Bt) nutrient broth culture—50 ml in an Erlenmeyer flask
1	plant sprayer
	sterile cotton swabs (page 250)
20	soybean looper larvae
4	plastic bags
4	rubber bands

[7]Later instars are more resistant to Bt.

[8]If you cannot obtain soybean loopers, you can substitute tobacco hornworm larvae, *Manduca sexta* and tobacco plants (page 250).

Teacher preparations prior to lab period

Before the semester begins

1. Obtain enough soybean seed to supply 4 plants per group.

2. Obtain a culture of *Bacillus thuringiensis*.

Twenty-one days (or more) before the lab period

1. Plant 2 to 4 soybean seeds each in 10-cm pots.

Three days before the lab period

1. Transfer a loopful of actively growing Bt culture to 50 ml of sterile nutrient broth in a sterile 125-ml Erlenmeyer flask.

2. Seal the mouth of the flask with a sterile cotton ball. Cover the cotton ball and the top of the flask with aluminum foil.

3. Incubate the broth cultures at approximately 28°C on a shaker for 1 to 3 days.

As near to the day of the lab period as possible

1. Obtain enough second or third instar soybean loopers to supply 20 larvae per group.

How to guide students

During class

1. Students should pour Bt broth cultures into a deep petri dish or wide beaker so they will be able to dip their soybean plants in the culture. Rubbing sterile cotton swabs over the leaves before they are dipped will cause leaf hairs to break and lead to better adhesion of the culture to the leaf surface.

2. After the plants have been treated, students should place approximately 5 soybean looper larvae on the leaves.

3. They should then cover the plant with a plastic bag and secure the bag to the pot with a rubber band. The pot should be incubated at room temperature until the next lab period.

4. Looper larvae placed on Bt-treated plants usually die within a few days and feeding damage to the soybean plants is minimal. Looper larvae placed on plants treated with broth-only or on untreated plants tend to feed extensively and grow much larger during the course of the week. Damage to plants is usually seen within 3 to 4 days.

Possible hypotheses students might want to test

1. Soybean loopers feed on soybean plants, causing damage to the plants.

2. *Bacillus thuringiensis* is toxic to soybean loopers.

3. Spraying soybean plants with Bt kills soybean loopers and keeps plants from being eaten.

4. Nutrient broth is toxic to soybean loopers.

5. Spraying soybean plants with nutrient broth kills soybean loopers and keeps plants from being eaten.

6. All bacteria are toxic to loopers.

Controls Some controls for this experiment might include placing loopers on untreated plants or on plants that have been dipped in uninoculated sterile broth, sterile water, or a suspension of another bacterium, such as *E. coli*. Additional treatments might include placing loopers on Bt culture plates or on plates with pet microbes.

> **Important:** Plants in treatment and control groups that do not require Bt should be dipped before dipping plants in the Bt culture to minimize the chances of bacterial contamination.

Data collection

For this experiment, students collect data to study the effects on loopers of treating or not treating plants with Bt and the effects on plants of controlling or not controlling looper infestation.

1. **Descriptive** - For loopers, compare size, color, and motion/activity; for plants, record appearance and evidence of looper damage.

2. **Quantitative** - Count the number of loopers that are alive or dead and the number of plant leaves damaged by the loopers. Calculate the percent or fraction of the plant damaged.

Troubleshooting and dealing with problems

Problem	Possible explanation	Solution
loopers die in untreated conditions	bacterial contamination	Be careful to avoid any contact between Bt and loopers. This is important if you plan to maintain a colony of loopers.

Questions to guide discussion

♦ What controls are necessary for you to be able to draw conclusions from your experiment?

♦ Do you think using Bt is preferable to synthetic insecticides for crop protection? What data would you like to see before answering this question?

♦ What might be the evolutionary advantage for Bt of producing the insecticidal toxin?

Sources of information

♦ Romoser, W.S. and J.G. Stoffolano, Jr. (1994) *The Science of Entomology*. Dubuque, Iowa: Wm. C. Brown Publishers. (See page 440 for discussion of biological control.)

II. *Bacillus cereus* (UW85) and *Pythium torulosum*

Introduction

Pythium is a genus of oomycete pathogens that includes species that attack a wide variety of plants in all stages of development, from the ungerminated seed to the fully developed fruit, causing seed rot, damping off, root rot, or soft rot. When seeds or seedlings are infected, as they often are in this experiment, the plant embryos succumb before or shortly after their emergence from the seed. Consequently, with damping off infections, we observe poor germination of seeds and reduced seedling emergence.

Oomycetes are a group of lower eukaryotes that were long thought to be fungi, but we now know that they are phylogenetically closer to the protists than to the fungi. Their motile spores are an indicator of this relationship, although their reclassification was based on 18S ribosomal RNA gene sequence. See the next page for an abbreviated life cycle of *Pythium*.

Pythium torulosum causes disease in alfalfa. A strain of *Bacillus cereus*, UW85, acts as a biological control agent, producing an antibiotic that affords protection of the emerging alfalfa seeds from damping off caused by *Pythium*. Students will propose and test hypotheses to test the relationships of alfalfa, *P. torulosum*, and *B. cereus* UW85.

Note: This experiment is a little more complicated to set up than the looper/Bt experiment. If you do not want to deal with a hemacytometer and zoospore production, then we suggest using the looper experiment instead. However, the *Pythium* life cycle is interesting to students and can be used to illustrate concepts in cell biology and development, as well as the ecological concepts that are the focus of the experiment.

Materials needed for teacher preparations

Pythium torulosum culture (page 251)
10% TSA plates (pages 231, 249)
50% TSA broth (page 249)
V-8 agar plates (pages 231, 249)

Materials needed for students

Number per group:

	vermiculite (steam sterilized)[9] 1 liter per flat (page 250)
1	seed flat
1	tray for seed flats (about 25 × 52 cm) containing about 4 liters of water
1,000	alfalfa seeds (page 251)
2	1-ml pipettes
	Bacillus cereus (UW85) culture (page 250)
	Pythium torulosum zoospores (200 to 500 per cell)

> Inexpensive seed flats and planting trays are available at garden stores. The flats may be divided into 48, 72, 96, or other numbers of cells. The exact number is not important as long as you have enough replications to detect differences between treatments. Our calculations for the number of seeds and zoospores and the concentration of *B. cereus* are based on 96-cell flats. If your flats contain a different number, you will need to adjust numbers and concentrations accordingly.

[9] If you use new, sealed bags of vermiculite and open the bags just before use, it is not necessary to steam sterilize the vermiculite.

Teacher preparations prior to lab period

Before the semester begins

1. Obtain cultures of *Pythium torulosum*, *Bacillus cereus* (UW85), and alfalfa seeds.

I. Preparing *Pythium* zoospores

Seven days before the first lab period

1. Using sterile technique, with a cork borer or similar tool, remove a small agar plug covered with mycelia from a *Pythium torulosum* culture plate and place it in the center of a V-8 agar plate. Prepare one V-8 agar plate for each group. Prepare an extra plate if you want to demonstrate counting and diluting zoospores using a hemacytometer (see step 4 below). Incubate the plates for 7 days at room temperature (24°C).

One day before the first lab period

If you teach a morning lab,

1. Before going home the night before lab, add 20 mls of distilled water to the surface of each culture plate. Let the plates stand for 30 to 60 minutes at room temperature. Then pour off and discard the water.

2. Put 20 to 25 mls of sterile water in an empty, sterile petri dish. Cut the agar of the original culture in half and place one half in the petri dish with the water.

3. Loosen the remaining half of the agar in the original plate and add 20 to 25 mls of sterile water. You have now created two petri dishes for zoospore production. Incubate both plates overnight at room temperature (24°C).

4. The next morning, decant and save the water from both plates. Calculate the concentration of zoospores in the water using a hemacytometer and dilute to about 500 zoospores per ml with sterile water. It takes about 20 to 30 minutes to count and dilute the zoospores.

If you have enough microscopes and lab time, you could have the students do this procedure. Alternatively, you can count and dilute the zoospores the students will use ahead of time, but prepare an extra culture plate to provide a demonstration of how to count zoospores with a hemacytometer and calculate dilutions.

If you teach an afternoon lab,

1. Do steps 1 through 3 above.
2. The next morning, pour off the water from both plates. (Save the water in case sufficient numbers of zoospores are not released by the next step.)
3. Add 20 to 25 ml of fresh, sterile water to each plate and incubate at room temperature 4 to 6 hours.
4. Count the zoospores using a hemacytometer and dilute to about 500 zoospores per ml (see step 4 above).

II. Preparing *Bacillus cereus*

Five days before the first lab period

1. Streak *Bacillus cereus* UW85 on trypticase soy agar (TSA) plates. Incubate overnight at 28° to 30°C.

Four days before the first lab period

1. Inoculate trypticase soy broth with *B. cereus* from the TSA plates. To provide a large surface area for oxygenation of the culture, culture 10 to 50 mls of broth in a 125-ml flask, 100 mls of broth in a 1,000-ml flask. Incubate the cultures on a shaker at 24° to 28°C for 4 days.

One day before the first lab period

1. Check for sporulation. At least 50% sporulation is desirable. Dilute the spore concentration to about 10^8 per ml. Most *Bacillus* cultures will reach a density of 1-5 × 10^8 cells per ml. Vegetative cells are larger and more nearly rectangular than spores. The spores are small, ovoid, and phase bright.

How to guide students

During the first lab period

1. Each group should: Fill the individual cells in one plant flat to about 1 cm from the top with vermiculite. Plant about 10 alfalfa seeds on the vermiculite surface of each cell. (Students may plant the seeds on the dry vermiculite up to a week before they conduct the experiment. They should not add water until it is certain a viable suspension of zoospores is available and until they are ready to begin the experiment.)

2. Add enough water to the tray so that when the seed flat is placed in the tray, the water level will come to the level of the top of the vermiculite (about 4 cm deep). (The zoospores need water to swim to the seeds and seedlings.) Place the flats in the tray to which the water has been added.

3. Students should use one pipette reserved for *Pythium* and another reserved for UW85. Pipette *Pythium* zoospores and/or UW85 over the seeds for appropriate treatment and control groups. For treatment or control conditions requiring *Pythium*, inoculate with about 25 to 50 zoospores per seed (or about 250 to 500 zoospores per cell). For treatment or control conditions requiring UW85, pipette 1 ml of broth culture over the seeds in each cell.

4. Add vermiculite to cover the seeds (up to the top of each cell in the seed flat). Allow the seeds to grow at room temperature. Keep the water level in the tray constant by adding water as needed.

   For an experimental layout, see the diagram on page 154. The students should mark off and label the treatment zones with a waterproof marker.

Experimental conditions that can be tested are as follows:

Treatment:
tx—alfalfa seeds + UW85 + *Pythium*
Controls:
c1—untreated alfalfa seeds (demonstrates that disease symptoms are related to infection by *Pythium* and not a manifestation of a physical condition such as having pots standing in water)
c2—alfalfa seeds + *Pythium* (tests the effect of *Pythium*)
c3—alfalfa seeds + UW85 (tests the effect of UW85)

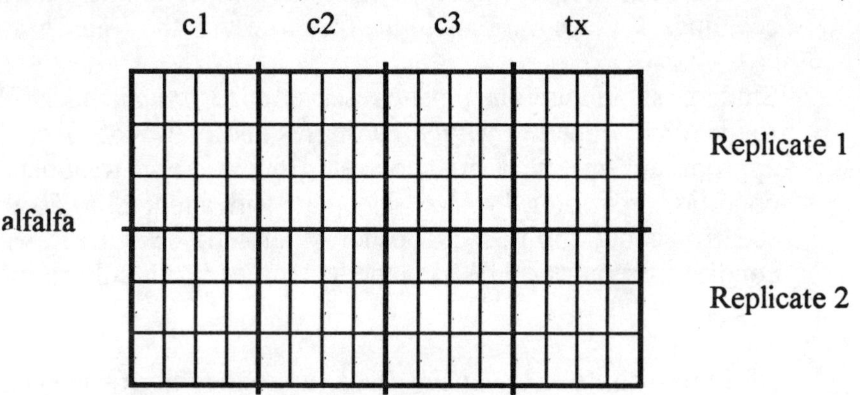

Diagram of treatment and control conditions

During the second lab period (one week after the first)

1. Students record seedling emergence for each treatment condition.

2. It is a good idea to add fertilizer to the water at this time if you intend to keep the plants growing.

During the third lab period (two weeks after the first)

1. Students again record seedling emergence and note the size of plants in each treatment condition.

Three weeks after the first lab

1. Students can again measure plant growth. Effects of *P. torulosum* or *B. cereus* on plant growth will be magnified after two weeks.

Possible hypotheses students might want to test

1. *Pythium torulosum* is pathogenic to alfalfa plants.

2. *Bacillus cereus* UW85 protects alfalfa plants from *P. torulosum*.

Data collection

Descriptive - Note the presence or absence of plants, symptoms of disease—color, size, vigor of plants, presence of lesions on stems or roots.

Quantitative - One week after planting - Count the number of alfalfa plants for each condition. Calculate the percent of seed germination ($n/120 \times 100$).

Three weeks after planting - measure differences in plant height or weight, leaf size, and root length for each treatment.

Both descriptive and quantitative data can be recorded on tables such as this one.

	No treatment	*Pythium*	UW85	*Pythium* + UW85
Iroquois				
Rep 1				
Rep 2				

Note: Whenever the students terminate the experiment, be sure they remove the plants and examine the roots. Often they will find that plants that look healthy above ground will have severely diseased and stunted root systems.

Troubleshooting and dealing with problems

Problem	Possible explanation	Solution
no disease	not enough zoospores	precheck with various levels of zoospores
no zoospores	culture not old enough to produce sporangia (check under microscope)	incubate longer
	culture not releasing zoospores	incubate with water longer
UW85 does not suppress disease	culture not old enough	make sure culture is sporulated
	too many zoospores	check at various concentrations of zoospores

Note: *P. torulosum* is most virulent at 16° to 20°C, and virulence decreases with increasing temperatures, being much reduced at 32°C. However, alfalfa seeds grow slowly at 16°C. *B. cereus* is more effective at 24°C. Overall, the experiment is most successful when conducted at room temperature (about 20° to 24°C).

Questions to guide discussion

◆ What effect does *Bacillus cereus* UW85 have on alfalfa plants that have not been infected with *Pythium*?

◆ What effect does *Pythium* have on the two strains of alfalfa plants not protected by *B. cereus* UW85?

◆ Can you see any differences in the plants that have been protected from *Pythium* by the UW85 and those that have not been infected with *Pythium*?

Sources of information

◆ Grau, C.R. (1990) *Pythium* seed rot, damping-off, and root rot. In: *Compendium of Alfalfa Diseases.* D.L. Stuteville and D.C. Erwin, eds., pp. 11–12. St. Paul, MN: The American Phytopathological Society.

◆ Handelsman, J., S. Raffel, E.H. Mester, L. Wunderlich, and C.R. Grau (1990) Biological control of damping-off in alfalfa seedlings with *Bacillus cereus* UW85. *Applied Environmental Microbiology*, 56: 713–718.

◆ Leath, K.T., D.C. Erwin, and G.D. Griffen (1988) Diseases and nematodes. In: *Alfalfa and Alfalfa Improvement.* A.A. Hanson, D.K. Baines, and R.R. Hill, Jr., eds. *Agronomy*, 29: 621–670.

◆ Van der Plaats-Niterink, A.J. (1981) Monograph of the genus *Pythium. Studies in Mycology*, 21: 1–242.

III. *Rhizobium* - root nodule demonstration - observation of root nodule formation on legume plants treated with *Rhizobium* bacterial suspension.

Materials

common bean seeds (*Phaseolus vulgaris* - green beans, kidney beans, or pinto beans)
seed pouches (page 250)
paper clips (large size)
5-ml pipette tips modified (pages 159, 250)
sterile paper towels
1-liter sterile beaker
sterile water
95% ethanol (EtOH)
40% chlorine bleach
aluminum foil
rack for holding pouches[10]
3-day-old *Rhizobium tropici* culture on nutrient agar (pages 228, 249, and 250)

Preparations

Twenty-four days before the lab period

1. To make a *Rhizobium* suspension, inoculate 2 ml of nutrient broth for each seed pouch with *Rhizobium* from a culture plate. Incubate at 28°C, with vigorous shaking, for 2 to 3 days.

2. Surface disinfest common bean seeds by soaking for 1 minute in 95% EtOH, followed by 3 minutes in 40% bleach. Rinse thoroughly in sterile water.

[10]A 45-rpm record rack makes an excellent rack for seed pouches.

3. Using a sterile forceps, arrange the disinfested seeds in a single row along the center of a sterile paper towel. The seeds should be oriented side by side with their long axes at right angles to the row and all pointing in the same direction. Snugly roll the paper towel containing the seeds from one end of the row to the other.

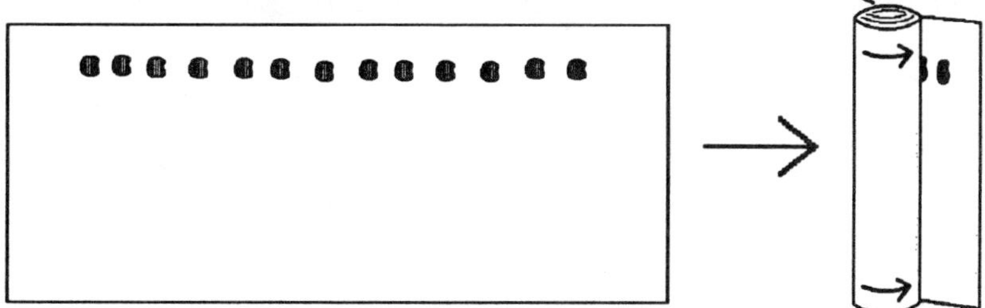

4. Place the rolled paper towel, with the root-forming part of each seed pointing downward, in a sterile beaker containing sterile water, 3 to 5 cm deep. Cover the beaker with aluminum foil and store at 28°C for 3 days while the seeds germinate.

Twenty-one days before the lab period

1. Each seed pouch consists of an autoclavable plastic envelope containing a paper wick liner with a perforated fold at the upper edge.

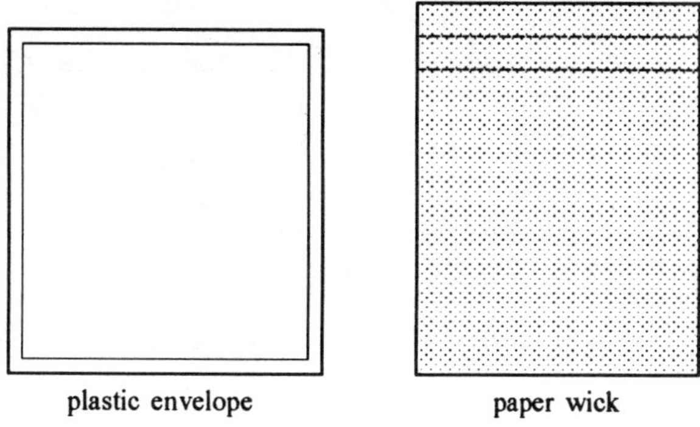

Set up the seed pouches as follows: Fold the paper wick along the perforated lines and slip it into the plastic envelope. Cut off the end of a 5-ml plastic pipette tip to form a tapered tube.

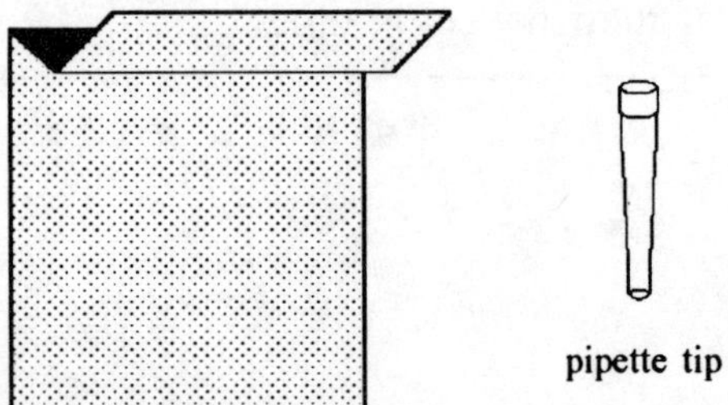

2. Open the envelope and insert the pipette tip along one side with the upper opening of the tip just extending outside the envelope. (The pipette tip will enable you to add liquids to the seed pouch without disturbing the bean seedlings.) Slide a large paper clip over the top edge of the envelope next to the pipette tip to hold the pipette tip in place. Add 20 mls of plant nutrient solution (PNS) (page 234) to the pouch through the pipette tip. Place the assembled pouches upright in a rack and autoclave at 18 psi, for 20 minutes. Exhaust the autoclave slowly. Allow the pouches to cool.

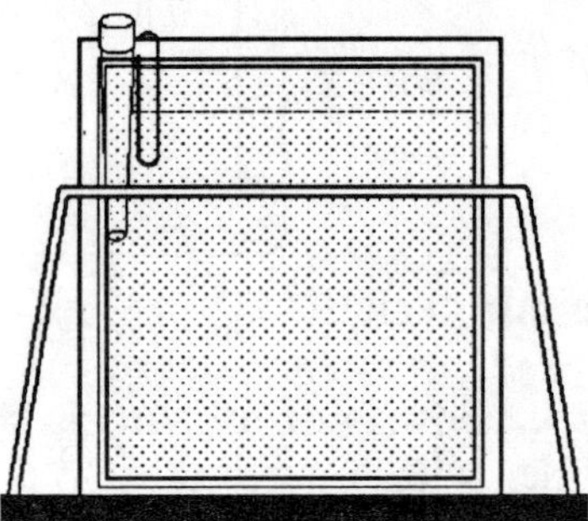

3. With a sterile forceps, open the pouch. Open the paper wick along the perforated fold to form a shallow trough at the top of the wick. With the forceps tip, make a small slit through the perforations at the center of the trough. Place one sterile bean seedling in the trough, and gently push the root through the slit so that it extends down into the pouch. (See the drawing on the next page.)

   Pipette 1 ml of *Rhizobium* suspension directly onto the seedling roots.

4. Cover each pouch with foil. Place the pouches upright in the rack and incubate at 24°C, in 12 to 16 hours of light.

5. As each plant in its foil packet begins to grow out of the pouch, open up the foil around the upper part of the plant to allow the leaves to be exposed to light but continue to keep the roots covered.

6. Nodulation will take place over 2 to 3 weeks. The students will be able to observe the root system with its nodules through the transparent sides of the pouch.

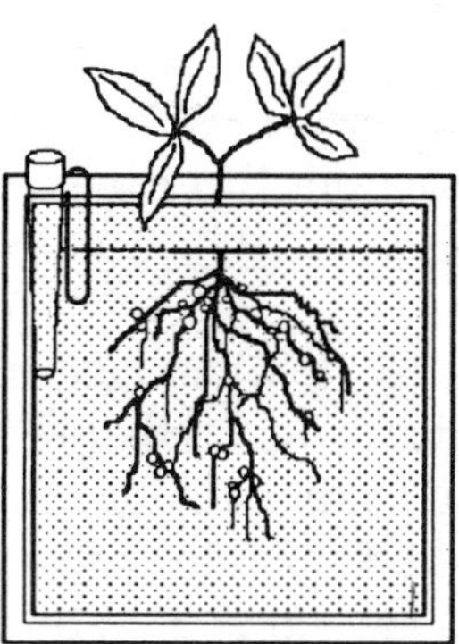

Note: This demonstration can be done as an experiment. Students can observe differences in nodulation in plants grown under different treatment conditions (for example, inoculated with *Rhizobium*, vs. not inoculated, or plants given supplemental nitrogen treatment vs. no supplemental nitrogen).

The plastic pouches are convenient and provide good viewing of the roots and nodules. However, if you cannot obtain pouches, you can grow the plants in vermiculite, between paper towels, or in petri plates. Remember the following to obtain good results:

- Fixed nitrogen (NH_3 or NO_3) inhibits nodulation.
- Roots exposed to light do not develop nodules.
- A few cells or even a single cell of *R. tropici* contaminating the roots of control plants will grow rapidly and may produce full nodulation.

Experiment 11: Biology in the real world
A lesson in field biology

Most life on Earth is found in forests, prairies, marshes, rivers, lakes, or oceans—in ecosystems that are managed by humans (such as agricultural fields or forests used for logging) or in unmanaged ecosystems (such as virgin rain forests). So far, the experiments in this book have focused on life in the laboratory. Studying life in the laboratory is a powerful approach to understanding biology because laboratory experiments can be well-controlled and the key variables can be manipulated. This is difficult to do in the field. Most laboratory biologists study problems that are interesting in the environment, but they use the power and relative simplicity of laboratory experiments to dissect biological phenomena in hope of contributing to knowledge of the natural world. But ultimately, to develop an understanding of the natural world, we need to apply the knowledge we have acquired in the laboratory to biological interactions in the field and to study interactions that occur in the field that cannot be reproduced in the laboratory.

It is the interplay between laboratory and field studies that gives the science of biology its excitement because while laboratory studies provide a high degree of precision and understanding at molecular and biochemical levels, field studies can integrate this knowledge into a meaningful picture of systems in the biological world. Some of the major advances in the history of biology have been made by scientists who integrated field observations with experiments conducted under controlled conditions. Perhaps the greatest field biologist of them all, Charles Darwin, developed the theory of natural selection as a mechanism of evolution. His great travels through the Galapagos Islands embody one of the most powerful field biology studies ever done. But key to the development of Darwin's theory was his earlier observation of populations of plants and animals bred by himself and others. Although not involving laboratory experiments, domestic breeding provided controlled genetic systems that stimulated Darwin's thinking about heritable traits, fitness, selection, and evolution when he observed the natural world.

The special challenge in field biology is to develop testable hypotheses. There are many interesting questions that we simply do not have the tools to answer either because we cannot construct appropriate controls, we cannot study enough organisms to provide a representative sample, or we cannot make observations without disturbing and altering the system we seek to study. Many interesting questions in the biological world can be addressed initially by observing and thinking. Field biology requires rigorous application of the scientific method and often requires clever approaches to gathering data.

There are two general approaches to exploring questions in field biology. One involves observing the natural system with as little disturbance as possible. The second involves deliberate perturbation of the system to determine the effect of specific change in the environment. For example, one might observe the behavior of gorillas in a troop to develop an understanding of their familial relationships without perturbation by the observer. In this example, it would be important for the observer to be as unobtrusive as possible so that conclusions about the behavior of the gorillas in the absence of human activity could be drawn. In contrast, if we were interested in determining the effect of birdfeeders on the foraging behavior of birds, the appropriate experiment would involve comparison of a population that had access to feeders with a population that did not have access to feeders. The feeders would be considered a perturbation of the "natural" system. The use of perturbations in field biology has been controversial in the scientific community. Some field biologists consider the use of perturbations a disruption to the natural system that results in observations that do not reflect the behavior of organisms in the world without human intervention. Other field biologists consider perturbations to be a necessary part of scientific experimentation, without which we are limited to simple observation and description of the natural world that will not result in isolating variables that influence it.

In this exercise, it is up to you to decide whether you wish to perturb your system or observe it in its unperturbed state. If you decide to perturb it, be sure to do so in an ethical manner. If you decide not to deliberately disturb it, then be aware of how you might inadvertently disturb it by your presence. Either approach is valid as long as you are sensitive to the ramifications of each.

Key concept

Field biology provides an understanding of the behavior of organisms in their natural environments.

Challenge

Your challenge is to go out into the field, make an observation, and develop a hypothesis to test. You will then devise an experiment or a set of measurements to test your hypothesis. Your "field site" may be a forest, a tree, a garden, a rock, a lake or stream, the beach, or a group of human beings in their "natural" habitat. Be sure to think about the aspects of the real world that may interfere with your experiment or that might cause you to misinterpret the results. Complex systems are much more difficult to study than are bacteria on petri plates or plants in a greenhouse!

You should notice that if you do not need a control, then you are not conducting an experiment. Often in field biology many careful observations are needed before an experiment can be designed. You may either conduct an experiment or make a careful set of observations that will provide the groundwork for experimentation. Be sure that you are clear about whether or not you are conducting an experiment. A valid part of field biology is descriptive -- simply making careful assessments of a behavior or trend but not necessarily conducting an experiment.

Key questions

☞ Is your approach an experiment or is it descriptive?

☞ What made you choose the organisms and the hypothesis that are the focus of your inquiry?

☞ How does the study of a system in the real world differ from a laboratory experiment?

☞ How might laboratory experimentation shed light on the problem you have chosen to study?

☞ What kinds of problems can you study out in the environment that you cannot study in the laboratory?

☞ What might be the selective advantage of the behaviors you observed?

Experiment 11: Biology in the real world
A lesson in field biology

In this experiment, students will observe the natural world and develop and test hypotheses about organisms in their natural environments. They may test their hypotheses using experiments (that include controls) or by making careful observations and measurements.

The experiment can be done outside in any environment. For example, in a rural area, the students might choose a field or a stream to observe; in a city, they might focus on a tree, urban birds, or squirrels. They may even choose to study human behavior, which might simply involve making observations about students on their campus.

What students will learn

observe, observe, observe! experiments vs. description; biology is all around us

The key objective of this exercise is to send students out into the world as more astute observers. By focusing on a defined question, they will be able to discern patterns and behaviors that were not apparent to them before. Whether or not they become scientists, they will leave your biology course with enhanced curiosity about the world around them and a better sense of how to find patterns of behavior in the complex natural world.

The students will also learn about the value of descriptive science. All of the previous exercises have relied heavily on the scientific method involving experiments. In this exercise the students may develop a testable hypothesis for which they can design an experiment, or they may make a set of observations that provide useful information about the system but do not constitute an experiment. This exercise provides an excellent opportunity to highlight the value of experiments and observations and to distinguish between them.

Even if you teach in an urban environment, one of the impressions your students are likely to get from this exercise is that biology is all around us. Whether they examine feeding behavior of butterflies, social interactions of sparrows, or habits of human beings, they will begin to notice that the world is full of organisms, and that there are patterns embedded in the behavior of all organisms.

Learning highlights and conceptual challenges

"You won't believe what I saw!" "Life's so complicated. . . ."

The highlight of this exercise will be the students' excitement at seeing new aspects of a world they thought they knew. They will go out into familiar territory, and simply by being observant and thoughtful they will find patterns and phenomena they never realized were there. If you have students who come from another type of environment (rural kids on an urban campus, for example), they may learn something about their new environment that makes them feel more at home in it. Regardless of how well they know their surroundings, all of the students should complete this exercise with a stronger sense of the environment and its order.

There are two difficult parts to teaching this exercise. First, there is no way to predict the observations and hypotheses the students will bring to the classroom. Although we cannot help with that (since we do not know the environment you will use), we can reassure you that this aspect gets easier after the first class. You will find that the students from class to class tend to find the same types of biological phenomena attractive, and you will begin to be able to predict the types of hypotheses, if not the actual hypotheses, they will test. This will help you prepare questions and pointers to assist future students with the exercise.

The second difficulty in teaching this exercise is helping the students design experiments or descriptions that will enable them to test their hypotheses. This is also a highlight of the exercise because it emphasizes the complexity of nature and therefore the difficulty of developing clear tests of hypotheses. For example, if students set out to test the hypothesis that butterflies prefer red flowers to yellow ones, how can they control for flower shape in their design? To handle this problem ask all of the students, "Are there any other variables that could influence the outcome of your experiment?" Then follow up with, "How can you control for that effect?" The students are likely to start out with much more complicated hypotheses than they can test effectively. Part of the class discussion process should be directed toward honing the hypotheses to be tested. Be sure to highlight the complexity as a challenge but also as part of the fun of doing field biology. It is like a very complex puzzle, and the biologist's challenge is find a small piece that fits.

Teacher preparations

The best way to prepare for this exercise is to do it yourself. Go out into the environment where you plan to take the students and make observations—as many as possible. Then go back to the classroom and develop hypotheses and experimental approaches to test them. By doing this, you are likely to arrive at many of the questions that will come up in class.

How to guide students

This exercise works best if split into two sessions. In the first session, students will spend time in groups outdoors making observations about the biological world. When the groups return to the classroom, have them develop hypotheses. Ask the groups to report their observations and hypotheses to the class as a whole. Then, have the groups begin to discuss their approaches to testing their hypotheses so that they can get a feel for the complexity of the system.

The following week students should come to class prepared with their experimental approach. Discuss the approaches briefly, requiring the students to identify variables that might confuse their results and describe the data they plan to collect. Then send them out to make their observations. When they return with the data, conduct a discussion of problems encountered and methods for handling the data.

Possible hypotheses students might want to test

1. Ants carry more material into their holes than they carry out.
2. Squirrels spend more time playing with each other than gathering food or eating it.
3. Bees, butterflies, and hummingbirds prefer red flowers to flowers of other colors.
4. Female ducks will fight more aggressively for food than will male ducks.

5. People will pick up quarters, but not pennies, nickels, or dimes on the sidewalk.

6. People will talk to strangers more readily if the strangers are male/female or wearing sunglasses/not wearing sunglasses.

Data collection It has been our observation in collecting data for field experiments that too much is far superior to not enough. It is a minor problem to leave out unnecessary detail when writing up an experiment. But it is a calamity that often cannot be remedied (short of redoing the experiment) to be missing vital data that were not collected or recorded.

Descriptive The specific data will depend on the nature of the investigations designed by the students. Encourage the students to carefully observe and describe physical details of the experimental setting, the organisms being studied, as well as behaviors and interactions.

Quantitative Students should record key elements, such as the number of observations they have made, the number of sites where they made observations, pertinent environmental conditions (temperature, rain or shine, dark or light). If they are studying humans they may want to record demographic information such as gender, rough age categories (adults or children), class rankings of students, or other relevant information.

Questions to guide discussion

- What type of data will you collect?

- What variables might interfere with the conclusions you would like to be able to draw at the end of your experiment?

- How might you eliminate or control for these variables?

- What conclusions can you safely draw from your results? What conclusions are you tempted to draw that would be beyond the data?

- Why do you think the organisms you observed evolved the behaviors you documented?

- What preconceptions did you bring to this experiment that might bias your data collection or interpretation?

Sources of information

- Martin, Paul and Patrick Bateson (1993) *Measuring Behavior, An Introductory Guide,* 2nd ed. Cambridge, England: Cambridge University Press. (See Chapter 3 for a thoughtful discussion of research design and experimenter effects).

Chapter 3 - Group Learning

Section 1: Cooperative learning for biology

Being part of a community helps students learn biology

Sharing the results of an experiment with peers in the laboratory, chatting with a colleague about a recent paper in *Science*, or learning a new experimental technique from a friend are common experiences for professional biologists. Rarely is a new idea in biology the product of a single mind. Biologists depend on colleagues to criticize ideas in seminars, manuscript reviews, and research proposal reviews. Participation in rigorous, open scientific debate is one of the most stimulating aspects of being a scientist. And yet introductory biology courses rarely capture the spirit of dialogue that is characteristic of the scientific enterprise. Students often think of biology as a science that comes from a textbook, rather than from a dynamic process that involves development and revision of ideas, experimentation, and debate. Participation in a community of biologists is key to understanding the process of science. Therefore, we must turn our biology classrooms into communities of scientists so that students engage in debate and experience the excitement of refining an idea by group process, thus teaching what it *really* means to be a scientist.

Learning and creative thinking require an open mind, confidence, and a challenging intellectual environment in which debate is honest and ideas are openly criticized. It is the teacher's role to create an atmosphere of support and nurture in which students feel accepted as young intellectuals. In such an atmosphere, students can respond constructively to criticism, because they feel intellectually, but not personally, challenged by disagreement. A nurturing environment enables students to develop the confidence to experiment with ideas and overcome the fear of being wrong, thus fostering creativity and imagination. Combining personal support with intellectual challenge encourages students to work cooperatively and to take an active role in the learning process and helps them discover the joy of scientific debate and inquiry. Classrooms that respect, value, and include the contributions of all students will be more likely to attract and retain women and minorities, who often express a sense of alienation, exclusion, and disenfranchisement in the traditional science classroom (Little Soldier, 1989; Okebukola, 1986a). We should be challenging ourselves to interest women and minorities in science, to attract them to our courses, and to provide them with a positive environment, the necessary stimulation, and the feeling that they are valued members of our educational community.

Pedagogical choices

Building a sense of community in the classroom can be accomplished through various pedagogies. Some that have been highly successful in the humanities are largely ignored in science teaching. The teaching philosophy that underpins this chapter is based broadly on cooperative learning, an approach that engages students in working together non-competitively toward a common goal (Johnson and Johnson, 1978; Watson, 1992), and feminist pedagogy, which promotes a non-hierarchical, egalitarian classroom in which each member is an equal, respected contributor (Schniedwind, 1983). In addition to providing a constructive environment for all students, these approaches encourage participation by students who are intimidated by competition or who avoid success if it necessarily requires demonstrating superiority over other students. Since the 1940s, the principles of cooperative learning have been described, tested, studied, and used successfully to build higher-order thinking skills and to reach students of diverse ability and backgrounds. Despite the proven success of these methods in other fields, most biology is still taught with individual and competitive modes of learning. One intent of this book is to introduce biology educators to alternative philosophies and methods of teaching.

Principles of building a classroom community

The biology teacher must play a central role in creating an environment in which students feel intellectually challenged and free to participate actively. The classroom must be both rigorous and nurturing. It must be rigorous to excite students, to ensure that they acquire accurate information, and to help them become critical thinkers who question and analyze the world around them. The classroom must be nurturing to provide students with the personal support to experiment with ideas, the freedom to be wrong, and the confidence to challenge others—including the teacher. The natural combination of rigor and support leads to a dynamic environment that fosters creativity and active learning. Rigor without support intimidates many students. Support without rigor is unfaithful to scientific and educational endeavors and is demeaning to students. The successful mixture can be achieved through many strategies. We describe some of the theoretical and philosophical underpinnings that provide a useful starting point for building a classroom community and then we offer tips and practical suggestions for building a good classroom environment. The final sections of this chapter present specific formats and exercises for cooperative learning in biology.

Cooperative learning - history and philosophy

Cooperative learning is not a new concept. It has endured as an important way of learning in some cultures for generations (Haynes and Gebreyesus, 1992; Jagers, 1992; Swisher, 1990). Socrates, engaging his disciples in group questioning and argument to develop their philosophical ideas, used a form of cooperative learning.

Early in this century when American students were schooled in a system based on authoritarian teaching and rote learning, educator John Dewey espoused a teaching philosophy that contained elements of cooperative learning. Dewey realized the importance of learning by doing and urged establishing laboratory and workshop courses to foster creativity and cooperation among students (Dewey, 1916).

Social psychologists began to study cooperation in the 1920s. In 1949, human relations specialist Morton Deutsch evaluated the effects of cooperation and competition on the functioning of small groups. Deutsch defined cooperative and competitive groups by basic differences in their goal structures. In cooperative groups, goals can be achieved by most or all group members; in competitive groups, goals can be achieved by some members but not by all. Comparing the two groups, Deutsch observed greater coordination of effort, obligation to participate, attentiveness to group members, diversity of contributions, sub-division of labor, understanding of communication, pressure to achieve, productivity per unit time, orientation, and orderliness in the cooperative group. Also, cooperative groups produced higher quality product and discussions, were friendlier during discussions, tended to evaluate the group and its products favorably, and perceived favorable effects on fellow members.

The cooperative learning methods used in contemporary education have evolved over the last 30 years. Though a number of researchers have contributed to the field, the work of a few especially stands out. In 1975, David and Robert Johnson of the University of Minnesota wrote *Learning Together and Alone: Cooperation, Competition, and Individualization* and established widely accepted definitions of the three learning modes. With competition, students wage a win-lose struggle to see who is best and reach their goals only if those against whom they are competing do not. With cooperation, members of small groups help each other master assigned material, and students reach their goals only if the others in their group also reach theirs. With individualistic learning, students learn independently, and the achievement of goals is unrelated to the successes or failures of others.

Living in a society that often places high value on the benefits of competition, the Johnsons exposed common societal myths about competition—that most human interaction in all societies is competitive; that the use of competition, under most conditions, will increase the quality of a student's work; that competition enhances the capacity for adaptive problem-solving; that competition builds character; that students prefer competitive situations; and that competition builds self-confidence and self-esteem. The Johnsons' research over more than two decades has served to dispel a number of these myths and has demonstrated the benefits of cooperative learning under a variety of conditions (Johnson, Johnson, and Scott, 1978; Johnson, Johnson, Scott and Ramolae, 1985).

During the past decade evidence has accumulated on the effectiveness of cooperative learning in classrooms from preschool to college and beyond, in a wide variety of disciplines. Cooperative learning methods have been applied in the physical sciences (Smith, Hinckley, and Volk, 1991), mathematics (Dees, 1991; Duren and Cherrington, 1992), and biology (Lazarowitz, Hertz, Baird, and Bowlden, 1988, Okebukola, 1986a & b), as well as in the social sciences (Lambiotte, Dansereau, Rocklin, Fletcher, Hythecker, Larson, and O'Donnell, 1987) and humanities (Barratt, 1992).

The value of cooperative learning as an educational tool lies in both its affective and cognitive impacts. For many students, the feelings of self-confidence and self-esteem they gain from learning cooperatively with their fellow students may be as important to their education as the specific knowledge they attain.

Proponents of cooperative learning often disagree on methodological details, such as whether groups must be heterogeneous or what specific course content best lends itself to a cooperative learning environment, but most do agree on basic requirements of the method. Though it has been a controversial point in the past, many leaders in the field now stress the importance of testing group members individually to ensure that each student will actively contribute to the group and not let others do all the work (Johnson and Johnson, 1993; Popp, 1987; Slavin, 1990). Other elements considered to be important for successful cooperative learning are recognition of group achievement (Popp, 1987) and providing group members with a worthwhile goal they have in common (Slavin, 1989). To spark motivation within a secure learning environment, competition is often encouraged between groups (Slavin, 1986), but it must not be interpersonal or take place within the group (Popp, 1987). Finally, students need to be trained in interpersonal and small group skills to be able to interact most effectively (Johnson and Johnson, 1993).

A continuing point of controversy surrounding cooperative learning is whether high ability students in heterogeneous cooperative groups are penalized by working with low ability students. In a somewhat narrowly focused study, Rewey and her colleagues (1992) showed that cooperative learning with knowledge map supplements can heighten learning among low ability undergraduate students without lessening the performance of high ability students. The Johnsons (1985) also found that constructive use of conflict in a cooperative setting promoted self-esteem and learning in both academically handicapped and non-handicapped students.

Cooperative learning in biology: Among the many studies that measure the effects of cooperative learning in biology, there is wide variation in quality, with some succumbing to the pitfalls of research involving human subjects, including small sample size, lack of random distribution and assignment to test conditions of students and teachers, and built-in bias in training teachers and teaching the material.

However, several good studies have shown that cooperative learning methods are effective for learning certain types of biological concepts. Lazarowitz and co-workers (1988) found that high school students in a cooperative classroom spent more time focusing on their assignment and achieved at a higher level in a cellular biology unit that demanded inquiry and high-level thinking than did students in a traditional competitive classroom. At the same time, students in the competitive classroom did better in a plant morphology and anatomy unit that required more observation and information gathering.

In an attempt to minimize bias in their studies, Peter Okebukola and his colleagues have conducted a number of large, controlled, and careful studies of middle-school biology students in Nigeria, in which the teachers were randomly assigned, carefully trained, and observed during the course of their teaching. Their results show that students who preferred cooperative learning benefitted most from it (Okebukola, 1986b, 1992); that cooperative learning is a powerful way to help students develop favorable attitudes toward lab work (Okebukola, 1986a); and that although students in a competitive environment were best at learning practical laboratory skills, those in a cooperative learning environment scored higher on cognitive achievement tests in science (Okebukola and Ogunniyi, 1984).

The work of these and other researchers points to the benefit of using cooperative learning in many classroom settings in biology. In addition to promoting academic achievement, cooperative learning has considerable value in affecting students' attitudes toward the subject matter and themselves. This cannot be overlooked as we search for new ways to make biology more accessible to all students who perceive the science classroom to be an alien and unwelcoming place.

The egalitarian classroom

It is well-documented that girls get off to a great start in elementary school, doing better academically than boys (Nelson-Le Gall and DeCooke, 1987). But by the end of high school, a disturbing transformation has taken place. By the time they graduate, the same girls who began their school years as eager young scholars are more likely to have taken fewer math and science courses, have had fewer hands-on experiences in science, have participated in fewer field trips, and are far less likely to pursue careers in science or technology than boys (Kahle and Lakes, 1983).

With a possible shortage of scientists and engineers predicted for early in the next century, we can no longer afford to continue turning this large segment of our population away from science careers (The Task Force on Women, Minorities, and the Handicapped in Science and Technology, 1988). We will need to rely on women and minorities to fill the gap. Furthermore, as science educators, we have a responsibility to make the knowledge and discipline of science appealing to a wide range of students.

Feminist educators, concerned about the loss of women from the sciences, have recognized that many women do not learn best in the traditional competitive, fact-oriented classroom and need to be taught in ways that will overcome barriers to their learning. The result of their efforts is a way of teaching science designed to include women as active contributors within a learning environment of trust and security. As an added benefit, teachers who have applied the method have found that what works well for women also works for many men, minorities, and students who feel alienated and disempowered in the science classroom (Rosser, 1990).

Five basic elements provide the foundation for this new way of learning (Schniedwind, 1983):

- Learning needs to take place in an environment of mutual respect and trust. When students know each other as human beings, speak freely, take risks with ideas, and offer mutual support, the classroom becomes a learning community that includes everyone. Developing democratic processes among students is important in establishing this sense of community and the right of all students to participate in classroom decisions.

- Leadership, not just of small groups, but of the class, should be shared. Although the teacher maintains primary responsibility for the design and structure of the course, students may help make many decisions, such as setting course objectives and determining the relative weight of assignments for final grades. The intent is to equalize, as much as possible, power differences between students and between teacher and student, while still recognizing the teacher's expertise and ultimate responsibility for the class. The teacher needs to seek feedback from students and be willing to become a learner in the classroom. As both teacher and students learn, students discover that knowledge is a dynamic entity, and that no one has all the answers.

◆ Use of cooperative learning strategies in the classroom improves cognitive and affective learning by students. Cooperative learning has been shown to benefit students in many educational settings. It is a central component of our method, and we will continue to discuss it throughout this chapter.

◆ Cognitive and affective learning should be integrated, enhancing students' self-esteem and confidence. A teaching environment in which concepts and ideas are emphasized connects science to the real world for students. They should be encouraged to contribute their own experiences to the learning activities. This will help students make connections between classroom learning and new scientific information after they leave the classroom.

◆ Active learning engages students' attention and imagination. Students become more fully involved with what they are learning and thereby learn more. Classes that involve active learning are more stimulating than those where teachers talk about ideas and students listen.

Individual teachers may combine these elements in varying proportions to suit the needs of their own students, and in doing so, they strive toward a common goal—creating an environment in which the widest spectrum of students can achieve and excel in science. These are students who take ownership of ideas and begin to identify themselves as scientists and who are more likely to remain interested in science either as active citizens or as career scientists.

Practical advice for building a classroom community

Everyday tips and tools: Many teachers would like to build a classroom community but lack specific strategies to confront the everyday situations and surprises that arise in the classroom. We often hear teachers comment that they would like to involve the students in more discussion, but the students simply will not talk. Other teachers are afraid of correcting students for fear the students will withdraw. Still others have trouble overcoming their students' feelings of not belonging in science. The following are a few proven tips and tools to build an environment in which students are vigorous participants and to help teachers deal confidently with the daily management of the classroom.

It is important to set the tone early in the semester. If the students receive the message clearly that they are expected to be active members of the classroom, and if they perceive immediately that their ideas shape the classroom, then a community spirit will naturally follow.

Start simple: The first time you attempt to elicit thoughts from the students, try something simple, open-ended, or personal. Remember that the students are afraid of being wrong and are convinced that they know nothing about the subject, especially if this is their first science course. If the first question they are asked is hard or has only one right answer that they may not know, they may not be eager to participate. Save the challenging questions for later when the students have more confidence or have learned that it is acceptable to be wrong. The first question could be something that makes a connection between the course and the rest of their lives. Some examples are:

- How does biology affect your life?
- Describe something you would like to understand about the biological world.
- What issues facing the world today involve biology?

It can also be useful to get the students thinking about what they wish to achieve in the course. Try having groups set objectives for the course and report back to the entire class. Have someone record the list and return to it every few weeks with the class to determine whether you are meeting the students' objectives and whether new objectives have emerged.

Alternatively, have the students collectively agree on a grading scheme for the course. Provide them with a list of assignments and have each group decide on the weight for each assignment. They can then report their scheme to the entire class or send a representative to a class council that will develop a consensus grading scheme. The grading topic is a good one because most students care about it and at first are thrilled with the opportunity to provide advice on how to weight assignments. Although this exercise can be very effective, the negative side is that it is time-consuming to achieve consensus, it is almost impossible to do so with a very large class, and it is of questionable value to reinforce the student obsession with grades by devoting an entire class period to them.

Making it personal: Students strive harder and achieve higher standards if they are thought of as individuals and not just identification numbers. It can be difficult in the large classes in which introductory biology is often taught to make personal contact with each student, but a few tricks can help: If at all possible, take pictures of the students with name cards on and learn as many names as possible. (To save film, pictures can be taken of groups.) If you call on even a few students in class by name, your classroom will have a more personal feel and the students will feel more committed to the class. If you do not have the resources, time, or memory to do this, at least ask students to say their names when they speak in class and then refer to their questions and ideas with their names associated. When students hear a teacher say, "as Heather pointed out," it sends the message that students are individuals and that individuals are responsible for ideas. Pride of ownership of ideas is an important emotion to reinforce in building a community of individuals who feel that their contributions to the group are unique and valued.

Even if you do not know your students' names, you can let them know that you notice them by addressing individuals with questions or comments. You might chat with a few of them individually for a minute before each class, stop certain students and comment if you have noticed they were not in class or were sitting in a different seat last time, or ask a student after class whether something you said in lecture was clear and understandable. These actions are easy to take, require little time, preparation, or follow-up but have a powerful impact on the willingness of students to participate in a class. Although these approaches to building a cohesive classroom may seem trivial or obvious, a comment we hear most often about our classes is that the students are astonished that a teacher would *care* about them and their opinions. This atmosphere, in turn, makes science seem more human, fun, and exciting to them.

Teacher takes risks: Sometimes students simply will not respond to a request for ideas. They may be too inhibited or they may not quite understand the material or the question asked. Often, gridlock can be broken by the teacher proposing an idea for the students to analyze or evaluate. If you have asked your students how they might test a certain hypothesis and are met with silence, you might propose an obviously silly experiment or a part of an experiment and ask the students if you are going in the right direction. For example, if you have asked them to design an experiment to learn about the proteins in muscle cells, you might suggest starting with grinding up a liver and ask them if that is the right place to start and why.

This approach can be humorous, but it serves the much deeper purpose of starting the students realizing that they do know something about the topic at hand even if it is simply that you do not go to the liver to isolate muscle cells. In addition, it is not surprising that it is much easier for people to volunteer criticisms of ideas than it is to volunteer ideas that might be criticized by others. It is valuable for the students to learn that the teacher's ideas are not always right and to practice criticizing ideas from any source. This is an important first step toward becoming a critical thinker. Once they take the first step, they are more likely to contribute their own ideas to the class and more willing to have them criticized.

Feedback: One of the simplest approaches to promoting participation is to be encouraging. This does not mean patting the students on the head and accepting all of their ideas. The key is to reinforce them as people while honestly evaluating their ideas and challenging them to evaluate their own and others' ideas. Students respond powerfully to what sometimes appear as trivial comments. We have found that simply saying, "Good question" before answering a question can put students at ease and encourage them to ask questions freely. When you think about it, all questions are good questions, but students are often fearful of demonstrating ignorance, confusion, or stupidity.

A technique as important as positive reinforcement is avoiding words and behavior that make students clam up. We emphasize this issue because we have heard from students that humiliation in science classes is common and a major reason that students do not participate easily in discussion. A particularly powerful inhibitor of participation is to imply that a student did not do assigned work. For example, one of our students asked a question that was answered in the reading assignment that the students were expected to do before coming to class. The teaching assistant in the class responded, "You would know the answer to that if you had done the reading." We heard from colleagues that the student was in tears later that day, claiming to have been humiliated in front of the class. He did not ask another question for weeks. The teaching assistant's response was wrong for two reasons. First, she did not know whether the student had read the assignment based on the student's question. The student might have simply not understood, not remembered, or not made a connection to the issue being discussed. Secondly, embarrassing a student in front of a class is unlikely to improve performance. If the goal was to point out what was in the reading, the teaching assistant could have gone through the reading and helped the students find the answer. If the goal was to assure that the student was doing the reading, a question asked in private would have been more effective.

Dealing with "wrong": One of the advantages of an open classroom community is that misconceptions are likely to be revealed quickly because the students participate actively *during* the learning process. The power of this result is that misconceptions can be dealt with immediately in class, instead of waiting until after an exam. It is essential that misconceptions be corrected so that they are not incorporated into students' thinking about the problem. However, students who have expressed wrong ideas have exposed themselves by sharing their ideas with the class, and it is important not to embarrass the students or to permit them to feel personally attacked. In managing a classroom community, it is essential to keep criticism of ideas separate from criticisms of people. In fact, the student who brings up an idea that is simply wrong (according to current scientific knowledge) may do a great service for the class and can be supported for doing so. By thanking the student for being brave enough to volunteer the idea, the teacher can provide personal support and respect for the person while making absolutely sure the idea is thoroughly evaluated and corrected. This is often easy to do, since every idea has some intrinsic merit. It may have historical value (if one of our students believes it, there was probably once a debate in which some great biologist defended the idea), it may be instructive as a contrast to the right idea, or it may simply be a common misconception that needs to be discussed.

The goal of many strategies for developing a classroom community is to show students that they are valuable members of the community despite (or sometimes because of) their mistakes and to show that everyone's ideas can be criticized or improved on by a group. This tends to teach the students that coming up with the idea is only the first step; honing and refining it with a group is where the fun in scientific debate really lies. A combination of approaches can be used to defuse the embarrassment of being wrong and to ensure that the right idea is transmitted.

For example, let us imagine that a student named Horton states that proteins are the universal hereditary material. Hearing this, most teachers would panic and wonder what they did wrong to instill such a wrong-headed idea, but once the panic subsides, a number of approaches could be used to arrive at the concept that nucleic acids are the hereditary material in biology. First, the other students might be asked if they agree with Horton's statement. This approach encourages the students to be critical of each others' ideas and provides the opportunity for Horton to be corrected by a peer instead of by the teacher, which may be less intimidating to him. If the other students do not correct the idea, then making the point that this is clearly a common misconception and it is a good thing Horton brought it up is a constructive way to show support for Horton and call attention to the fact that many of the other students probably need to learn some information that is about to be presented. Whether a student or the teacher corrects the misconception, Horton's pride can be protected by discussing the fact that although all current evidence shows that proteins are *not* the universal hereditary material, there was a substantive debate about the chemical nature of hereditary material involving many great biologists in the early part of the 20th century. Finally, Horton or anyone else in the class can be invited to imagine why nucleic acids might make better hereditary material than proteins, or how cells would function differently in transmission or expression of genes if genes were proteins. This takes the emphasis off the "wrongness" of Horton's idea and turns it instead into the basis for a creative, educational exercise.

Formats for cooperative learning

Cooperative learning is effective in large or small groups, formal and informal settings, and for short and long duration. The same exercise or problem can serve different educational goals used in different situations. For example, in a lecture setting, particularly with large classes, a cooperative exercise may be used primarily to help the students be active participants and provide the instructor with immediate feedback, and in a laboratory setting the same exercise could be used to build cohesiveness among groups.

It is important that cooperative learning not be used as a forum for a few students to dominate, to turn the class into a free-for-all, or to feel they can present sloppy or wrong ideas without being challenged. Cooperative learning should be highly managed and the goal should be to evaluate and analyze ideas as a group. Keep two principles in mind at all times when managing cooperative learning exercises. First, it is essential to build the expectation that ideas will be rigorously evaluated. The second principle is that all participants need to feel a right to and pride in their own ideas.

Lecture format: In lecture, cooperative learning exercises help students be active learners instead of simply passive recipients of information. Providing an opportunity for each student to make a decision or evaluate and comment on information encourages students to think about the material they are learning. Being asked for their ideas and opinions also makes students feel that they are necessary members of the class—they are empowered because the content of the lecture material is shaped by their presence and participation. This is a likely reason for the observation that cooperative learning used regularly in lectures improves attendance. In addition, students are more likely to come to class on time, and they are more likely to be alert and involved when they are in class.

The simplest and least disruptive approach to cooperative exercises in lecture is to present a problem to the class as a whole, instruct the students to consult with the students sitting on either side of them in groups of three for no more than three to five minutes and then report to the entire class. Each group is then asked to report the results of their group's consultation and the results are recorded on the blackboard. In large classes, the process can be shortened by asking for answers that differ from those already reported after the first ten groups report. If this approach is used, it is essential to start the reporting process with groups from a different part of the classroom each time cooperative learning is used so that all groups have the opportunity to report their results over the course of the semester.

The approach described here for cooperative learning in lectures minimizes the amount of time dedicated to the exercises while maximizing student involvement. Most in-lecture exercises can be completed in ten minutes from set-up to final reporting. The benefit is that students feel that their ideas are valued, they are challenged to think and not simply absorb information, and they experience the satisfaction of seeing their ideas direct the course material.

Project format: Group projects are one of the best strategies to encourage students to engage with each other intellectually and personally. Projects can involve laboratory experiments or library research. The key is to provide a common goal that can only be achieved with participation by all group members. The goal might be to design and execute a successful experiment, solve a problem, or develop a research strategy. It is important that the goal be presented as a group product in some forum to provide practice and support for students' learning to function as a group. In addition, we find that students also appreciate the opportunity to present their individual vision of the group effort. Therefore, we often require both a group presentation and a written report from each student. For example, in laboratory sections conducting experiments, the members of each group will describe to the entire class the hypothesis they developed and their experiments designed to test it. Then each student will submit his or her own written lab report describing the experiment, results, and interpretation.

Exam format: One of the most surprising uses of cooperative learning for many teachers is group exams. It is surprising because most of us have been taught that exams must be individual, competitive experiences to measure learning. If, however, our goal is to *promote* learning, instead of just measuring it, we must consider the value of group exams. Group exams are most effective with open-ended, complex questions that do not have right or wrong answers. The group process, interactions between students, and vigorous debate are intensified by an exam structure and the grade associated with it. These can be used to generate creative ideas and build the critical and logical thinking skills needed for biology. Our own experience and that reported by others (Johnson and Johnson, 1975; Duren and Cherrington, 1992) shows that students are willing to tackle much more difficult problems in groups than they will attempt individually. We find that students respond best to being required to work with a group (we ask for a list of their group members) but then to generate a written answer individually for which they receive an individual grade. This approach capitalizes on both group process and pride in individual accomplishment.

Examples of group learning exercises

Group hypothesis development: To help students become curious, creative thinkers, they must be challenged to explore many possible answers to problems. A brainstorming exercise that is directed at generating a wide range of possible answers encourages students to think broadly and helps them come to grips with the notion that there are not always (if ever) simple answers to most problems in biology.

Group exercises are effective ways to reinforce application of the scientific method. Students can be presented with an observation about the natural world and then asked to confer in small groups to develop hypotheses that would explain it. One fun and practical example is to bring a sick plant to class and explain that you have not been able to isolate in culture a microorganism that induces similar symptoms on a similar plant. Ask each group to develop three hypotheses to explain the symptoms of the plant. After a few minutes, each group should report back to the entire group and a list of possible causes can be generated. Many of the students are likely to suggest the same causes (chemical damage, nutrient deficiency, a virus) but there will be some answers that may be a surprise in their creativity and insight (multiple organisms required to induce the symptoms, the new test plant is the wrong age to develop symptoms with the microorganism isolated in culture, wrong conditions for infection). One of the rewards of this exercise is that collectively, the students are likely to generate a list of possible causes that exceeds what any one of them alone or the teacher could generate. The list of possible causes can then be used as the basis for future lessons in the causes of disease.

A similar approach can be used with any part of the scientific method. The students can be presented with a hypothesis and be asked to devise experiments, in groups, to test the hypothesis. They can be presented with an experiment and data, and they can generate interpretations of the results.

Group exercises flourish in an atmosphere of mutual trust and respect. Even shy students are willing to risk expressing their ideas if know they will be listened to and taken seriously.

Collective brain-storming: Giving a broad, open-ended problem to the whole class to discuss and solve as a group is one of the most effective exercises. Because it **is** so open-ended, it generates a wide variety of thinking and responses from students. This exercise works especially well in a lecture setting and has the advantage of requiring little advance preparation time and no supplies or materials. Many of the ideas that come from collective brain-storming sessions go beyond the instructor's own imagination. And, not infrequently, ideas contributed by students serve as the basis for future lectures, which both contributes to the depth of learning in the class and promotes student self-esteem.

Some examples of collective brain-storming topics are:

- Imagine you are a cell. What is your greatest challenge?
- Come up with some new uses for genetic engineering in medicine or agriculture.
- Think of some examples of natural selection.
- What are the similarities or differences between . . . and . . . ?

Collective decision making: Acquiring the power to make decisions that affect the lives of others and being held accountable for those decisions is a strong inducement to ask questions and to learn and evaluate facts about an issue. Groups of students can be asked to imagine that they are policy-makers who must make tough decisions that require biological information. The desire to appear responsible and rational will induce them to become experts on the issue, which will require learning information, thinking critically, and developing a creative solution. It is important to remind groups that every member of the group must participate and that each member is likely to bring different skills and strengths to solving the problem.

Some examples of the types of decisions students can be asked to make are:

◆ You are the U.S. Secretary of the Interior. You must decide whether or not to save the old forests of the Northwest and thereby preserve or destroy the biological diversity of the region. To save the forests, you must reduce or eliminate logging there, thus alienating the powerful lumber industry and putting local people out of work, severely affecting the economy of the region. What will be your policy? Why? How will you mitigate the social and environmental impacts of your policy?

◆ You are the head of a major blood bank, and there is a world-wide blood shortage. You are offered a shipment of blood that might be contaminated with a new retrovirus that has not been well studied. Will you allow the blood to be used? Why? What would you like to know before you make your decision?

◆ You are the Executive Director of the National Pesticide-Free Food Network. You learn that a chemical company is about to register a new fungicide. The fungicide reduces accumulation of aflatoxin, a highly carcinogenic toxin produced by a fungus that often grows on peanuts. You must decide whether your group should protest the use of the fungicide on peanuts. What questions will you ask and what process will you use to decide whether or not to fight the use of the fungicide?

◆ You are the director of research for an agriculture biotechnology company. You have been asked to develop a research plan for the next five years. What products for agriculture will you develop with genetic engineering? Defend your plan.

Grading: Many cooperative learning exercises can be used in the classroom with no evaluation system except the verbal evaluation of ideas. However, it is useful to reinforce the importance of group work by providing grades for certain assignments that are performed at least in part by groups. Two principles are useful in devising grading schemes for group projects. First, the point of our teaching should be learning first, then evaluation. The second principle is that balance must be achieved between reinforcing group effort and providing opportunities to evaluate students individually and opportunities for students who dislike group work to feel that they have a chance for self-determination.

There are two approaches to grading. The strict cooperative learning approach suggests that students are motivated to ensure that all group members contribute to and understand the group effort only if every member of the group receives the same grade for the assignment. Some instructors find that students are motivated to do their best by individual rewards, such as grades. If they are graded individually, they will use the group as a springboard for their efforts, but will not be limited by the group activity or process. We find that a combination of grading strategies is probably best to motivate the largest cross-section of students and to provide a good measure of individual achievement while reinforcing group effort. For example, students might conduct their lab experiments in groups, discuss the results and interpretation, but write the reports individually. For group projects, they can be asked to make an oral presentation for which all members of the group will receive the same grade, but then they can be asked to write about a specific aspect of the project for an individual grade.

Ethics of group work: Encouraging or requiring group work will act as an invitation to some students to cheat, perhaps by copying another student's assignment, using lab results from an experiment they did not perform, or by simply not contributing to the group effort. The best method to prevent this is to make expectations clear. Cooperative work provides the substance for useful discussions about ethics in science, giving and sharing credit, and the difference between fair exchange and exploitation. To prevent abuses of the system, make the rules clear by writing them down in course handouts. A separate handout on ethical conduct, explaining what is acceptable and what is not, is very much appreciated by the students. Consider asking students to sign a contract for ethical conduct that states the requirements of your classroom (see Appendix V, page 240 for a sample contract). Committing in writing to uphold ethical standards is probably enough to prevent most students from cheating. If you find that a few students do cheat, remember that even if you and class have been violated by the behavior of a few, the rest of your students have benefitted from these teaching strategies.

References - cooperative learning

♦ Barratt, Leslie B. (1992) Cooperative learning in the college classroom. *Contemporary Education*, 63: 201-202.

♦ Dees, Roberta L. (1991) The role of cooperative learning in increasing problem-solving ability in a college remedial course. *Journal for Research in Mathematics Education*, 22: 409-421.

♦ Deutsch, Morton (1949) An experimental study of the effects of co-operation and competition upon group process. *Human Relations*, 2: 199-231.

♦ Deutsch, Morton (1949) A theory of co-operation and competition. *Human Relations*, 2: 129-152.

♦ Dewey, J. (1916) *Democracy and Education*. New York: The Free Press, MacMillan, Inc.

♦ Duren, Phillip E. and April Cherrington (1992) The effects of cooperative group work versus independent practice on the learning of some problem-solving strategies. *School Science and Mathematics*, 92: 80-83.

♦ Haynes, Norris M. and Sara Gebreyesus (1992) Cooperative learning: a case for African-American students. *School Psychology Review*, 21: 577-585.

♦ Jagers, Robert J. (1992) Attitudes toward academic interdependence and learning outcomes in two learning contexts. *Journal of Negro Education*, 61: 531-538.

♦ Johnson, D. W. and Johnson, R. (1978) Cooperative, competitive, and individualistic learning. *Journal of Research and Development in Education*, 12: 3-15.

♦ Johnson, D.W. and Johnson, R. (1975) *Learning Together and Alone: Cooperation, Competition and Individualization*, (1st ed.), Engelwood Cliffs, NJ: Prentice-Hall.

♦ Johnson, David W. and Roger T. Johnson (1993) Implementing cooperative learning. *The Education Digest*, 58: 62-66.

♦ Johnson, David W. and Roger T. Johnson (1985) Classroom conflict: Controversy versus debate in learning groups. *American Educational Research Journal*, 22: 237-256.

♦ Johnson, D.W., R. Johnson, and L. Scott (1978) The effects of cooperative and individualized instruction on student attitudes and achievement. *Journal of Social Psychology*, 104: 207-216.

♦ Johnson, Roger T., David W. Johnson, Linda E. Scott, and Beverly A. Ramolae (1985) Effects of single-sex and mixed-sex cooperative interaction on science achievement and attitudes and cross-handicap and cross-sex relationships. *Journal of Research in Science Teaching*, 22: 207–220.

♦ Kahle, Jane Butler and Marsha K. Lakes (1983) The myth of equality in science classrooms. *Journal of Research in Science Teaching*, 20: 131–140.

♦ Lambiotte, Judith G., Donald F. Dansereau, Thomas R. Rocklin, Bennett Fletcher, Velma I. Hythecker, Celia O. Larson, and Angela M. O'Donnell (1987) Cooperative learning and test taking: Transfer of skills. *Contemporary Educational Psychology*, 12: 52–61.

♦ Lazarowitz, R., R.L. Hertz, J.H. Baird, and V. Bowlden (1988) Academic achievement and on-task behavior of high school biology students instructed in a cooperative small investigative group. *Science Education*, 72: 475–487.

♦ Little Soldier, Lee (1989) Cooperative learning and the Native American student. *Phi Delta Kappan*, 71: 161–163.

♦ Nelson-Le Gall, Sharon and Peggy A. DeCooke (1987) Same-sex and cross-sex help exchanges in the classroom. *Journal of Educational Psychology*, 79: 67–71.

♦ Okebukola, Peter Akinsola (1986a) Cooperative learning and students' attitudes to laboratory work. *School Science and Mathematics*, 86: 582–590.

♦ Okebukola, Peter Akinsola (1986b) The influence of preferred learning styles on cooperative learning in science. *Science Education*, 70: 509–517.

♦ Okebukola, Peter Akinsola (1992) Concept mapping with a cooperative learning flavor. *The American Biology Teacher*, 54: 218-221.

♦ Okebukola, Peter A. and Meshach B. Ogunniyi (1984) Cooperative, competitive, and individualistic science laboratory interaction patterns—Effects on students' achievement and acquisition of practical skills. *Journal of Research in Science Teaching*, 21: 875–884.

◆ Popp, Jerome A. (1987) If you see John Dewey, tell him we did it. *Educational Theory*, 37: 145–152.

◆ Rewey, Kirsten L., Donald F. Dansereau, Sandra M. Dees, Lisa P. Skaggs, and Urvashi Pitre (1992) Scripted cooperation and knowledge map supplements: Effects on the recall of biological and statistical information. *The Journal of Experimental Education*, 60: 93–107.

◆ Rosser, Sue (1990) *Female-friendly Science*. New York: Teachers College Press.

◆ Schniedwind, Nancy (1983) Feminist values: Guidelines for teaching methodology in women's studies. In: *Learning Our Way: Essays in Feminist Education*. Charlotte Bunch and Sandra Pollack, eds. Trumansburg, NY: The Crossing Press.

◆ Slavin, Robert E. (1986) *Student Team Learning: An Overview and Practical Guide*. Washington, D.C.: National Education Association.

◆ Slavin, Robert E. (1989) Cooperative learning and student achievement. *The Education Digest*, 54: 15–17.

◆ Slavin, Robert E. (1990) *Cooperative Learning: Theory, Research, and Practice*. Englewood Cliffs, N.J.: Prentice Hall.

◆ Smith, Mark E., C.C. Hinckley, and G.L. Volk (1991) Cooperative learning in the undergraduate laboratory. *Journal of Chemical Education*, 68: 413–415.

◆ Swisher, Karen (1990) Cooperative learning and the education of American Indian/Alaskan native students: A review of the literature and suggestions for implementation. *Journal of American Indian Education*, 29: 36–43.

◆ The Task Force on Women, Minorities, and the Handicapped in Science and Technology (1988) *Changing America: The New Face of Science and Engineering*. Washington, DC: The Task Force on Women, Minorities, and the Handicapped in Science and Technology

◆ Watson, Scott B. (1992) The essential elements of cooperative learning. *The American Biology Teacher*, 54: 84–86.

Section 2: Learning skills for success in biology

The challenge

Many students are at risk of failure in their college courses not because of a deficiency in ability or intelligence but because they lack the fundamental skills required to learn the material presented in their classes. Young students are not taught how to study. Instead they are expected to have somehow assimilated learning skills during their primary and secondary school careers. By the time they reach college, they are supposed to **know** how to study and be successful at learning. But many do not. The story of the student who "spent hours studying for the exam" but who performed poorly is all too familiar to teachers. Such a student equates learning with time spent but has not learned how to learn.

A lack of basic learning skills can pose significant problems for students enrolled in science courses, especially those who are not typically "good at science." In our experience, students who have trouble learning science often lack fundamental skills in note-taking, study practices, and exam-taking that are essential for learning and achieving satisfactory grades. Personality, culture, and previous learning experiences also contribute to academic success or failure. Recent work suggests that key cognitive and personality traits are often associated with study competence (Waters and Waters, 1992). Our goal is to teach all students who need them the basic skills of learning and help students build the awareness and personal characteristics to be enthusiastic and successful learners. Attributes associated with good learners consist of two groups—practical skills such as notetaking, reading, writing, and exam-taking, and the personal characteristics that make the learning process fulfilling and efficient, including such traits as confidence, independence, and logical thought processes. The goal of this section of the book is to present methods for enhancing both the practical skills and the personal characteristics associated with good learners.

Including learning skills exercises in science course curricula can be particularly meaningful to women, minority, and other students who do not have role models in science or who believe they will not do well in science courses. The combination of learning skills and cooperative learning can be particularly powerful for people who do not have role models that enable them to see themselves as scientists or who do not have the confidence in science classes to reach out to their teachers or peers. Often their lack of faith in themselves as science students prevents these students from engaging in the very activities that would help them be successful, such as forming study groups, asking questions, or imposing their own framework on new information.

They often withdraw, become tense and self-conscious, and fulfill their own prophesy that they do not "fit" in science. Discussing the key activities and strategies for successful learning with such students and providing a non-threatening environment in which they can try out new activities can reverse the negative sequence of events and turn these students into fine learners.

The study skills and personal characteristics of successful students*

Study skills:

Note-taking	Reading a text
Sifting out the important	Previewing
Shortening sentences	Underlining and note-taking
Using symbols and abbreviations	Mastering terminology
Reformatting	Drawing inferences
Integrating material	

Writing papers	Taking exams
Using the library	Forming study groups
Finding main ideas	Consolidating and reviewing
Paraphrasing	Managing time
Thinking and writing clearly	Concentrating
	Improving memory
	Reducing nervousness

Personal characteristics:

Affective	Cognitive
Self-aware	Logical thinkers
Self-confident	Critical questioners
Positive in their attitude	Able to impose their own framework on study data
Able to have an adult relationship with teachers	Willing and able to teach themselves
Independent and pro-active	Independent-minded

* Based on a schema by Waters and Waters, 1992.

Research on cognitive styles reveals diversity in the ways people learn. Some students tend to see their environment in its entirety rather than its component parts, some prefer intuitive rather than either deductive or inductive reasoning, some tend to rely on both nonverbal and verbal cues, and some respond only to verbal cues (Chinien and Boutin, 1992/93). Some research has suggested that these differences are influenced by culture and ethnicity (Brown, 1980), but anyone who has taught a large class with a narrow ethnic base knows of the tremendous diversity that is found even in students of the same cultural heritage. Building learning skills in analytical and critical thinking and reformatting course material graphically (we describe a number of helpful exercises in this section) can help students of diverse cognitive styles learn effectively from a single teaching style (Delpit, 1988, 1992).

We do not need to understand the process by which our students learn in order to provide the opportunity for them to find their own cognitive style. Recognizing that there are many cognitive styles and then providing a classroom format in which students can piece biological information together in their own ways by whatever process is effective for them can help us reach a wide range of students in an efficient manner. The teacher needs to provide the starting information and to evaluate the verbal or written product that students construct, but the process by which they arrive at logical arguments that are based on current knowledge should be a personal one for each student.

Strategies for developing learning skills in biology

We have found that exercises to enhance learning skills can be incorporated directly into a course in biology or they can be offered in an adjunct course or discussion section dedicated to teaching learning skills. You may find that some of the exercises fit into your lectures, labs, or discussion sections. For example, the use of index cards to increase the students' awareness about their learning (see page 194), or the reformatting of information in a new graphical style (see page 210) are exercises that fit naturally into standard teaching and can help all students. Other exercises, especially those that appear more contrived, such as strip sequence (page 199) or jigsaw (page 204), may be more appropriate to use in a homogeneous group of students who are searching for help in learning biology. We have found that students who are struggling with a biology course are the most likely to be willing to try new types of exercises if they believe the exercises will enhance their learning.

If you choose to develop a course in learning skills, it is essential to link it to the biology course as an "adjunct" course and not offer it as an isolated course. We have found the adjunct approach to be effective for a number of reasons. First, the learning skills course makes students immediately more successful in the biology course. Students' success strengthens their self-confidence because they have mastered what they perceive as a difficult subject area. Students often tell us that a good grade in a science course is a big boost to their self-image because they view science courses as difficult, intimidating, and unfamiliar.

Second, it is easier to convince students to take a learning skills course associated with a science course than a general learning skills course because their anxiety about science may be high and their pride about being able to learn without special help is often less in science than in other areas. The learning skills course should be presented to the students as an enrichment course, not as a remedial experience. It is an occasion to learn new skills and provides a unique opportunity for instructors to help students learn science. Most students are reluctant to admit that they lack the skills to do well in college, whereas many are willing to admit that they just cannot learn science.

Finally, the attachment of the learning skills course to the science course provides an incentive to the students to work diligently in the learning skills course since it has a direct impact on their grades in the science course. The guidance provided by the learning skills instructor, the support that is derived from shared experience among the students, and the immediate application of newly acquired skills to material in the biology course contributes to confidence-building and reinforces the skills required for success in this course. Success in the biology course, in turn, helps build the confidence the students need to continue to apply their new skills in future courses.

One key component of the learning skills course is that it should empower the students to take an active role in their education. The students are expected to work together to identify problem areas and develop their own solutions. They are encouraged to share and learn from each other's successes and failures. In teaching learning skills, it is especially important to build a sense of community and employ cooperative strategies for active learning.

Beginning of the semester

The beginning of the semester is typically a time of nerves and confusion for students, with new courses, unknown professors, and a heap of intimidating syllabi. Science courses will be particularly threatening to those who think they cannot learn science. Therefore, it is essential to show the students immediately that they can. The first few class sessions must be used to put students at ease and increase their self-confidence by showing them they can be successful cooperative learners. It is also critical to build their self-awareness. If students know themselves, they will at least have one fewer unknown to deal with. Furthermore, self-aware students will address their own inadequacies before serious problems arise. Several exercises for self-analysis are productive early in the semester:

Learning skills survey: On one of the first days of class, students can be asked to examine and analyze their own study habits on a survey. (See Appendix VI, page 241 for a sample survey.) Answering the survey questions in private at home, students can honestly admit what they do and do not do and thus become aware of the strengths and weaknesses of their study habits. Students can discuss the survey with each other and compare study styles. The questions on the survey also provide a good preview of desirable learning skills and what students need to learn during the semester. It is both important to the process of building self-awareness and informative to the teacher to follow up on the survey as the semester progresses, asking the students whether, in fact, they are making changes in their habits in all their classes.

A logical consequence of the learning skills survey is to devise a study schedule. Students can plot out their classes, study time, job hours, relaxation time, and other daily responsibilities on a grid with blocks of time. The purpose of blocking this information out on a grid is to help students maximize the efficient use of their time. Setting up a study schedule along with another good study habit, previewing a text, are standard fare in study skills manuals. The list of references at the end of this section provides further guidance and samples of both.

Collecting your thoughts: A quick but important early activity is to ask students to collect their thoughts on the area of biology they are about to study. They can do this orally in class or it can be added to the survey. Questions could include: What have you studied about biology in the past? What interesting things did you learn? What did you like about the material? What didn't you like? What was easy about it? Difficult? Such questions make students more aware of both themselves and the course content and can be particularly meaningful if students make a connection between their new knowledge and other learning experiences.

What kind of thinker are you? Students may never have considered the fact that people have different learning and thinking styles, yet recognizing one's own style is a key element of intellectual self-awareness. It is important that students realize there is no inherently superior thinking style and that learning biology requires the ability to both remember facts and interpret them. An activity that allows students to assess their own thinking styles, such as the one described below, can thus be very enlightening and lead students to study in ways that build on their strengths and compensate for their weaknesses.

For this exercise, students are given a copy of Table 1 and instructions to look at it for three minutes. At the end of that time, the students hand in their copies of the table, and the class begins to discuss what they learned from it. The teacher makes a list of responses on the board and points out that some responses fall more into the category of factual, detailed information and others more into interpretation or analysis. (Alternatively, students could be asked to analyze and classify the responses.) If a pattern develops in the type of observations made by individual students, they can discuss whether or not they feel this is typical of their thinking style. Since both data and interpretation of data are important in the sciences, students can try to compensate in the future for any imbalance in their focus, or they may recognize the role they are more likely to play in cooperative groups—the fact-finder and recorder or the analyst and synthesizer.

It is essential that this exercise not be used to damage the confidence of students but rather to point out tendencies and preferences. It is important not to introduce a judgmental tone into this exercise, which might make students feel less confident or inadequate in dealing with either facts or concepts. This is a good time to stress the need—in learning groups, in science, and in society—for diversity of all kinds, including diversity of thinking style.

Table 1: Numbers of described species of living organisms

Common name of group	Number of described species
viruses	1,000
bacteria	4,760
fungi	46,983
plants	248,428
insects	751,000
reptiles	6,300
birds	9,040
mammals	4,000
TOTAL (all organisms)	1,392,485

Source: NRC Report on Conserving Biological Diversity

Index card questions: A technique that offers students an active role in learning and that can be used at the beginning of the semester to build self-awareness and self-confidence is index card questions. Because the answers to index card questions are short (short enough to fit on a 3 × 5-inch card), they provide a non-threatening way for students to experiment with using the language and terminology of biology. The cards offer students regular writing practice and the chance to learn how to express ideas about biology without adding a huge reading burden for the instructor. Moreover, they build students' confidence by providing a "success," showing students that they can contribute valued ideas to the dialogue of science.

A question is posed in class and each student must write an answer to it on an index card. (Practical details: Class routine can be established so that students pick up any class handouts and an index card at the front of the room on their way into class. They drop off their index cards in boxes marked with their lab section number on the way out of class. The cards are not graded, but the students should put their names on them. This helps the teacher be aware of individual students who may need extra help with the material). A good question to ask to encourage self-awareness, for example, is: What concept presented in class this week was difficult for you? The answer to this question can be illuminating to both students and teachers. The simple act of writing down the answer may lead a student to realize that s/he should review that concept or see the instructor for help. A large number of students citing the same point may likewise lead the instructor to recognize the need to return to the concept during the next class meeting.

In addition to raising consciousness, the index card technique is effective later in the semester to encourage critical thinking and to show students the relevance of biology and its connections to their everyday lives. A good example for mid-semester might be: If you were an official for the EPA, what three questions would you ask about registering a new pesticide? This develops students' ability to think logically and ask well-directed questions. Here are more examples of questions to develop self-awareness and critical thinking skills:

- Describe the connection between the content of today's lecture and your life outside the classroom.

- Describe how your own personal bias, shaped by your background, ethnic origins, culture, experience, religion, education, or gender might affect your interpretation of the material presented today.

- What was the most interesting part of today's lecture for you? What do you think other students or the professor found most interesting?

- What was the key concept in today's lecture?

- What more would you like to know about today's topic?

Index card questions can promote the kind of thinking and writing skills students need to do well in their biology classes and to succeed in their academic work overall. And if the teacher makes use of people's answers in the next class meeting, those little white cards can be very important for students, who realize they are playing a role in setting the agenda for the class.

Middle of the semester

The middle of the semester is a time of demands for students. If they are to be successful, they must manage the conflicting and sometimes overwhelming requirements of their different courses. Homework, reading, exams, papers—these are some of the obvious, easily identifiable requirements. Yet an equally important and more subtle need also exists—the need for students to recognize that their teachers cannot simply implant information into their brains but rather that they themselves must take responsibility for learning. (The ability to teach oneself has been identified as one of the key characteristics of successful learners; see page 190.) To meet the many demands on their time, energy, and intellectual willingness and ability, students need many skills, foremost among them the capacity to think clearly, carefully, and analytically.

Critical and analytical thinking in science classes requires an understanding of the connections between scientific concepts as they are presented both in lecture and in the required reading. Research has shown that both oral and written science discourse relies heavily on five major patterns (Horowitz, 1985). If students are to succeed in science, they must be able to recognize and use these patterns appropriately. The five patterns are:

- time order - steps in a process or procedure, directions
- list order - lists of materials needed, reports of data
- compare/contrast - comparisons, analogies
- cause/effect
- problem/solution

The last three are seen as higher-order patterns and thus require higher-order thinking skills than do the first two patterns.

The exercises and activities described in this section are designed to make students better able to meet the demands of learning science, both in class and out, by making them more adept at and comfortable with the thinking processes underlying these five basic patterns.

Paraphrasing: Paraphrasing is a critical skill but one that is often not taught. It seems that teachers in the American school system always say, "Explain *in your own words*," but seldom show students how to do just that, assuming that simply saying it should make it happen. By regularly paraphrasing and internalizing material from lectures and readings, students take responsibility for their own learning and for teaching themselves. It is essential that students be able to paraphrase the key concepts from a lecture or reading as a means of thinking through the material and of making that information their own. Paraphrasing is equally essential if students are to be successful writers and avoid the pitfall of plagiarism. A student's ability to articulate the key questions and issues in her/his own words is a true expression of biological literacy (BSCS, 1993, pages viii-ix, 21–22).

Students need regular, repeated practice in paraphrasing. This is especially true for those who are non-native speakers of English, in part because paraphrasing requires the sophisticated use of vocabulary and syntax in a second language, and in part because their previous educational experience may not have emphasized paraphrasing at all. Routine practice for all students may involve asking them to restate, either orally or in writing, the key concept from a particular portion of the lecture or reading material, especially material in one of the five basic rhetorical patterns outlined above. It may take some prompting or leading questions from the instructor or small contributions of a word or phrase from other students in the class to complete such a restatement. This kind of practice does not require any special preparation on the part of the teacher, but it must be done regularly so that students acquire the habit of doing it by themselves as they read their assignments, listen to lectures, review after class, and write papers using sources.

Two variations on the simple request for individual students to paraphrase are these more structured class activities: For the first, the class is divided into pairs, and students work with a partner to paraphrase a few sentences of spoken or written text selected by the instructor. One member of each pair is then asked to write their paraphrase on the blackboard. The class can examine and compare all the sentences on the board, looking for similarities in content but variety in form and language. Here are examples of short paraphrases:

Original text: "Although Robert Koch was not the first to use experimental animals for the study of infectious disease, he was the first to use them in an integrated way with other methods." (From Brock, Thomas D. (1988) *Robert Koch: A Life in Medicine and Bacteriology.* Madison, WI: Science Tech Publishers, and Berlin: Springer-Verlag.)

Paraphrase 1: Many scientists used animals in their experiments, but Robert Koch was the first to use animals together with other methods to study contagious disease.

Paraphrase 2: Robert Koch was the first scientist to combine the use of animals with other techniques in studying infectious disease.

Once students are adept at paraphrasing shorter bits of information, they need practice with longer pieces of text. In this second activity, two students again work together to discuss the meaning and key points of a written text. Next, each student prepares a written paraphrase. Finally, the partners can engage in an interesting comparison of what they have produced. Such practice is valuable to students not only in their science classes but also in other classes that require library research and writing from sources. Here are examples of longer paraphrases:

Original text: "By the mid-19th century, the French scientist Louis Pasteur had conducted extensive studies of the role of bacteria in fermentation, and he had shown conclusively that while germs could travel through the air, they were not capable of spontaneous generation. There was also a prevailing assumption at the time that microbes were in some way connected with disease, but whether their presence was a requirement for disease or a result of disease was not clear. Furthermore, many infected tissues contained more than one type of microorganism. This made it difficult to define with certainty the role played in disease by any particular type of bacterium.

The work of Pasteur and others, improved techniques in microscopy, and perhaps most important, the discovery of semi-solid culture media all paved the way for a German physician, Robert Koch, to demonstrate for the first time in 1875 that a specific type of bacterium was responsible for a specific disease." (From Experiment 5: Koch's postulates and experimental evidence, pages 63–64.)

Paraphrase 1: In the 19th century, scientists struggled to work out the relationship between bacteria and disease. Louis Pasteur studied bacteria extensively and showed that they could be passed through the air, but Pasteur and the scientists of his day did not prove that bacteria caused disease or resulted from it. They were unable to definitively link specific diseases with specific bacteria. However, Pasteur's work, improved microscopic techniques, and the discovery of semi-solid media for culturing bacteria enabled a German scientist, Robert Koch, to prove in 1875 that a particular disease was definitely caused by a particular bacterium.

Paraphrase 2: In 1875, Robert Koch was the first to identify conclusively a specific bacterium as the cause of a specific disease. Koch achieved success in an area that had long frustrated scientists trying to understand the role of microbes in the disease process. Many suspected that microbes were associated with disease, but they didn't know whether the microbes were causes or by-products of disease. Their work was hindered because seldom could they isolate just one type of organism from a disease site, making it difficult to link a particular bacterium to a disease.

Koch reaped the benefits of advances in microscopy, the discovery of semi-solid culture media, and results of the exacting research of Louis Pasteur to facilitate his research. Pasteur, working in the mid-19th century, studied the role of bacteria in fermentation. Pasteur established without doubt that microbes are not produced by spontaneous generation, as was commonly thought, and that they can be transported through the air.

Students should be carefully guided and gently encouraged in paraphrasing tasks. They should be told to read the text more than once if necessary and to think about it and discuss it with their books closed, to force them to find their own words rather than depending on the words on the page in front of them. If students get stuck, saying, "I understand what it says, but I can't explain it," they can be prompted with questions such as these: "What do you think it says?" "Tell me in a few words what it is about." "Pretend you're explaining this to someone who knows less about it than you do, like your roommate or younger brother." Paraphrasing exercises may be slow at first and take time, but they are more cost-effective than they first appear to be, because students do three things simultaneously when paraphrasing: (1) see that there is not just one correct way to paraphrase, (2) identify and review key concepts, with one student often demystifying for others what the teacher or text said, and (3) push themselves to use higher-level thinking skills, including analysis and synthesis.

Strip sequence: A fun class activity to strengthen students' logical thinking processes is the strip sequence. Step-by-step processes lend themselves well to this technique, but other material could also be used. The teacher prepares before class by typing up one copy of the steps in a process (see the example on the next page) and then cutting that copy into individual strips with one step on each strip. The challenge for the students in class is to work together to reconstruct the proper sequence. Students sit in a circle and each one picks a strip, let us say, from a brown paper bag. They then take turns reading aloud what is written on their strip. In something of a free-for-all, someone proposes a possible first step, then the next. When a faulty sequence is suggested, students can say why it is incorrect and move on to a more logical sequence. Through collaborative effort and thoughtful trial and error, the correct sequence emerges.

The strip sequence can sometimes make the class a bit rowdy, but everyone seems to enjoy it and nobody seems to be embarrassed if they blunder. If the class is too large to work as a single group, two groups can work simultaneously on the same process or on two different processes and then "perform" for each other. The strip sequence offers the fun and satisfaction of cooperative learning, practice in the logic of time order, and subtle reinforcement of the notion that trial and effort is part and parcel of science.

Strip sequence example - Gene expression

(cut into strips on dotted lines)
(assign one student per strip)

The first step in the process of gene expression is transcription.

In this step, DNA is used as the template for synthesis of RNA (mRNA).

Base pairing between one strand of DNA and RNA bases, following the rules of base complementarity, defines the base sequence of the mRNA.

The enzyme RNA polymerase is required for mRNA synthesis.

In the next step, known as translation, mRNA bases pair with transfer RNA molecules (tRNA).

Each mRNA contains many 3-base units called codons; each tRNA has a unique 3-base unit called an anti-codon.

Each tRNA carries a particular amino acid.

As the tRNAs line up along the mRNA in the order defined by codon/anti-codon recognition, they define the sequence of amino acids in the protein.

The enzyme peptidyl transferase detaches the amino acids from their tRNAs and links them together to form a protein.

The string of amino acids makes up a protein, and proteins give an organism its distinguishing characteristics.

Order! order! A variation on the strip sequence is to provide each student with a copy of a short text with the sentences in scrambled order and have students unscramble them. This lends itself particularly well to processes but is also appropriate for more descriptive texts. Students can work in pairs and then compare their solution with that of another pair. If the teacher prepares two short texts, students can swap and review a text different from their own. The purpose, as with the strip sequence, is to help students discover the patterns of scientific writing and encourage clear, organized, analytical thinking. On the next page is an example:

Order! Order! example - Antibiotic resistance by bacteria (scrambled)

Each time antibiotics are used to treat an infection, most, but not all, bacteria are eradicated. The remaining population of bacteria cannot be controlled by the antibiotic. Once hailed as wonder drugs, antibiotics were expected to eliminate human bacterial infections. Continued elimination of susceptible bacteria and multiplication of resistant bacteria results in a new population with a larger percentage of resistant bacteria than was present in the original population. Antibiotics are a powerful selection pressure for resistant bacterial strains. The remaining bacteria are genetic mutants that are resistant to the antibiotic. Fifty years later this has not happened. Since the 1940s, antibiotics have seen increasingly widespread use to control bacterial disease in humans. These bacteria can pass the trait for antibiotic resistance on to their progeny.

Antibiotic resistance by bacteria (unscrambled)

Since the 1940s, antibiotics have seen increasingly widespread use to control bacterial disease in humans. Once hailed as wonder drugs, antibiotics were expected to eliminate human bacterial infections. Fifty years later this has not happened. Antibiotics are a powerful selection pressure for resistant bacterial strains. Each time antibiotics are used to treat an infection, most, but not all, bacteria are eradicated. The remaining bacteria are genetic mutants that are resistant to the antibiotic. These bacteria can pass the trait for antibiotic resistance on to their progeny. Continued elimination of susceptible bacteria and multiplication of resistant bacteria results in a new population with a larger percentage of resistant bacteria than was present in the original population. The remaining population of bacteria cannot be controlled by the antibiotic.

The missing link: This exercise is designed to help students analyze the underlying relationships between ideas and also master the linguistic forms associated with these basic patterns in scientific inquiry. Students are given a paragraph or two of text (one page maximum) from which all the connecting words and transitions have been deleted. The passage may be an extended elaboration of just one of the five major patterns (page 196) or it may contain more than one. Students must then read and "edit" the text, inserting appropriate connections, i.e., supplying the missing links. This exercise can be given as homework or it can be done in class in small groups. If individual or group answers are compared, students will quickly see that a variety of alternatives exist in English to express the relationships between ideas (e.g., therefore, consequently, as a result) and also to explore subtle differences between them (e.g., however, on the other hand, on the contrary).

Missing link example - Possible connecting phrases to use: however, on the other hand, on the contrary, moreover, furthermore, as a result, therefore

Connecting phrases missing

Why is it that some habitats bustle with a variety of creatures while others are home to only a few species? Habitats that are large enough are likely to be populated by a diversity of organisms. -----, not only the size but also the number of potential ecological niches that are available to a variety of organisms is important in establishing diversity within a habitat.

Lack of accessibility of a habitat, -----, can present challenges for population diversity. The isolation of an island offers protection from outside predators and disease. -----, just as predators may find it difficult to reach an island, so may all new species that could diversify a population. An island may also provide limited food resources. -----, in years of famine or natural disaster, island species that face local extinction are unlikely to be replenished from the outside. -----, isolated habitats such as islands or spring-fed lakes are less likely to be diversely populated than are more accessible habitats.

A greater diversity of organisms is likely to be found in hospitable environments. -----, the cold and dark of the ocean floor provides a hostile habitat that few organisms brave. -----, in the extreme ocean depths that are near steam vents, still dark but no longer cold, an astonishing diversity of organisms thrives.

Connecting phrases added - (In most cases, more than one connecting word will work. Students should choose a connector that makes logical sense in the sentence.)

Why is it that some habitats bustle with a variety of creatures while others are home to only a few species? Habitats that are large enough are likely to be populated by a diversity of organisms. **Moreover**, not only the size but also the number of potential ecological niches that are available to a variety of organisms is important in establishing diversity within a habitat.

Lack of accessibility of a habitat, **on the other hand**, can present challenges for population diversity. The isolation of an island offers protection from outside predators and disease. **However**, just as predators may find it difficult to reach an island, so may all new species that could diversify a population. An island may also provide limited food resources. **Furthermore**, in years of famine or natural disaster, island species that face local extinction are unlikely to be replenished from the outside. **Therefore**, isolated habitats such as islands or spring-fed lakes are less likely to be diversely populated than are more accessible habitats.

A greater diversity of organisms is likely to be found in hospitable environments. **As a result**, the cold and dark of the ocean floor provides a hostile habitat that few organisms brave. **On the other hand**, in the extreme ocean depths that are near steam vents, still dark but no longer cold, an astonishing diversity of organisms thrives.

As with many of the activities we describe, this is not a one-time-only exercise. It should be repeated, especially if the teacher chooses to work on one rhetorical pattern at a time. By focusing on the organizational patterns of scientific discourse,

students can become more familiar and comfortable with both the thinking processes and the style of science. These exercises also provide an opportunity for students to put scientific information together by whatever process makes sense to them, thereby learning in the context of their own cognitive style.

Deductions that add up: Drawing logical conclusions is a dangerous business. We all, at times, jump to conclusions, because we are in a hurry or because we know how we would like things to be. Making logical deductions in science can be particularly tricky for students. They are not experts and do not have an extensive body of information to work from. They may feel pressured in lab, for example, to substantiate their hypotheses or they may be used to having their instructor or text lay it all out for them and not at all used to reaching conclusions by themselves.

A simple way to begin work on drawing inferences is to present students with a piece of information and several alternative inferences that could be drawn from it and have students evaluate each inference for validity. There could be more than one valid conclusion or just one correct one for the students to select. A particularly valuable way to do this exercise is with data from the desk-top experiments, asking students to consider the validity of various conclusions drawn from the data. Use of experimental data has double value because it offers practice in the broader need to draw inferences as well as the more immediate need to write lab reports. (See the examples on the next page.)

Deduction examples

Statement: In the Ames test, no mutant colonies grew around a disk soaked in a bathroom cleaner.

Inferences:

a. The bathroom cleaner is not a mutagen.
b. The cleaner killed all of bacteria around the disk.
c. A non-viable bacterial culture was used for the test.

Statement: A week ago a student's pet microbe was dark pink and shiny. This week it appears to be grayish white and fuzzy.

Inferences:

a. A contaminant has taken over the culture plate.
b. The pet microbe has entered into a new growth phase.
c. The pet has different growth characteristics on different media.
d. The student mixed up the plate with one belonging to another student.
e. The student didn't take good notes and doesn't really remember what the pet looked like a week ago.

Statement: When half a culture plate has been inoculated with a pet microbe suspension and the other half of the plate has been inoculated with a *Penicillium* culture, a clear band with no growth is visible between the two organisms.

Inferences:

a. The pet microbe is secreting a substance that inhibits the growth of *Penicillium*.
b. The *Penicillium* is secreting a substance that inhibits the growth of the pet microbe.
c. An antagonistic relationship exists between the two organisms.
d. The culture medium contained an inhibitory substance that was confined to the area of the band.

Jigsaw: First developed in 1978 by E. Aronson and his colleagues, Jigsaw is one of the most widely used and, we feel, most clever and adaptable techniques of cooperative learning. Cooperative learning teaches students to rely on themselves and their peers in the learning process, and Jigsaw activities send that message most clearly. Students can teach themselves almost any body of information using the Jigsaw method.

Students work in home groups of three or four. The home group is responsible for teaching itself a body of information. Each member of the group is assigned a piece of the information to be learned, contained in a paragraph, chart, table, or page of text. When all of the pieces are assembled, they will form the whole body of information. The class, when assigned to home groups, looks like this:

All of the A people are assigned the same piece of information, all of the B people have another piece of the puzzle, and C people have their respective pieces. Now, the A people get together and form an "expert group." In the expert group, students discuss their information, decide what is most important, and how to best explain/teach it to their home group. When they have finished consulting with their expert group, they return to their original Jigsaw home group and take turns teaching their material to that group. After all the pieces have been assembled, the students demonstrate their success by answering a question or questions, in class or at home, on the material.

What does the teacher do all the while? As in other activities we have described, the teacher's role during the Jigsaw activity is to move from group to group, observing, clarifying, explaining, or facilitating when necessary. S/he should note how well the information is being communicated; what, if anything, has been slighted (and needs to be presented later); and what the group dynamics are (what kinds of roles students are taking, which groupings work well together and should be reused, and which should not).

Teachers clearly have a more direct and interactive relationship with students during Jigsaw than during a lecture presentation of material. An example of a Jigsaw exercise is presented below. For a more detailed description of Jigsaw and the role of the teacher in it, see Elizabeth Coelho's chapter in Carolyn Kessler's resource book (1992).

Jigsaw example - (This is a short version of the sort of information students might learn by this method. You could also give your students more lengthy and detailed information and ask them to select and emphasize the most important information to teach to their home group. In a modification of the jigsaw method, you could give your students an outline of the information they will need to learn in their expert group along with source books to fill in missing information from the outline. The students will work with the other members of their expert groups to find and learn the information they will ultimately teach to the members of their home group.)

Challenge: Tell the story of late blight. When your group reassembles, construct the story of late blight, including the history of the disease, the biology of the pathogen, and the current outlook for control.

***Phytophthora*, potato late blight pathogen**

Expert group A - General information: *Phytophthora* is a member of a group of organisms called water molds, which are lower eukaryotes. *Phytophthora* can reproduce both sexually and asexually. It grows best in cool, damp conditions and is responsible for causing a number of stem and root rots, including late blight of potatoes. Over a period of several years in the 1840s, potato late blight swept Ireland and caused the Irish Potato Famine. Infected potatoes rotted in the fields before they could be picked. Estimates of the number of people who starved during the famine vary from 750,000 to over one million. Thousands of others left Ireland in search of better lives in other countries including the United States.

Expert group B - Reproductive biology in *Phytophthora*: In spring, when the soil is wet and temperatures are favorable, the *Phytophthora* mycelium begins to grow. The mycelium is the mat-like structure of the fungus, consisting of strands called hyphae. The mycelium grows over soil or plants, digesting food and absorbing nutrients.

When the mycelium finds abundant food and good growing conditions, its hyphal tips swell, and the tips grow into new structures called zoosporangia. Tiny, motile zoospores form within the zoosporangia. When conditions are right, the zoospores are released. They swim through water in the soil, and if they come in contact with susceptible roots, the zoospores may encyst and infect the roots. Each zoospore germinates and grows into new mycelium. Both mycelia and zoospores are produced in abundance during wet, cool weather, and more plants become diseased than when the weather is warm and dry.

Sexual reproduction occurs during adverse conditions when the weather is very dry, hot, or cold. During sexual reproduction, male and female nuclei fuse and an oospore develops. The oospore germinates forming a zoosporangium that produces infective zoospores. The zoospores are released, and they begin to swim through water in the soil. If they come into contact with susceptible roots, the zoospores may encyst and infect the roots. Each zoospore germinates and grows into new mycelium. Oospores and mycelia can overwinter in infected roots. Oospores also survive the winter in soil.

Expert group C - *Phytophthora* control: Control of potato late blight in agriculture is usually accomplished through a number of preventive measures. When growing plants susceptible to the fungus, the surest way to prevent disease is to choose plants from uninfected stock and plant in soil that is free of the pathogen. Infection can be reduced by growing plants in light, rapidly draining soils. In the greenhouse, soil and pots should be steam sterilized, and fungicides can be applied as seed and soil treatments, at transplanting, and in sprays in irrigation water. Some disease control has been achieved by planting seedlings in soils containing microorganisms that are antagonistic to the fungus.

In spite of all attempts to eradicate potato late blight, highly virulent strains of the pathogen are currently gaining a foothold in North America. Researchers fear that in cool, moist years that provide ideal growing conditions for the pathogen, late blight could devastate the potato crop.

Information gap: Information gap is another useful cooperative technique to help students become more self-reliant in their learning. Students work on a problem-solving activity in groups of two or three, with each student having part of the key to the problem's solution. It is only by pooling their resources that the students can succeed in solving the problem.

Take, for example, a problem in diagnosis and treatment of a crop disease. One student has either a sick corn plant or a description of the symptoms of a sick plant. The next student has a table of all the diseases corn is susceptible to and the symptoms of each. A third student has a list of diseases and their treatments. This group of students can propose a strategy for treating the disease if they work together and share their "expertise."

An information gap activity can also be built around protein synthesis problems. One student may have information about a codon string but does not have a codon chart. A classmate can fill in the gap and by working together they can transform that string.

Information gap activities lend themselves to problem-solving situations. Students should be encouraged to talk to each other, to truly collaborate, and not just swap papers. As they discuss and share information in this structured setting, students review and reinforce their own knowledge. They also gain confidence in their ability to find solutions and to present scientific material clearly.

Taking notes: A skill universally recognized as critical to success in college is the ability to take good notes. Most study skills texts include general tips and practice for taking notes on lecture and reading material. (Consult the list of references on page 217 for citations that describe note-taking techniques). The Cornell Note-Taking System, which involves recording lecture notes, key words and phrases, and a page summary in three separate areas of each notebook page (Pauk, 1989), is one system students find especially helpful when they study for exams. The students can cover up all parts of the page but the key word area and see if they can remember the important points in their notes just from looking at the key words.

Taking notes for science classes can be a particularly intimidating prospect for students because of the detail and precision required, the subtlety of the concepts, and the extensive terminology. Since so much published material is readily available on note-taking, we will present only the three keys to successful note-taking in science lectures that we have found most useful to our students. These are: (1) knowing what to write, (2) shortening sentences, and (3) reformatting.

Knowing what to write: How do you teach someone what to write and what not to write? The first reaction of anyone who has been a good student is, "Well, you just know what's important and what's not." But how do you know? Knowing what to write can become almost automatic from years of practice doing it and from thinking clearly and rationally about what the key points are and how much supporting detail is worth scribbling down. All of our exercises and activities in the rhetorical patterns and logical thinking of science contribute to the student's ability to understand the connections between ideas and to distinguish key concepts from details. Moreover, students can be given focused practice in note taking. The teacher can deliver small chunks of lecture material and students can take notes. The class can then discuss which points were worth writing down and which were not. The simulated lecture material should include the commonly used transitions and conventions of good lecturing (for example, first of all, now this is important, moving on to the next point, or let me say that again) and students should learn to pay attention to and take advantage of those useful road signs to help them make their way through lecture.

Shortening sentences: Students can practice shortening sentences and using symbols and abbreviations in simulated note-taking. The instructor can deliver short pieces or sentences of lecture material and give students a few seconds to write them down, either on paper or on the board. The group can then consider whether the notes are intelligible and/or whether they can be further streamlined. Here is another time when paraphrasing is important. Students may be able to express a long, complicated thought more simply and quickly in their own words, rather than trying to copy the professor word for word. As part of this process, the group can identify those words and expressions that are most likely to recur and generate a list with a clear, simple symbol or abbreviation for each. Alternatively, students can be provided with such a list, though they need to be reminded that they will have to make their own lists for their other classes.

Examples of symbols for note-taking short cuts

Word	Abbreviation	Symbol
increased/rose	incr	↑
decreased/fell	decr	↓
led to/caused		→
greater, larger		>
less, fewer		<
genus	g.	
species	sp.	

Reformatting: In the course of a semester, students will see many different types of material, each of which may be most effectively presented, formatted, or organized in a different way. Students should be encouraged to reformat important material appropriately. For instance, lecture notes on modern methods of plant disease control lend themselves to an outline format:

I. Cultural methods
  A. tillage methods
  B. weed control
  C. spacing
  D. other

II. Regulatory methods
  A. quarantine
    1. advantages
      a.
      b.
    2. disadvantages
      a.
      b.
  B. elimination
  C. other

Lecture notes on key characteristics of bacteria, viruses, and fungi are well-suited to summary on a table:

	fungus	bacterium	virus
structure			
cell wall			
nucleus			
reproduction			
size			
other			

Because of the diversity in students' thinking styles, one student may be able to propose a reformatting style that other students or the instructor might not have considered. For example, after studying the geographic spread of diseases in tropical crops, one of the students in our learning skills section suggested a full-page map of the world with different patterns of dotted lines representing the spread of various diseases, such as rust in coffee, witches' broom in cacao, and leaf blight in rubber. The class as a whole then embellished her idea by suggesting a set of symbols (a coffee cup, a candy bar, or a car tire) to add to each of the dotted lines. We produced just such a world map, and one student's inspiration became a clear and valuable visual study aid for the entire class.

Concept mapping: Another technique that is becoming increasingly popular is concept mapping. Concept maps are graphic representations of the relationships between concepts, somewhat like a hierarchical flow chart. Concept maps can be drawn by students in cooperative groups following these steps: (1) identifying the key words, phrases, and notions of the concepts to be mapped; (2) enclosing those key pieces in circles or boxes; (3) connecting the ideas with lines or arrows and any brief linking words necessary to make the relationship between the parts clear; (4) providing an example, if appropriate. (See page 213 for an illustration of what a concept map of evolutionary theory might look like.)

One way to begin training in concept mapping is to give students pieces of a potential map and have them conceptualize the relationships between ideas and lay the pieces out. This can be done in the following simple way:

- (before class) Take index cards and write a key concept or point on each card.

- (in class) Tape a large sheet of clean paper to the students' work space.

- Shuffle the cards.

- Deal out or hand out the whole pack of cards to small groups of students.

- Tell the students to start sorting and arranging the cards on the large sheet of paper and to start drawing lines, arrows, or any other marks they like to show the connection between them. As they work, point out that they should feel free to make changes and move the cards around.

- Compare the maps that different groups produce, with one member of each group explaining what they have done. Make clear, as appropriate, that different maps may be equally valid.

One bonus of this activity is that it gets students on their feet, actively involved, huddled around the table, using their hands and heads to talk about ideas. The students will need to practice this activity several times, but the time invested is well worthwhile. With guidance and practice, they will learn to generate useful concept maps on their own. (See Taylor, 1993, for more information about using concept maps in biology.)

Since they were first developed in 1972 at Cornell University, concept maps have been proven by many researchers to "improve problem solving skills, . . . reduce anxiety level, . . . and promote meaningful learning of science concepts" (Okebukola, 1992). Moreover, Okebukola's study showed that students who mapped cooperatively achieved higher test scores than those who mapped individually, and members of both of those groups scored higher than students with no mapping experience. For students who are confused or students who have only a vague grasp of an important concept and how its parts fit together, developing a concept map in class can be very helpful. These students may come into class feeling "lost," produce a map through cooperative effort, and leave class with a navigational tool, feeling they are "on the right road" once again.

Outlines, tables or charts, and concept maps are three ways we have discussed to reformat material. Different students may have different preferences or they may have other creative ways to reformat. What is important is that students have the opportunity to try out different formats and that they learn to choose the format that suits both the material and their own learning style.

Concept mapping:

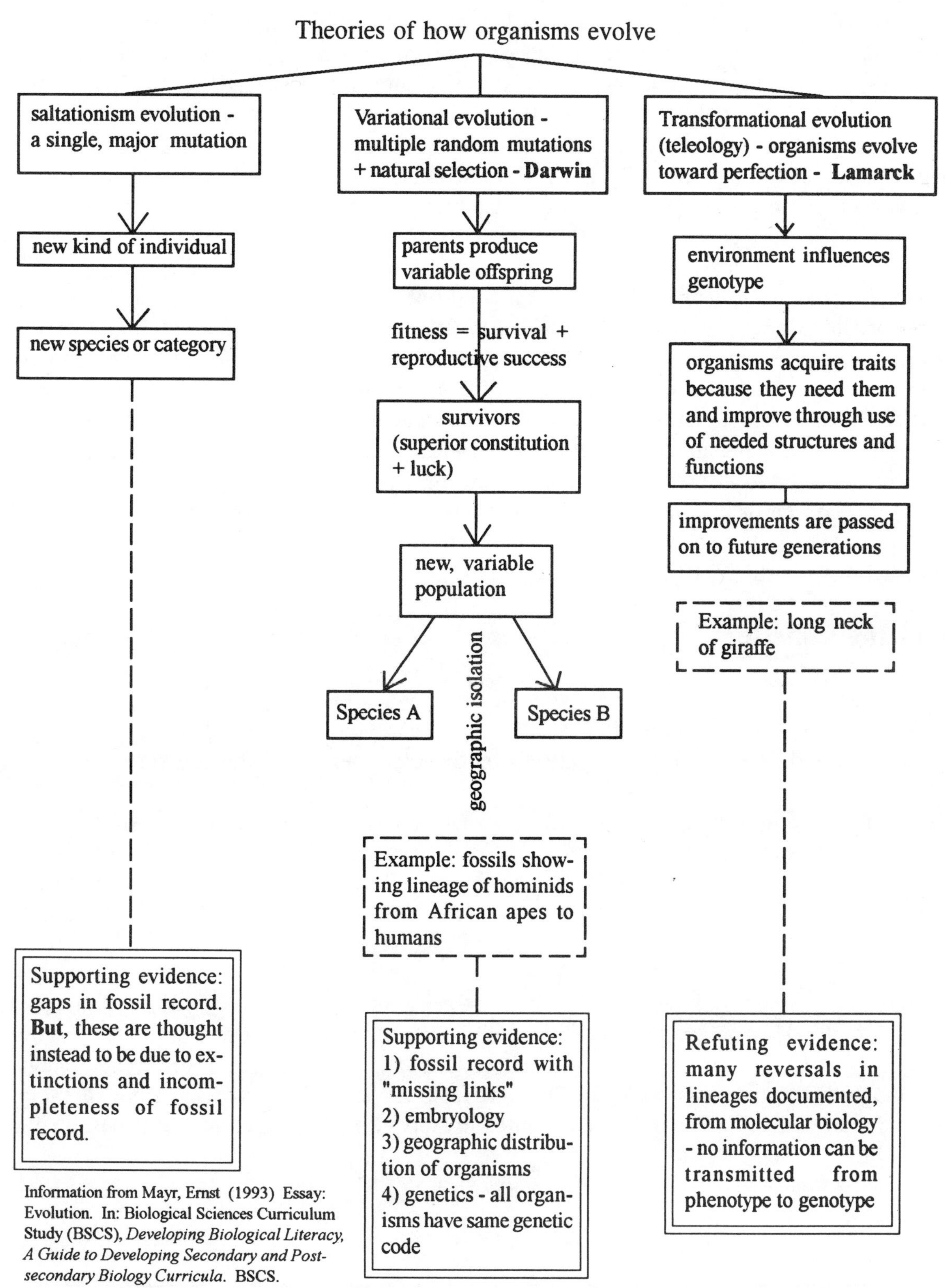

Information from Mayr, Ernst (1993) Essay: Evolution. In: Biological Sciences Curriculum Study (BSCS), *Developing Biological Literacy, A Guide to Developing Secondary and Post-secondary Biology Curricula.* BSCS.

Writing a lab report

Lab reports are an essential part of enhancing logical, analytical, and critical thinking skills. The process of describing an experimental design, recording data, separating observations from conclusions, and evaluating hypotheses in light of results requires students to sharpen their thinking processes. We suggest having students write many short lab reports, rather than a few long ones. Repetition of the process will help students recognize the similarities and differences among experiments. Emphasizing brevity will encourage the students to focus sharply on the key ideas rather than filling pages with vague language.

Because the lab report is a major vehicle for communicating the findings of experiments, it is important for students to learn how to write a good one. A good lab report should be concise and well-organized and contain all essential information about the experiment. Many students are able to write brief reports. However, the reports are often poorly organized and incomplete. As an aid, we present our students with an outline to follow for creating a comprehensive lab report in a standard format. In addition, we give the students a handout, "How to Write a Better Lab Report," that explains in detail what is needed in each section of the report. We have found these handouts to be most useful if we give them to the students **after** they have tried writing a few lab reports on their own. Then the concepts involved are no longer abstract and have direct application to the students' own lab report writing. (For a copy of the lab report format and instructions for students, see Appendix IV, page 236).

End of the semester

"Eek! The semester is almost over! How can I help my students prepare well for the final and leave the class with something they'll remember?" Here are two answers: 1) Make sure they're studying right, and 2) guide them in synthesizing the key concepts of the course.

Studying smart: Students often do not have a realistic picture of the effectiveness of their study habits. Good students as well as less successful ones may feel they possess appropriate strategies to prepare for exams, or at least strategies they think work well for them. Or perhaps they have the vague feeling their study habits are not what they should be, but they do not know exactly how or what to change. Once again, a little introspection may be helpful.

Have your students take an honest look at the nitty-gritty of how they study. What do they eat before an exam? How much sleep do they get? How many hours at a time do they study? Which questions do they answer first? The advantages and disadvantages of different strategies can be compared by students working in small groups or by a whole-class discussion. A sample questionnaire to help focus discussion is included in Appendix VII, page 246. It is designed to produce some surprises and food for thought. Also in Appendix VII is a set of follow-up questions and insightful comments for the instructor to use. Time spent helping students prepare for exams in your course is a good investment in helping them succeed in all their academic course work.

Putting it all together: The prospect of reviewing a whole semester's worth of material may be daunting to professor and student alike. And no one wants to simply rehash the same old stuff. An interesting alternative for review may be a thematic rather than a chronological approach.

Identify themes that run through the fabric of the course. Such themes may have been explicitly discussed in a section of course content or when dealing with specific topics. They may have also been present, though not explicitly pointed out, in others. Assign a theme or key concept to each student or to a pair of students, who can then search their notes, readings, and memory for all its appearances. If time allows, students can present their findings to the group and pool their knowledge.

Themes may be major concepts of biology as a whole (for example, natural selection, evolution, or the relationship between science and society) or concepts more specific to an individual course (such as genetic vulnerability or genetic engineering in a course in issues in agriculture).

One advantage of this scavenger hunt approach is that it gives students a focus to their review. Instead of simply re-reading their notes passively, students have something important to look for and a sense of Eureka! when they find their pet theme in an unexpected spot.

Meet the real world: Is it not our true goal, after all, to prepare students to deal in an effective and intelligent way with their world, whether their role is to be a researcher in a laboratory or a citizen of planet Earth? To accomplish this, the end of the semester should provide some activities that connect students' new knowledge of biology with unsolved research problems or practical problems faced by society. Students can be asked to identify biological problems that demand attention from the research community. They can propose research strategies or technological solutions to address real world problems. Alternatively, they can apply their new knowledge to evaluation of issues in science and technology.

Local newspapers are a rich source of material for end-of-semester projects. They often run articles that illustrate key concepts covered in biology courses, such as bovine growth hormone, molecular forensics, or the process of FDA approval of new drugs. These can provide the springboard for discussion and the focus for applying critical thinking and biological principles. For example, when a poorly informed citizen writes something outrageously unscientific to the editor, students can be asked to criticize. When a controversy is under way, students can be asked to analyze and weigh. When a public-policy decision is made that affects us all, students can be asked to judge. An up-to-date collection of such newspaper clippings provides a valuable tool for promoting reflection and review. And if the students' criticism, analysis, and judgment are well-reasoned and based on the best information available, we know they are ready to take what they have learned into the world as scientifically literate citizens.

Conclusion: In this manual we have avoided providing a comprehensive course in study skills teaching. That has already been done quite thoroughly elsewhere. We have focused on techniques that are particularly useful for or unique to biology. For those who want more information about the basics of teaching study skills, though, we refer you to the many books that have been written on the subject. The education section of your library or your college bookstore are also good places to find more information on specific study skills techniques.

References - teaching learning skills

◆ Biological Sciences Curriculum Study (BSCS) (1993) *Developing Biological Literacy: A Guide to Developing Secondary and Post-secondary Biology Curricula.* BSCS.

◆ Brinton, Donna, Marguerite Ann Snow, and Marjorie Bingham Esche (1989) *Content-Based Second Language Instruction.* New York, NY: Newbury House.

◆ Coman, Marcia and Kathy Heavers (1993) *What You Need to Know About Developing Study Skills, Taking Notes and Tests, Using Dictionaries and Libraries.* Lincolnwood, IL: National Textbook Company.

◆ Galica, Gregory S. (1991) *The Blue Book: A student's guide to essay exams.* San Diego, CA: Harcourt Brace Jovanovich.

◆ Kean, Elizabeth and Catherine Middlecamp (1986) *The Success Manual for General Chemistry.* New York, NY: Random House.

◆ Kessler, Carolyn (1992) *Cooperative Language Learning: A teacher's resource book.* Englewood Cliffs, NJ: Prentice Hall.

◆ Pauk, Walter (1989) *How to Study in College.* Boston, MA: Houghton Mifflin.

◆ Roberts, James (1989) *Bud's Easy Note Taking Kit.* Lawrence, NY: Lawrence House.

◆ Taylor, Martha (1993) *An Introduction to Concept Mapping for Campbell's Biology, Third Edition.* New York: The Benjamin Cummings Publishing Company, Inc.

References - learning and cognitive styles

◆ Brown, Anthony D. (1980) Cherokee culture and school achievement. *American Indian Culture and Research Journal*, 4: 55–74.

◆ Chinien, Chris A. and France Boutin (1992/93) Cognitive style FD/I: An important learner characteristic for educational technologists. *Journal of Educational Technology Systems*, 21: 303–311.

◆ Delpit, Lisa (1988) The silenced dialogue: Power and pedagogy in educating other people's children. *Harvard Educational Review*, 280–298.

♦ Delpit, Lisa (1992) Education in a multicultural society: Our future's greatest challenge. *Journal of Negro Education*, 61: 237-249.

♦ Horowitz, Rosalind (1985) Text patterns: Part I. *Journal of Reading*, 28: 448–454.

♦ Okebukola, Peter Akinsola (1992) Concept mapping with a cooperative learning flavor. *The American Biology Teacher*, 54: 218–221.

♦ Waters, Mary and Alan Waters (1992) Study skills and study competence: Getting the priorities right. *English Language Teachers' Journal*, 4613: 264-273.

Appendix I: Organisms used in desk-top experiments

Experiment	Microorganism	Plant/Animal
#1 Pet microbes	Fungal cultures *Botrytis cinerea* *Fusarium graminearum* *Rhizoctonia* spp. *Saccharomyces cerevisiae* *Trichothecium roseum* Bacterial cultures *Bacillus thuringiensis* *Erwinia carotovora* *Pseudomonas aureofaciens* *Rhizobium tropici* *Xanthomonas campestris*	Plants and animals used in other experiments.
#2 Ice	*Pseudomonas syringae*	Bean leaves (any frost-sensitive plant)
#3 Bread mold	*Penicillium notatum*	Bread
#4 Stimuli	---	Nematodes or soybean loopers
#5 Koch's version 1	*Xanthomonas campestris* pv. *campestris*	Wisconsin Fast Plants
Koch's version 2	*Erwinia carotovora*	Potato (tuber)
Koch's version 3	*Botrytis cinerea*	Onion (bulb)
Koch's version 4	*Rhizoctonia solani*	Pea seedlings
#6 DNA	*Agrobacterium tumefaciens*	Sunflower seedlings
#7 Chemicals	*Escherichia coli*	---
#8 Vulnerability	*Colletotrichum trifolii*	Alfalfa plants
#9 Diversity	---	---
#10 Mutual/Antag	*Rhizobium tropici* *Bacillus thuringiensis* *Bacillus cereus* & *Pythium torulosum*	Bean plants Soybean plants & soybean loopers Alfalfa seedlings
#11 Field biology	---	---

Appendix II: Instructions from the student manual

Pure cultures from single colonies

A common method for establishing the purity of bacterial cultures is to isolate **single colonies**. A colony that is physically isolated or separate from other growth is usually derived from a single bacterial cell. This was first observed by Robert Koch, who noticed that when he left a cut potato open to the air, isolated colonies would develop on it. He found that each contained a pure culture. Koch figured out that each colony was initiated by a single cell that landed on the potato. This led to the development of solid culture media placed in petri dishes, which is now the most common method for culturing bacteria.

One way to isolate single colonies is the **three-way streak method**. The principle underlying this method is that when the bacteria are sufficiently diluted, individual cells will be deposited on the surface of the agar. After the single cells divide, a colony will be visible. A colony contains a **pure culture** because it is derived from a single cell.

The three-way streak method involves the following steps:

1. Gently spread the material to be streaked over about 20% of the agar surface of a petri plate with a glass rod, a toothpick, or a microfuge tube. This will be referred to as Area #1.

2. Drag a sterile toothpick across the end of the spread area. Spread this material across a clean area of the plate, which will be Area #2. Do not reenter Area #1.

3. Drag a fresh sterile toothpick across the end of Area #2. Spread the material over a new region of the agar. This will be Area #3.

4. Incubate the plate 1–3 days at room temperature. Examine it for single colonies.

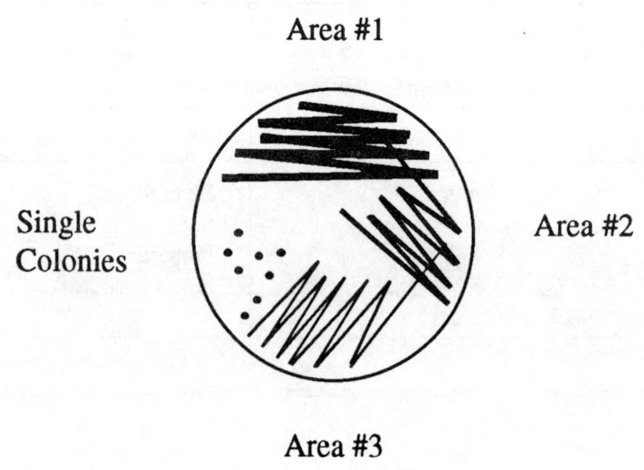

Growth of a bacterial colony

When a bacterial cell is deposited on a solid surface and provided with nutrients, it can form a colony. A colony is a group of cells that are derived from a single cell, and thus, cells in a colony are usually genetically identical to each other and to the original cell that gave rise to the colony. Many bacteria grow very rapidly so that a single cell on a rich nutrient medium can form a colony visible to the human eye in a few hours or days. For example, the common gut bacterium, *Escherichia coli,* can divide every 20 minutes when it is grown under optimal conditions. A single cell of *E. coli* will divide forming two cells, the two cells divide forming four cells, the four cells divide forming eight cells, and on and on until they run out of nutrients. In just 10 hours, or 30 generations, one cell can grow to be one billion cells!

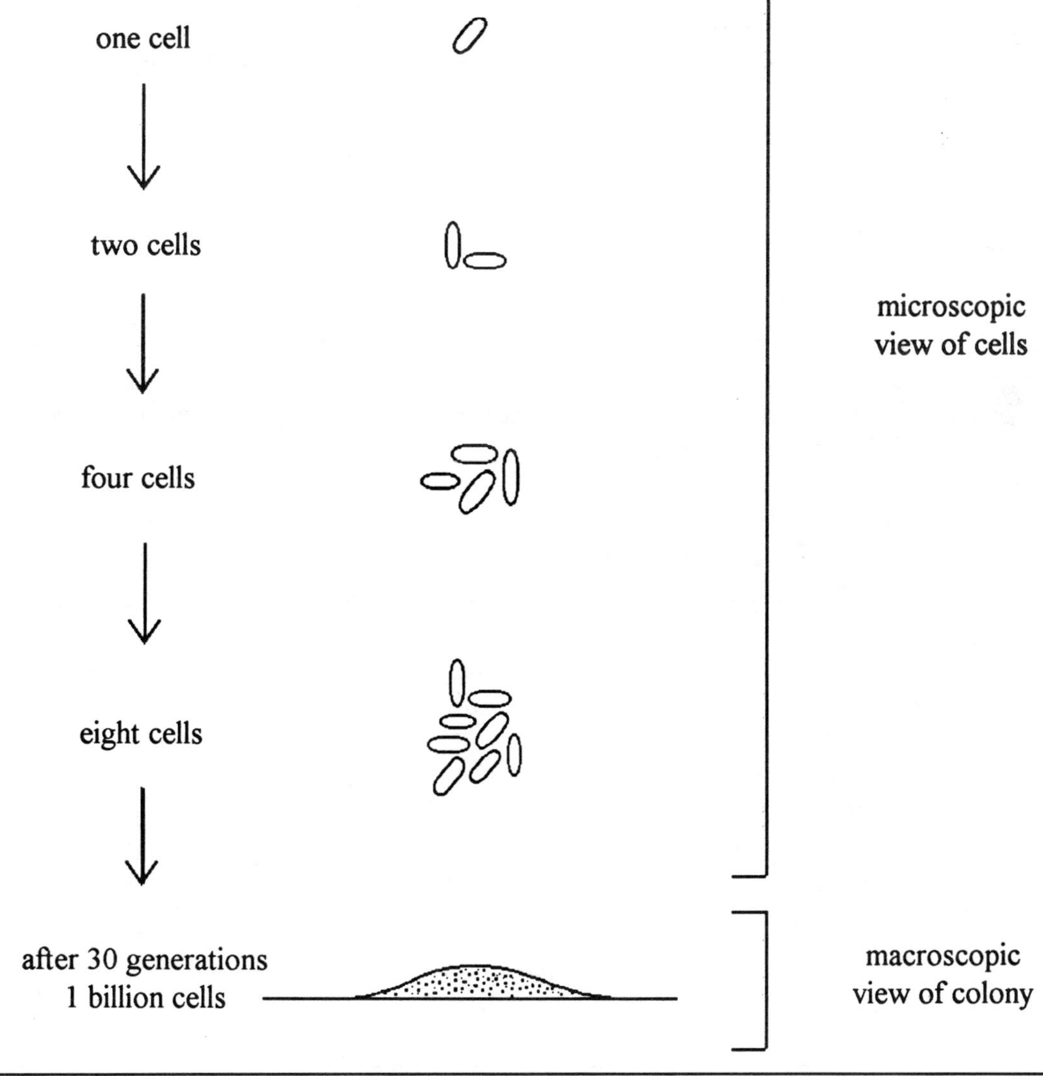

Methods for testing microorganisms

Characterizing a microorganism often involves testing it for its ability to influence the growth or development of a plant, animal, or another microorganism. The following are a few tips and standard techniques for such testing. Feel free to adapt them, change them, or make up your own.

Inoculating plants with microorganisms

Decide what part of the plant you want to inoculate. If you think that the organism you are testing might infect leaves, then you might apply it to the leaves. If you suspect that your microorganism infects roots, then you might apply it to the roots.

Next, you will need to decide on the method of application. Many pathogens of plants, particularly bacteria, require a wound to infect the plant. Therefore, you may want to wound your plant gently to enhance infection. You can introduce the microorganism by scooping a colony off an agar plate with a toothpick and stabbing the toothpick into the plant tissue. You can also scrape the microorganism off the agar, suspend it in water, and apply the mixture by dipping, spraying, or drenching the plant. For organisms that infect roots, drenching the soil with the microorganism works well.

Finally, you need to decide how to incubate your plant after inoculation. Since microorganisms require water for growth, and the surfaces of plant tissue often dry out rapidly, you might consider placing your plant in a moist environment. A plastic bag provides a simple, moist chamber that can be used for most plant material.

Inoculating animals with microorganisms

In these experiments, we will use only lower animals, such as insects and nematodes. Therefore, we will not discuss methods for inoculating higher animals with microorganisms. Experimentation with mammals is subject to federal regulations and should only be conducted in a laboratory that is licensed for that purpose, by trained personnel.

The simplest method of inoculation of insects and lower animals is to mix the microorganisms with their food. Some insects will grow well on agar and the solid media that are used for the culture of microorganisms, so you may want to spread bacterial or fungi on an agar plate and then add the insects. Be sure to put parafilm around the plate so the insects do not escape.

Testing microorganisms against microorganisms

Many microorganisms produce substances that either enhance or inhibit growth of other microorganisms. The most common example of this is the production of antibiotics. If you place an antibiotic-producing microorganism on an agar plate near a microorganism that is sensitive to the antibiotic produced, then the sensitive organism will not grow in the area nearest to the producing organism. This is because the antibiotic diffuses through the agar, and it will be at its highest concentration at the source. The concentration will become progressively lower at points on the plate further from the source.

A simple method to test for growth inhibition or enhancement is to streak two organisms near each other and perpendicular to each other on an agar plate. With this method, you can test a number of organisms on a single plate. Streak the organism you want to test for production of an inhibitor or enhancer in one direction (we will call this the test organism), and streak the strains to be tested for their sensitivity to the inhibitor or enhancer perpendicular to the first streak (we will call these organisms the target organisms). If the test organism produces a substance that inhibits growth of a target organism, then the target organism will not grow in the part of the streak closest to the test organism. If the test organism produces a substance that enhances the growth of the target organism, then the target organisms will grow more vigorously near the test organism.

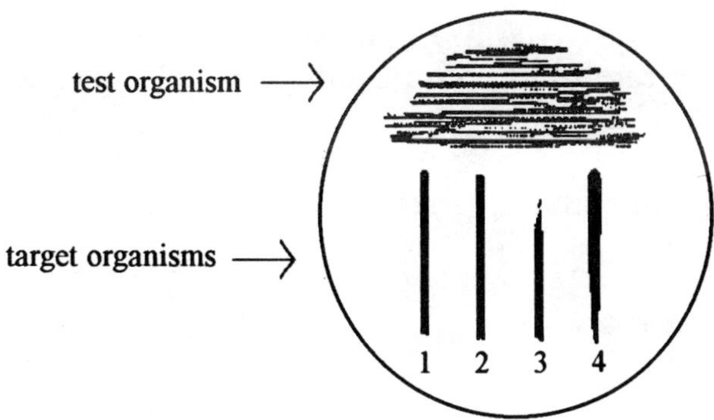

The growth of target organisms 1 and 2 appears unaffected by the test organism.

Growth of target organism 3 appears to be inhibited by the test organism.

Growth of target organism 4 appears to be enhanced by the test organism.

Safety tips for students

The experiments you do in this course are intended to be fun and safe. You will not work with any toxic chemicals or organisms that are pathogenic to humans, but there are a few precautions you should follow.

1. Do not eat or drink in the room where you conduct experiments. This is just good practice when you are working with substances or organisms that you are better off not ingesting.

2. Wash your hands when you leave the lab. The microorganisms you will work with are not pathogenic to people, but it is still a good idea not to eat them. You will work with soil and soil contains many human pathogens, so it is best to treat the microbes with respect and take some basic precautions.

3. Some people have allergies to mold spores. If you find you have allergic reactions to molds or any of the materials you work with, let your instructor know.

4. Although none of the organisms you will use are pathogenic to healthy people with normal immune responses, many microorganisms can cause health problems if they are inhaled or ingested by people who are immunosuppressed. If you know that you have a weakened immune system, please let your instructor know and be careful not to inhale or ingest the microbes.

5. You may occasionally work with flames to sterilize equipment or boil water in the lab. Use appropriate care around flames and be careful to keep flammable liquids, such as alcohol, far from the flame.

6. When you are finished working with cultures, please put them in the place designated by your instructor so they can be sterilized.

After the lab

Since scientific research is usually a cooperative effort involving many types of collaboration and cooperation, scientists must learn to work together. An important part of working in a group of scientists is being respectful of other people's time and space. In many laboratories, scientists share space, equipment, and supplies. It is therefore essential for all members of a group to learn basic rules of cleanliness and consideration in the laboratory for the scientific group to be successful. One simple way that each member of the group can show consideration for others is to clean up the lab after use.

Please adhere to the following simple rules in the laboratory:

1. Place your experimental materials in the place marked for your use and label all materials with your name, group, and lab section.

2. Make sure petri plates are properly stored so that they do not dry out; put Parafilm around your experimental plates and be sure that unused plates are in sealed bags.

3. Place all reusable materials that need washing in the designated place, and discard used disposable materials. Place glass in the container designated for glass and other sharp objects.

4. Return pieces of equipment or borrowed items to their original places.

5. When you are finished with biological materials (plants, microbes, or animals), place them in the appropriate container for sterilization and disposal.

6. Wipe your work space with a damp cloth and make sure you leave it as you found it.

7. Ask your instructor whether there is anything else you can do to help clean up your lab.

Experimental notes

Title of experiment

Observations

Hypothesis

Experiment

Controls

Treatments

Techniques needed to conduct experiment

Data collected/observations made

Conclusions/interpretations

Appendix III: Instructions for lab preparations

Media types

Medium	Effect
King's B	detection of fluorescent microbes
Luria-Delbruck Broth (LB)	favors *Escherichia coli*
Nutrient Agar (NA)	favors bacteria
NA + cycloheximide (cyc)	inhibits fungi
NA + streptomycin (strep)	inhibits bacteria
Potato Dextrose Agar (PDA)	favors fungi
PDA + cycloheximide (cyc)	inhibits fungi
PDA + streptomycin (strep)	inhibits bacteria
Pectinase Detection Agar (Pectin)	detects microbes that produce pectinase
Rose Bengal (has chloramphenicol - RNA synthesis inhibitor)	inhibits bacteria, some fungi
Tetrazolium Chloride (TCZ)	diagnostic - bacteria range from pink to red
Triple Sugar Iron Agar (TSIA)	diagnostic/pH; *Pseudomonas aureofaciens* develops a metallic sheen
Tryptic Soy Agar (TSA)	broad spectrum medium for bacteria
V-8	favors fungi and oomycetes; some bacteria will grow
Water Agar (WA)	good for antagonism experiments
Weak PDA	favors fungi, minimizes contamination

Recipes for culture media and antibiotics

Culture media

1. King's B (used to detect fluorescent *Pseudomonas*)

15 gm	Bacto agar
10 ml	glycerol
1.5 gm	$MgSO_4.7H_2O$
1.5 gm	K_2HPO_4
20 gm	protease peptone #3

Make up to 1000 ml with distilled water; adjust pH to 7.2.

2. LB (Luria-Delbruck) broth (for *E. coli*)

1 l	distilled water
10 g	tryptone
5 g	yeast extract
5 g	NaCl

Adjust the pH to 7.5 using NaOH. Autoclave at 121°C for 30 min.

3. Nutrient agar (NA)

1000 ml	distilled water
18 gm	Bacto agar
3 gm	beef extract
10 gm	peptone

4. Nutrient agar with glycerol (NAG) (used to grow *Pseudomonas syringae* on slants)

80 gm	nutrient broth
20 gm	agar
20 ml	glycerol
1000 ml	distilled water

5. Nutrient broth (NB)

Prepare nutrient agar as above, but omit agar.

6. **Pectinase detection agar** (Some pathogens produce pectinase, an enzyme that breaks down pectin, a long-chain polysaccharide found in plant cell walls.)

6.0 gm	Na_2HPO_4
3.0 gm	KH_2PO_4
0.5 gm	NaCl
1.0 gm	NH_4Cl
5 ml	glycerol
1.0 gm	yeast extract
5.0 gm	sodium polypectate (Sunkist)
900 ml	distilled water

Adjust pH to 7.5 for pectate lyase assay

Add:

15 gm	Bacto agar

Autoclave at 121°C for 20 minutes.

Then add:

1 ml	1 M $MgSO_4$	
0.2 ml	1 M $CaCl_2$	Add slowly to 100 ml sterile water, then add to rest of media.

Grow microbes in agar tubes as stab (works best using 24- to 72-hour cultures). One week later, overlay with saturated copper acetate solution (filtered) for 15 minutes. Pour off solution. If pectinase is present, a halo will be visible around the bacterial growth where pectin has been broken down.

7. **Potato dextrose agar (PDA)**

PDA	Weak PDA	
250 gm	40 gm	potatoes (peeled and sliced)
15 gm	15 gm	Bacto agar
20 gm	7.5 gm	dextrose
1000 ml	1000 ml	distilled water

1. Cook potatoes in half of the water for 1 hour.
2. Melt agar in the other half of the water.
3. Strain potato liquid through 2 layers of cheesecloth.
4. Add dextrose and dispense.
5. Autoclave at 121°C for 30 minutes.

8. **Rose Bengal agar** (inhibits growth of bacteria and some fungi; used for fungal selection; keep in dark, pH 7—will produce material toxic to all fungi when exposed to light)

15 gm	Bacto agar
10 gm	glucose
0.5 gm	$MgSO_4.7H_2O$
5 gm	papaic digest of soybean meal
1 gm	KH_4PO_4
0.05 gm	Rose Bengal
10 ml	chloramphenicol solution (1%)
1000 ml	distilled water

Add all ingredients but chloramphenicol to 990 ml water. Mix thoroughly. Heat to boiling. Autoclave at 121°C for 15 minutes at 15 psi. Cool to 45°C. Aseptically add chloramphenicol solution. Pour into plates or tubes.

9. **TES 8**

50 mM	glucose
25 Mm	Tris· Cl (pH 8)
10 mM	EDTA (pH 8)

10. **Tetrazolium chloride (TZC)** (some bacterial strains will grow red colonies; some will grow pink colonies with white edges)

5 gm	glucose
10 gm	peptone
1 gm	casamino acids
18 gm	Bacto agar
1 gm	yeast extract (supplement)
1000 ml	distilled water

Autoclave at 121°C for 30 minutes. Add 2 ml sterile filtered TZC plus solution—1% 2,3,5-triphenyltetrazolium chloride—1 gm/100 ml. Wrap in foil and store in refrigerator.

11. **Triple sugar iron agar (TSIA)**

500 ml	distilled water	2.5 gm	NaCl
6.5 gm	agar	10 gm	peptone
1.5 gm	beef extract	0.012 gm	phenol red
0.1 gm	ferrous sulfate	0.15 gm	sodium thiosulfate
0.5 gm	glucose	5.0 gm	sucrose
5.0 gm	lactose	10 gm	yeast extract

Combine all ingredients. Adjust pH to 7.3. Autoclave at 121°C for 20 minutes.

12. Tryptic soy agar (TSA) (broad spectrum medium for bacteria)

3 gm	tryptic soy broth
18 gm	Bacto agar
1000 ml	distilled water

1. Adjust pH to 7.2 after dissolving powder.
2. Autoclave 20 minutes at 121°C.

13. V-8 agar (favors fungi and some bacteria)

20 gm	Bacto agar
3 gm	Calcium carbonate ($CaCO_3$)
200 ml	V-8 juice
800 ml	distilled water

1. Add V-8 to warm water.
2. Mix $CaCO_3$ and agar together and add.
3. Melt and autoclave.

14. Water agar (WA)

1000 ml	distilled water
12 gm	regular agar **or**
20 gm	Bacto agar

Antibiotic solutions

1. Chloramphenicol solution (1%)

0.1 gm/10 ml
Filter sterilize.

2. Cycloheximide (inhibits growth of eukaryotes)

Stock: 12.5 mg/ml
Add 4 ml to 1 liter of medium for a final concentration of 50 μg/ml.

3. Streptomycin (inhibits prokaryotes and some eukaryotes)

Streptomycin stock: 30 mg/ml
Add 1 ml to 1 liter of media for final concentration of 30 μg/ml.

Methods

Freezing bacterial cultures

Materials: dimethyl sulfoxide (DMSO)
1.5 ml microfuge tubes (sterile)

Grow bacteria in NB cultures overnight to get a good, rich suspension. Add DMSO to culture to a final concentration of 15% DMSO. Quickly mix and pour into labeled microfuge tubes. Freeze immediately by placing the tubes in an ice/ethanol bath. Store in ultracold (-80°C). If DMSO is unavailable, 80% sterile glycerol may be substituted. Use equal volumes of glycerol and bacterial suspension. Freeze quickly and store at -80°C.

Inoculating healthy plants with isolated bacteria or fungi

1. Perform a three-way streak to isolate single colonies of bacteria or fungi (see page 220).

2. Use a sterile toothpick to collect a mass of bacterial cells from a single colony or fungal hyphae from a pure culture growing on the isolation plate.

3. Puncture or rub a healthy plant with the bacteria or fungal material on the toothpick.

4. Store the inoculated plant under conditions conducive to disease, which usually mean optimum growth conditions and high humidity.

5. The length of time for symptoms to develop and appearance of the plant will vary according to the plant type and organism inoculated as follows:

Plant	Pathogen	Days post inoculation	Symptoms
alfalfa	*Colletotrichum trifolii*	10	leaves spotted, plants wilted, withered
cabbage	*Xanthomonas campestris*	4-7	necrotic lesions with yellow margins
onions	*Botrytis cinerea*	7-10	brown, mushy onions covered with white to gray, fuzzy fungal growth
peas	*Rhizoctonia solani*	~7	brown, mushy roots
potatoes	*Erwinia carotovora*	1-3	creamy, tan, slimy rot

Isolating bacteria and fungi from diseased plants replace with PageMaker mortar.pm5

One lab period before microbial colonies are needed -

1. Use a sterile razor blade or scissors to cut a disk of plant tissue approximately 0.5 cm in diameter from a given area on the plant.

Grind the plant tissue in 0.5 ml of sterile water in the sterile micro mortar and pestle (see below).

Carefully remove the pestle from the mortar so that a drop of the plant and water suspension clings to the outside of the pestle. Using sterile technique, place the drop on a petri plate that contains an appropriate culture medium. Complete a three-way streak using sterile toothpicks.

2. Pieces of plant tissue may also be placed directly onto plates of culture medium.

3. Seal plates with Parafilm (page 250), invert, and incubate at room temperature until the next lab period.

4. **Note:** Examine all plates after 3 to 4 days for the presence of especially fast growing fungi. If plates appear to be in danger of being overwhelmed by fungal growth, transfer the plates to a 5°C refrigerator until they are to be used in the next lab.

Micro mortars pestles

1. Cut the lid and rim portion off of a sterile 0.5-ml microcentrifuge tube (page 250) and insert a sharpened pencil into the tube to form the pestle.

2. Fit the tube with the pencil into a 1.5-ml microcentrifuge tube (the mortar) that contains a small amount of liquid and the material to be ground.

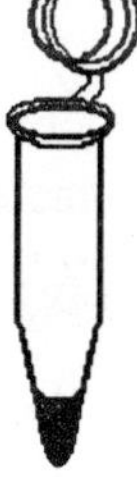

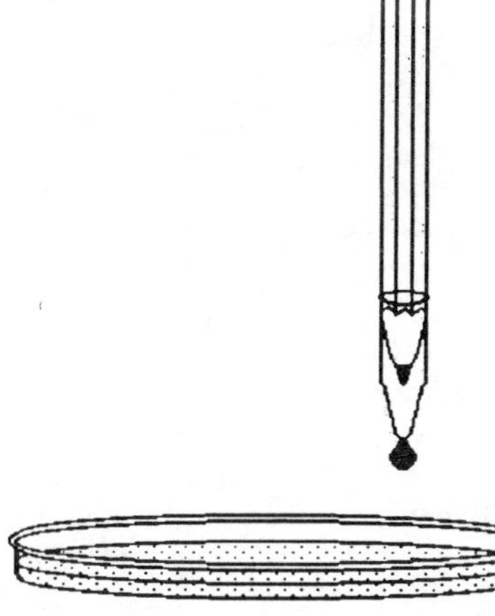

3. After grinding, carefully remove the pestle from the mortar so that a drop of the ground suspension clings to the outside of the pestle. Using sterile technique, place the drop on a culture plate. Complete a three-way streak with sterile toothpicks.

Plant nutrient solution (PNS)

Chemical	Solution amount			
	1 L	4 L	8 L	16 L
distilled H_2O	1 L	4 L	8 L	16 L
K_2SO_4	0.077 g	0.307 g	0.613 g	1.22 g
K_2HPO_4	0.023 g	0.092 g	0.184 g	0.368 g
KH_2PO_4	0.137 g	0.547 g	1.093 g	2.187 g
$CaSO_4$ ($\cdot 2H_2O$)	0. 343 (0.438) g	1.373 (1.753) g	2.747 (2.506) g	5.493 (0.701) g
$MgSO_4$	0.247 g	0.987 g	1.973 g	3.947 g
NaFeEDTA	0.040 g	0.160 g	0.320 g	0.640 g
micro-nutrient solution	1 ml	4 ml	8 ml	16 ml

Micronutrient solution:

1 L	distilled water
0.15 g	$CuSO_4 \cdot 5H_2O$
0.44 g	$ZnSO_4 \cdot 7H_2O$
0.40 g	$MnSO_4 \cdot 7H_2O$
0.02 g	$(NH_4)_6Mo_7O_2 \cdot 4H_2O$
1.43 g	H_3BO_3

Steam sterilization

Autoclave Sterilize media and other liquids for 20 minutes at 18 pounds of pressure. When sterilization is complete, let the autoclave cool before exhausting to avoid having the liquids bubble out of their flasks. For non-liquids use the same time and pressure but exhaust the autoclave as soon as sterilization is complete to avoid condensation wetting the materials you are sterilizing.

Pressure cooker A pressure cooker provides an excellent alternative for sterilizing materials, if you do not have access to an autoclave. You will need the kind that comes with a rack. Place the rack in the bottom of the cooker. Add enough water so that the bottom of the pan is covered but the surface of the rack is out of the water. Place the materials to be sterilized on the rack. Following the instructions for your pressure cooker, sterilize at 15 pounds of pressure—instruments, heat resistant plastics, and utensils for 15 minutes; liquids for 30 minutes. When sterilization is complete, remove the pan from the heat and allow the pressure cooker to cool gradually to room temperature before opening.

Surface disinfestation of seeds and fruits

1. Make a 10% solution of chlorine bleach.

2. Soak seeds or fruit for about 2 minutes, making sure all surfaces are in contact with the solution.

3. Rinse 3 times in sterile water. Be sure the seeds or fruits are well rinsed. Otherwise, remaining bleach may inhibit seed germination or microorganisms.

4. Place seeds on moistened, clean filter paper in petri dishes and incubate 2 to 3 days at 28°C for germination.

Appendix IV: Lab reports - Format

Name ______________________

All write-ups must be typed and must not exceed one page. Include the following:

Title—brief, clear, descriptive

Hypothesis—state it clearly and concisely

Treatments and Controls—list your treatments and controls; explain why you chose to include each control

Results—state briefly what you observed; provide a table or graph with data if you made measurements

Conclusion—explain why your results support or refute your hypothesis

Key question—answer one of the key questions included in the lab manual

How to write a better lab report

Note to teachers: We have not included this in the student manual, since you may not want your students to have it until after they have conducted the bread mold experiment.

Title

1. Make it brief—short enough to be **centered** on one line. If you really feel the need to make it longer, try a few words of the most important information followed by a colon and a subtitle with details or explanation.

   Examples: Mold and the Disease Triangle
   Bread Mold: The Effects of Environment

2. Be sure it relates clearly to the main point or process of the lab.

3. Use humor sparingly. Try a funny, cute, or catchy title once you know the instructor will appreciate it.

4. Use a title given in the manual or a slight variation on it, if all else fails.

Hypothesis

1. Try to get all the important information into your hypothesis in as few words as possible.

2. Remember that a hypothesis should be stated as a "truism" or statement of how things generally work rather than a "prediction" of how things will come out in your experiment or of what you think is going to happen. It is very tempting to write a hypothesis in the future tense ("Bread will get moldy if. . .") but it is more meaningful and true to the scientific method if it is written in the present tense ("A warm environment favors the growth of mold. . .") .

3. Be patient with yourself. Formulating hypotheses can be complex and difficult, but you will get better at it with practice.

Treatments and controls

1. Include *all* your treatments and controls. Make sure you show clearly which are the treatments and which are the controls.

2. Consider using a list or table to do this.

Example 1:

Experimental condition:

treatment	bread type	incubation condition
1 slice spore-sprayed	sourdough	37°C

Spore-sprayed bread has been sprayed 6 times with a spore suspension of *Penicillium notatum.*

Controls:

treatment	bread type	growth condition	isolates effects of . . .
1 slice spore-sprayed	sourdough	4°C	temperature
1 slice spore-sprayed	sourdough	24°C	temperature
1 slice water-sprayed	sourdough	37°C	spore inoculum
1 slice water-sprayed	sourdough	4°C	spore inoculum
1 slice water-sprayed	sourdough	24°C	spore inoculum

Water-sprayed bread was sprayed 6 times with pure water. All 6 slices were stored in closed plastic bags.

Example 2:

	incubation condition			
bread type	warm	cool	room temp	treatment/control
spore-sprayed sourdough	X			experimental condition
spore-sprayed sourdough		X	X	control - effect of temperature
water-sprayed sourdough	X	X	X	control - effect of spore inoculum

Spore-sprayed sourdough was . . . .
Water-sprayed sourdough was . . . .
All 6 slices were stored. . . .

Results

1. State just what the result were, what you observed. **Describe** them: "a blue-green fuzzy growth" not just "a mold." A simple and clear way to include all results is to plug them into the table or list you generated for your treatments and controls. Make sure to separate your observations from your interpretation of the observations. This will enable others who read your report to form their own conclusions based on your data. Save the interpretation of what the results mean for the next section, "Conclusion."

   Example:
   Results: I see a blue fuzz vs. Conclusion: I believe it to be *Penicillium.*

It may seem to you that this is too obvious, too easy, but simple description is all that is required here and is really the most difficult and important part of science. Making good observations and recording them accurately is the crux of good experimental biology.

2. Quantify your results, if possible. Use a standard scale or count, or devise a simple numerical scale of your own.

   Example:
   fraction of bread covered with mold: 0 = no mold, 1 = ¼-covered, 2 = ½-covered, etc.

Conclusions

1. Explain why your results *support* or *refute* your hypothesis. Use expressions like, "The results support/refute the hypothesis" or "This evidence is/is not consistent with the hypothesis." **DO NOT** say, "This proves our hypothesis," because it is possible to disprove a hypothesis but not to prove it.

2. Relate your conclusion directly to your hypothesis. If your hypothesis has more than one part, make sure your conclusion deals with each part.

3. Propose an explanation or multiple explanations of why your data do not support the hypothesis, if, in fact, they do not. You are not a failure and you do not need to cover it up or hide it when your data and hypothesis do not match up. Some of the greatest discoveries in science have been made when the initial hypothesis was shown to be wrong! Honesty is another essential part of good science.

4. Suggest a follow-up experiment or question to answer based on what your treatments and controls have revealed. Remember that science is a *process* of inquiry, so it is good if your experiment leads to another experiment.

Key question

1. Identify which question you are answering. Give both the number and a brief restatement of the question.

2. Be concise. Have you noticed how often the instructions tell you to be "concise," "clear," and "brief?" Science writing places high value on brevity and clarity. This is one way scientists let the data speak for themselves.

Appendix V: Ethical contract for students participating in a cooperative classroom

Learning in a cooperative environment should be stimulating, demanding, and fair. Because this approach to learning is different from the competitive classroom structure that many other courses are based on, it is important for us to be clear about mutual expectations. Below is the code of conduct that is expected of students in this class. This code is intended to maximize debate and exchange of ideas in an atmosphere of mutual respect while preserving individual ownership of ideas and written words. If you feel you do not understand or cannot agree to these expectations, you should discuss this with your instructor and classmates.

1. I will work cooperatively with other members of the class, showing respect for the ideas and contributions of other people.

2. When I work as part of a group I will strive to be a good contributor to the group, I will listen to others in the group and try not to dominate, and I will recognize the contributions of others. I realize that everyone contributes in different ways to a group process.

3. I will conduct experiments, discuss group exams, and develop projects as part of a group, but when I write a lab report, exam, or paper, I will write it by myself and not copy from anyone else. I will also not copy from published sources without appropriate attribution.

Signed,

Appendix VI: Learning skills survey

The purpose of this questionnaire is to help you think about your study habits. Please answer each question truthfully. Give your own honest opinion and not what you think someone else (like the teacher) might want to hear.

Please circle your answer in terms of the percentage of time you do whatever is asked. For example, if you always do it, circle 100% of the time. If you do it most of the time, circle 75% of the time. If you do it half the time, circle 50% of the time. If you do it sometimes, circle 25%. If you never do it, circle 0% of the time.

MOTIVATION

1. Do you like to study?

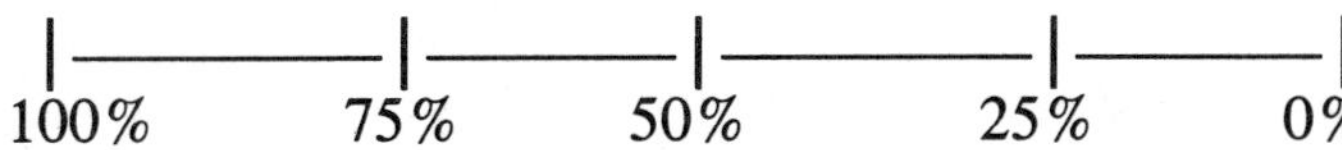

2. Is it important to you to do well in school?

100% 75% 50% 25% 0%

3. Do you try to **understand** the material for your courses or just memorize it?

100% 75% 50% 25% 0%

PLANNING/ORGANIZATION

4. Do you make a list of priorities, of the things you have to do (study, go to the store, etc.)?

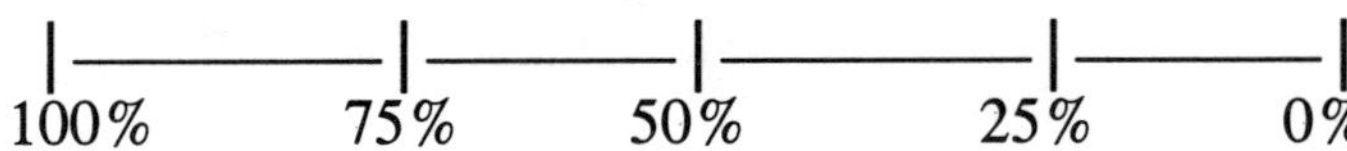

5. Do you use free time you have between classes to study?

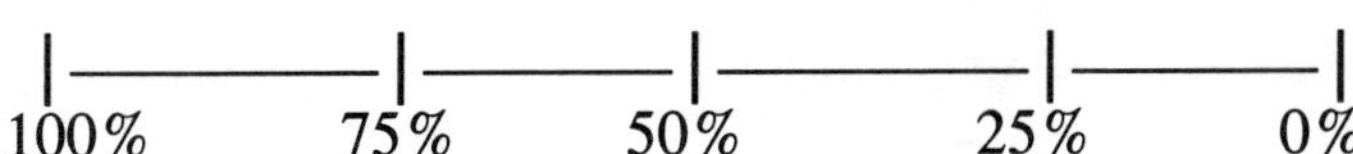

6. Do you study at least 2 hours for each hour of class during a week (e.g., for 15 credits, do you study 30 hours a week)?

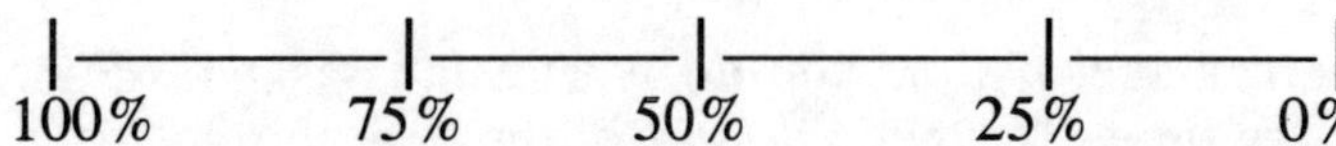

7. Do you periodically review the material for each class you're taking?

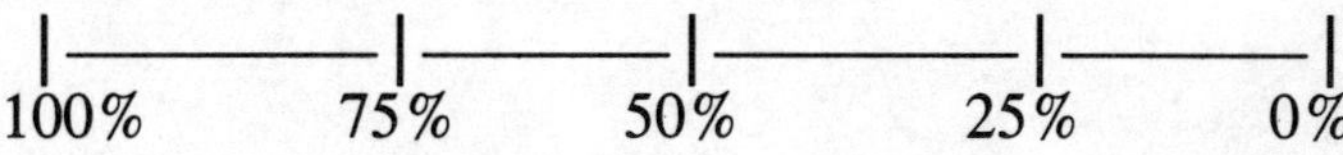

8. How often do you study just because the next exam is coming?

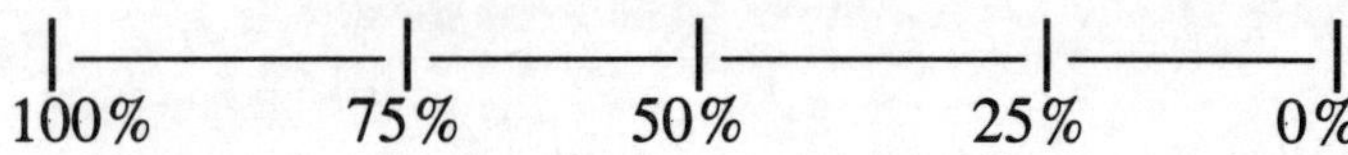

9. Do you keep up with your study assignments (get them done when you're supposed to)?

|————|————|————|————|
100% 75% 50% 25% 0%

CONCENTRATION

10. How often do you feel that your study time has not been very productive and that you haven't accomplished much?

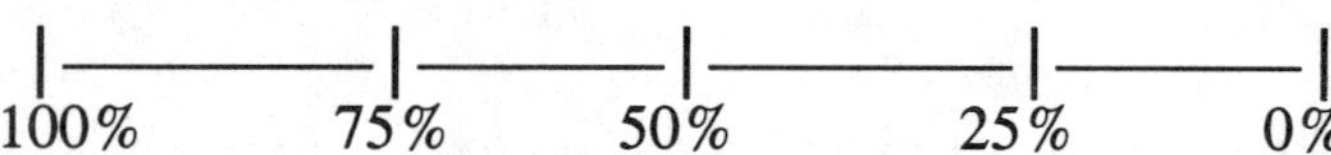

11. How often do you have problems sitting down to study?

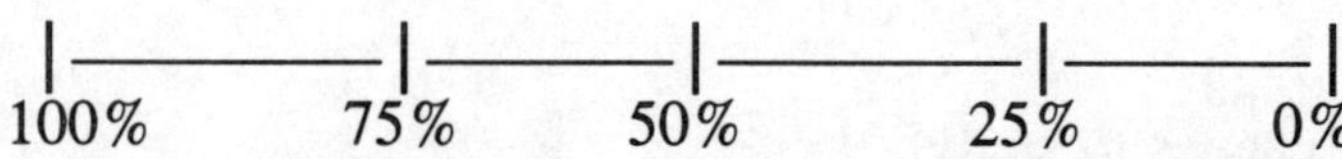

12. When you study, how often do you daydream or waste time?

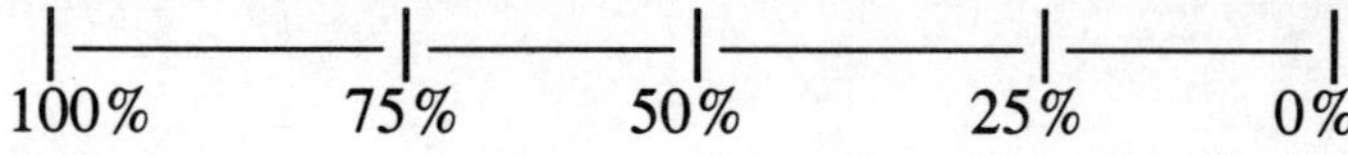

READING

13. Before using a textbook, do you preview it?

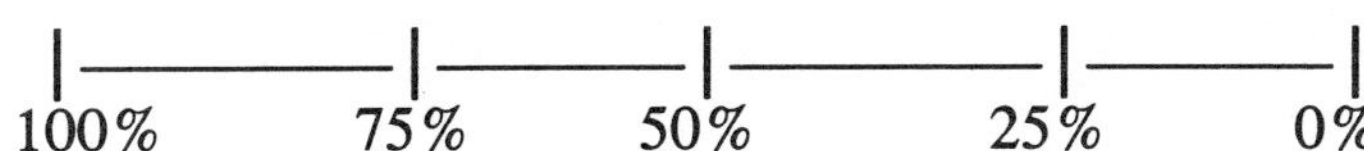

14. Before reading a chapter, do you look over the topic headings, illustrations, and chapter summaries?

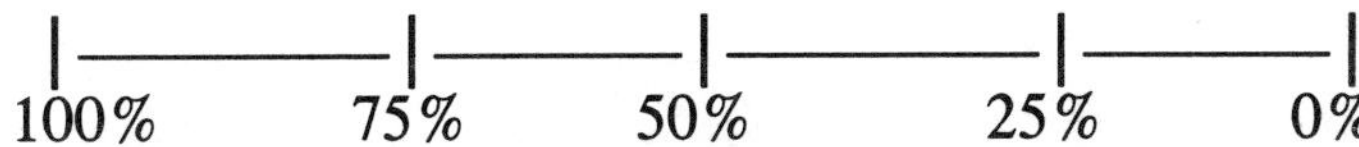

15. Do you try to find the main ideas in what you read?

|————|————|————|————|
100% 75% 50% 25% 0%

16. Do you underline and/or make notes in your textbook?

|————|————|————|————|
100% 75% 50% 25% 0%

17. Are you selective in underlining important points?

|————|————|————|————|
100% 75% 50% 25% 0%

18. Do you think about what you read after you finish the assignment?

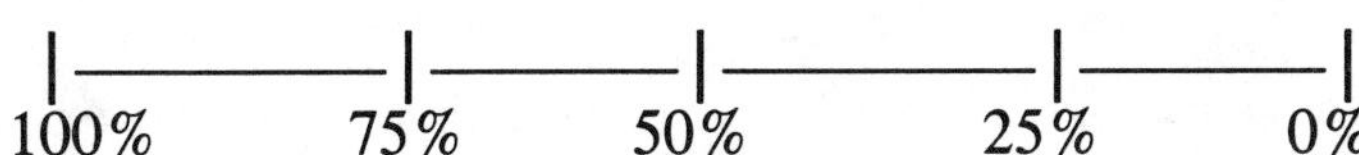

NOTE-TAKING

19. When you take lecture notes, do you try to identify the main ideas?

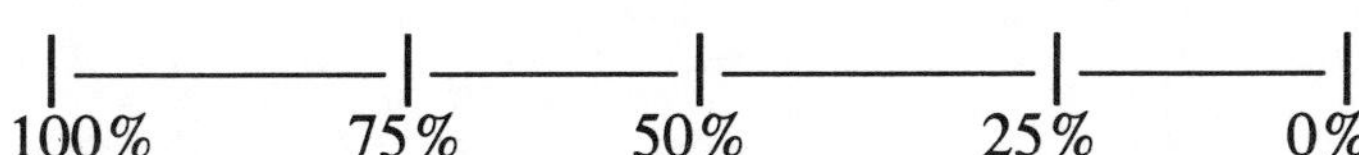

20. Do you review your notes soon after you take them?

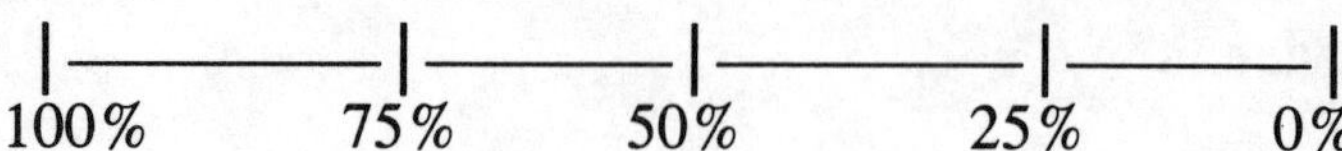

21. Before you go to class, do you review your notes from the last class?

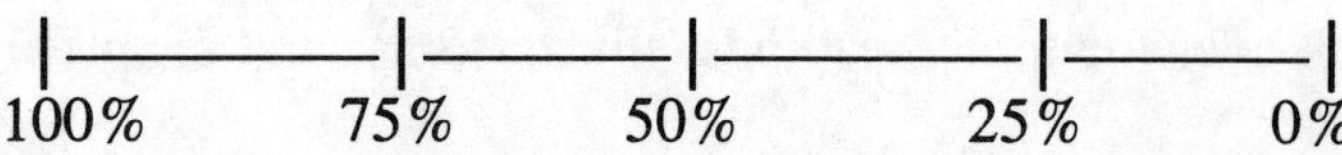

22. How often do you miss writing down something important because you were still busy writing down the last thing?

|———|———|———|———|
100% 75% 50% 25% 0%

EXAMS

23. On the day of an exam, how often are you tired because you stayed up too late studying the night before?

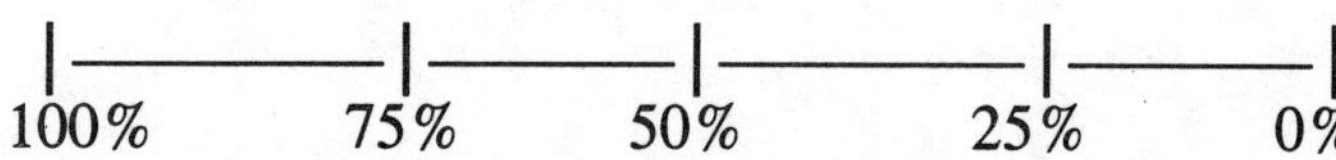

24. Do you condense the important information from your textbook and lecture notes into summary sheets when you study for an exam?

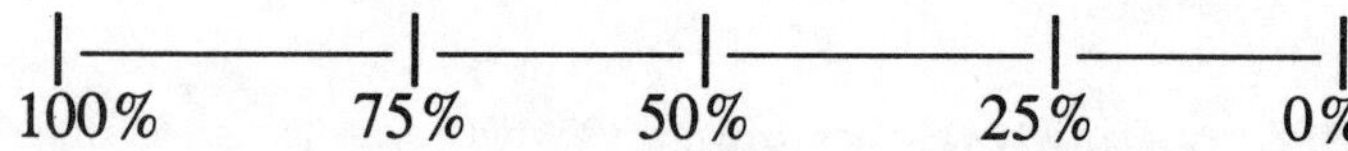

25. When you prepare for an exam, do you predict possible questions and try to answer them?

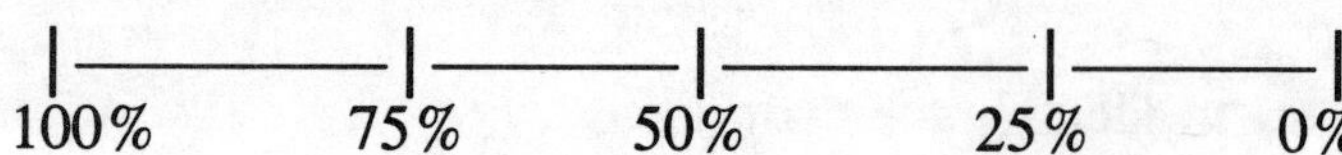

26. When you take an exam, do you read the directions and questions carefully?

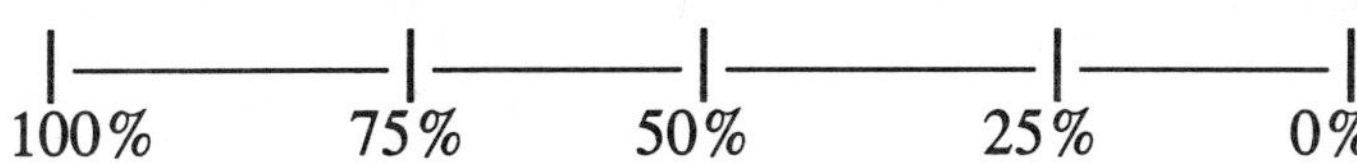

27. When you take an exam, do you tend to make careless mistakes that lower your grade?

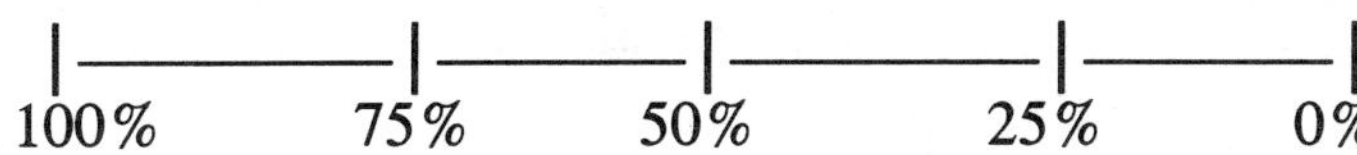

28. On an essay exam, do you make an outline of what you are going to say before you begin writing your answer?

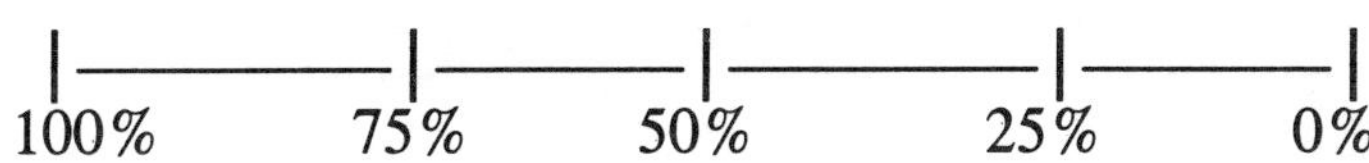

29. When you take an exam, do you consciously divide up your time among the questions?

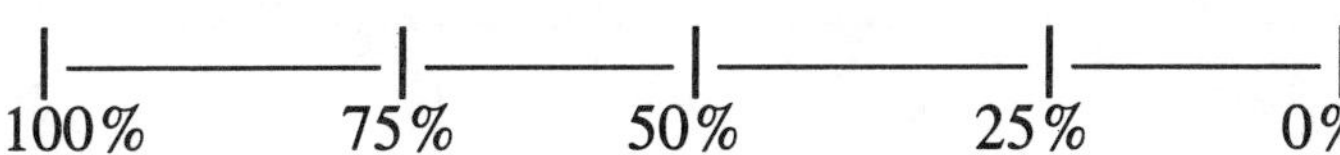

LIBRARY USE

30. Do you know how to use the library for research purposes?

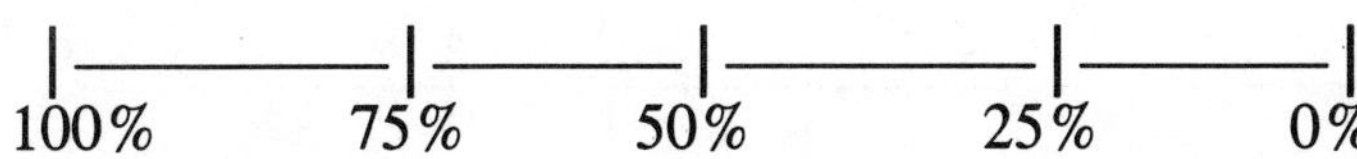

Review your answers to these survey questions. What three changes in your study habits do you think would have the greatest effect on your performance and learning?

1.

2.

3.

Appendix VII: Exam preparation

Analyze how you study for exams and what you do when you take them. Answer the questions below. Discuss them in your group and think about how you might improve upon your present strategies.

	Yes	No	Change?
1. Do you study with friends?			
2. Do you do most of your studying on the night before the exam?			
3. Do you study for more than 2 hours before allowing yourself a break?			
4. Do you re-read all the material in the textbook?			
5. Do you re-read your class notes?			
6. Do you make summary sheets or study sheets?			
7. Have you written out answers to questions asked in class?			
8. Do you often find yourself looking around the room or distracted when studying for an exam?			
9. Do you go to an exam on less than 6 hours of sleep?			
10. Do you go to an exam with just coffee in your stomach?			
11. Do you sometimes go to an exam thinking that you're going to fail?			

12.	Have you ever had the experience of making a mistake on an exam because you didn't read the directions carefully?			
13.	Do you look over the whole exam before you start?			
14.	Do you read each of the exam questions once carefully before you begin to write?			
15.	Do you start writing your answer immediately after reading the question?			
16.	Do you answer the easy questions first?			
17.	Do you use the key words and terms from the lectures and readings in your answers?			
18.	If you are running out of time and the exam is almost over, do you write furiously until the bell rings?			

COMMENTS ON "STUDYING SMART" (keyed by question number)

#1. A 1991 study conducted at Harvard University shows students who study with other students do better on exams than those who study alone.

#2. Spread your studying out over 2 to 3 nights. Try alternative systems: Go over all the reading, then all your class notes, or use an integrated plan going over reading and notes, topic by topic.

#3. Research shows the optimum length of a block of study time is 1½ to 2 hours followed by a short break. Don't expect your brain to do the impossible and don't feel guilty about refreshing it!

#4. What about highlighting and marginal notes?

#5. Are you familiar with the Cornell system for taking notes? (See Pauk, 1989, page 217.)
Do you try to anticipate what is coming next in your notes as a way of seeing if you really know the material?

#6. Do you make summary sheets as you go through the semester or leave them all until the last minute?

#7. Or at least some notes!

#8. For people who can never seem to concentrate, who go to the library intending to study but wind up looking around at the other students: Work on extending your ability to concentrate. Go to the library. Sit down and start to study. FORCE YOURSELF to concentrate for 5 minutes. Do not allow yourself to look up before 5 minutes has passed (or 2 minutes if that is a challenge for you). Keep doing 5 minute stints until you are really concentrating for those 5 minutes (not just looking at the clock and counting) and gradually extend your time frame.

#9. Most American adults require more sleep than they get. Most people think more clearly when they are well-rested.

#10. Studies show that eating breakfast improves academic performance.

#11. Have you ever heard of a "self-fulfilling prophecy?" How can you combat it?

#12. Here is an all-too-common story: A student walks out of lecture hall at the end of an essay exam feeling pretty good about what he wrote. He overhears the two students in front of him discussing the exam: "Which one did you do—the one on evolution or the one on genetic vulnerability?" "Aargh!" thinks our now unhappy student. "There was a choice and I did them both!"

#13. Is this a waste of time? Not! Look over the whole exam to get an idea of how to budget your time. If you do, you'll be less likely to wind up with a #18.

#14. How about **twice**? You definitely don't want to answer the wrong question.

#15. Reflect! Outline!

#16. What are the advantages of this system?

a) It is more efficient—you don't waste time trying to figure out what to write for the things you're not sure about—do that at the end.

b) You ensure getting points for what you know well.

c) You control your nerves and build your confidence as you go.

#17. It shows you understand the materials if you can use the terminology correctly.

#18. Does anyone have a better idea? Like maybe:

a) Save a few minutes to re-read your answers and fix any silly mistakes.

b) Outline or make brief notes on what your answer would be. You may be given partial credit for your sketch of the answer.

Appendix VIII: Commercial sources of supplies

Culture media, chemicals, and antibiotics

$CaCO_3$

Chloramphenicol [DIFCO - sold as Rose Bengal antimicrobial supplement C; SIGMA]

Cycloheximide [SIGMA]

Bacto agar [DIFCO]

Beef extract [DIFCO]

Dextrose [DIFCO]

100% ethanol (not denatured)

King's B agar [DIFCO - sold as *Pseudomonas* agar F]

ICR-191 acridine mutagen [SIGMA]

Nutrient agar (NA) [DIFCO, VWR, WARD'S]

Nutrient agar + streptomycin

Nutrient broth (NB) [DIFCO, VWR, WARD'S]

Peptone [DIFCO]

Potato dextrose agar (PDA) [DIFCO, VWR, WARD'S]

Potato dextrose agar + streptomycin (PDA+strep)

Proteinase K [SIGMA]

Rose Bengal agar base [DIFCO]

SDS [SIGMA]

Streptomycin [SIGMA]

Tetrazolium chloride agar (TZC)

Triple sugar iron agar (TSIA) [DIFCO]

Tryptic soy agar (TSA) [DIFCO, VWR, WARD'S]

Tryptic soy broth [DIFCO, WARD'S]

V-8 agar [DIFCO sells tomato juice agar]

Yeast extract [DIFCO]

General supplies

Unless otherwise specified, most are available from general scientific suppliers, such as Fischer or VWR.

Cotton swabs (sterile)

125-ml Erlenmeyer flasks

Filter paper disks - 0.5 cm diameter, 9-cm diameter

Filters - 10 μm diameter

Glass spreaders

Microcentrifuge tubes 0.5 and 1.5 ml

Parafilm M

Petri plates

Pipette tips (5 ml)

Seed-pack Growth Pouch [VAUGHAN'S]

Vermiculite [GARDEN SUPPLY STORE]

Insects

Cabbage loopers - *Trichoplusia ni*
Soybean loopers - *Pseudoplusia includens* (Lepidoptera: Noctuidae)
Tobacco hornworm larvae - *Manduca sexta* [CAROLINA]

Microbes

- Many microorganisms can be obtained from any state's land-grant university through plant pathology or microbiology departments. Also check the Carolina Biological Supply catalog for organisms that have been added since this printing.

Bacteria

Agrobacterium tumefaciens [WARD'S]
Bacillus cereus UW85 [ATCC]
Bacillus thuringiensis [CAROLINA, WARD'S]
Erwinia carotovora [CAROLINA, WARD'S]
Escherichia coli [CAROLINA, WARD'S]
Pseudomonas aureofaciens
Pseudomonas syringae
Rhizobium tropici
Xanthomonas campestris

Fungi and oomycetes

Botrytis cinerea
Colletotrichum trifolii
Fusarium graminearum
Penicillium notatum [CAROLINA, WARD'S]
Pythium torulosum
Rhizoctonia solani [CAROLINA]
Saccharomyces cerevisiae [CAROLINA, WARD'S]
Trichothecium roseum

Nematodes

Caenorhabditis elegans [WARD'S]

Seeds

alfalfa seeds [AUSTIN CAMPBELL, FARM SUPPLY STORE, WARD'S]

pea seeds [GARDEN SUPPLY STORE, WARD'S]

soybean seeds [FARM SUPPLY STORE, WARD'S]

striped sunflower seeds [GARDEN SUPPLY STORE]

Wisconsin Fast Plants [CAROLINA]

Names and addresses of sources

American Type Culture Collection (ATCC)
12301 Parklawn Drive
Rockville, MD 20852

Austin Campbell
USDA/ARS/PSI/SARL
Building 002, Room 12
10300 Baltimore Avenue
Beltsville, MD 20705-2350
301-504-5638

Carolina Biological Supply
2700 York Road
Burlington, NC 27215
800-334-5551
919-584-3399 FAX

Difco Laboratories
P.O. Box 331058
Detroit, MI 48232-7058
800-521-0851
313-462-8517 FAX

Fisher Scientific
1600 West Glenlake Avenue
Itasca, IL 60143
708-773-3050
800-776-7000
800-926-1166 FAX

Millipore Corp.
Bedford, MA 01730

Sigma Chemical Company
P.O. Box 14508
St. Louis, MO 63178
800-325-3010

Vaughan's Seed Company
5300 Katrine Avenue
Downers Grove, IL 60515-4095
708-969-6300
708-969-6373 FAX

VWR Scientific (many regional offices)
P.O. Box 66929
O'Hare AMF
Chicago, IL 60666
800-932-5000

Ward's Natural Science Establishment, Inc.
5100 West Henrietta Road
P.O. Box 92912
Rochester, NY 14692-9012
1-800-962-2660
800-635-8439 FAX

Appendix IX: APHIS form for importing pathogens into a state

U.S. DEPARTMENT OF AGRICULTURE
ANIMAL AND PLANT HEALTH INSPECTION SERVICE
PLANT PROTECTION AND QUARANTINE
PLANT IMPORTATION AND TECHNICAL SUPPORT
HYATTSVILLE, MARYLAND 20782

APPLICATION AND PERMIT TO MOVE LIVE PLANT PESTS

☐ Arthropods ☐ Other *(Specify)*
☐ Pathogens

SECTION A - TO BE COMPLETED BY THE APPLICANT

1. NAME AND ADDRESS *(Include Zip Code)*

2. TELEPHONE NO.

A. SCIENTIFIC NAMES OF PESTS TO BE MOVED	B. CLASSIFICATION *(Order, Family Other)*	C. LIFE STAGES IF APPLICABLE	D. NUMBER OF SPECIMENS OR UNITS	E. SHIPPED FROM *(Country or State)*	F. ARE PESTS IN U.S.	G. WHAT HOST MATERIAL WILL ACCOMPANY PEST?	H. USDA USE PEST CATEGORY
3.							
4.							
5.							

6. DESTINATION

7. PORT OF ARRIVAL

8. APPROXIMATE DATE OF ARRIVAL OR INTERSTATE MOVEMENT

9. NO. OF SHIPMENTS

10. SUPPLIER

11. METHOD OF SHIPMENT
☐ Air Mail ☐ Air Freight ☐ Baggage ☐ Auto

12. INTENDED USE *(Be specific)*

13. METHODS TO BE USED TO PREVENT PLANT PEST ESCAPE

14. METHOD OF FINAL DISPOSITION

15. SIGNATURE OF RESIDENT, APPLICANT OR AGENT

16. DATE

SECTION B - TO BE COMPLETED BY STATE OFFICIAL

17. STATUS
☐ Approve ☐ Disapprove
☐ Accept USDA Decision

18. CONDITIONS RECOMMENDED

19. SIGNATURE

20. TITLE

STATE

21. DATE

SECTION C - TO BE COMPLETED BY FEDERAL OFFICIAL

PERMIT

22. PERMIT NO.

(Permit not valid unless signed by an authorized official of the Animal and Plant Health Inspection Service)

Under authority of the Federal Plant Pest Act of May 23, 1957, permission is hereby granted to the applicant named above to move the plant pests described, except as deleted, subject to the conditions stated on, or attached to this application. *(See standard conditions on reverse side.)*

23. SIGNATURE OF PLANT PROTECTION AND QUARANTINE OFFICIAL

24. DATE

25. LABELS ISSUED

26. VALID UNTIL

PPQ FORM 526
(SEP 79)

Previous editions are obsolete.

STANDARD SAFEGUARDS OF PERMIT

1. All organisms must be shipped in sturdy, escape-proof containers.

2. Upon receipt of plant pests, all packing material and shipping containers shall be sterilized or destroyed immediately after removing organisms.

3. Organisms shall be kept only within the laboratory at the permittee's address.

4. No living organisms kept under this permit shall be removed from confined area except by prior approval from State and Federal regulatory officials.

5. Without prior notice and during reasonable hours, authorized PPQ and State regulatory officials shall be allowed to inspect the conditions under which the organisms are kept.

6. All organisms kept under this permit shall be destroyed at the completion of the intended use, and not later than the expiration date, unless an extension is granted by this issuing office.

7. All necessary precautions must be taken to prevent escape of pests. In the event of an escape, notify this office.

Index